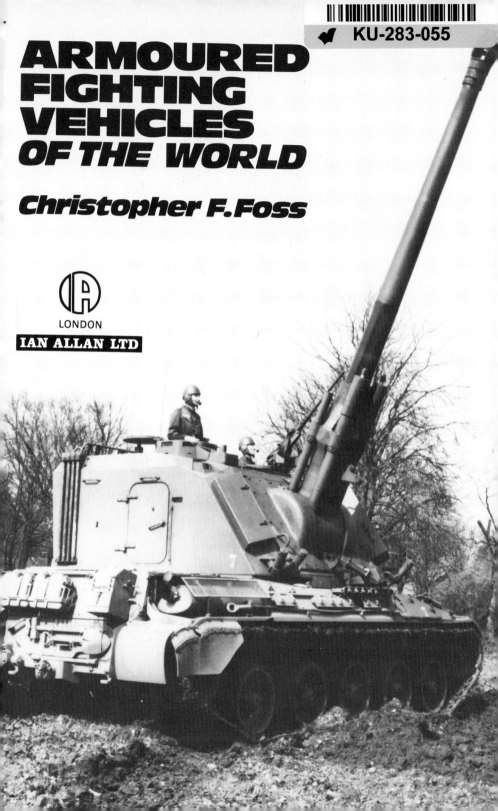

# ARMOURED FIGHTING VEHICLES OF THE WORLD

## Christopher F. Foss

LONDON

IAN ALLAN LTD

First published 1971
This edition 1982

ISBN 0 7110 1105 2

© Christopher F. Foss 1971, 1974, 1977, 1982

Published by Ian Allan Ltd, Shepperton, Surrey;
and printed by Ian Allan Printing Ltd at their works
at Coombelands in Runnymede, England

Cover: *Leopard C1 of the Canadian Royal Dragoons
at the Canadian Army Trophy meet in June 1981.*
Martin Horseman

Back cover, top: *FV438 Swingfire ATGW vehicles in
travelling order.* MoD (Army)

Back cover, bottom: *155mm SP gun Mk F3 is based
on the AMX-13 chassis.* Creusot-Loire

Below: *M730 Chaparral low altitude surface-to-air
missile system which is based on a modified M548
tracked cargo carrier chassis.* Ford Aerospace

# Contents

# Abbreviations

| | | | |
|---|---|---|---|
| **AA** | Anti-Aircraft | **HEAT-MP-T** | High Explosive Anti-Tank Multi |
| **AEV** | Armoured Engineer Vehicle | | Purpose Tracer |
| **AFV** | Armoured Fighting Vehicle | **HEI** | High Explosive Incendiary |
| **AML** | Automitrailleuse Légère | **HEP** | High Explosive Plastic |
| **AMP** | Amphibious | **HESH** | High Explosive Squash Head |
| **AMX** | Atelier de Constructions | **hp** | Horse Power |
| | d'Issy-les-Moulineaux | **HVAP** | High Velocity Armour Piercing |
| **AP** | Armour Piercing | **IAFV** | Infantry Armoured Fighting Vehicle |
| **APC** | Armoured Personnel Carrier | **ICBM** | Intercontinental Ballistic Missile |
| **APDS** | Armour Piercing Discarding Sabot | **IFCS** | Integrated (or Improved) Fire Control |
| **APFSDS** | Armour Piercing Fin Stabilised | | System |
| | Discarding Sabot | **IFV** | Infantry Fighting Vehicle |
| **APG** | Aberdeen Proving Ground | **inc** | Including |
| | (United States) | **IR** | Infra-Red |
| **APHE** | Armour Piercing High Explosive | **IS** | Internal Security Vehicle |
| **API** | Armour Piercing Incendiary | **ITV** | Improved TOW System |
| **APS** | Armour Piercing Shot | **kg** | kilogramme |
| **ARSV** | Armoured Reconnaissance Scout | **kg/sq cm** | Kilogramme per square centimetre |
| | Vehicle | **km** | Kilometre |
| **ARV** | Armoured Recovery Vehicle | **km/h** | Kilometre per hour |
| **ATGW** | Anti-Tank Guided Weapon | **LLLTV** | Low Light Level TV |
| **AVGP** | Armoured Vehicle General Purpose | **LMG** | Light Machine Gun |
| **AVLB** | Armour Vehicle Launched Bridge | **LVT** | Landing Vehicle (Tracked) |
| **AVRE** | Vehicle Royal Engineers | **m** | Metre |
| **BAe** | British Aerospace | **max** | Maximum |
| **BAOR** | British Army of the Rhine | **MBT** | Main Battle Tank |
| **BARV** | Beach Armoured Recovery Vehicle | **MICV** | Mechanised Infantry Combat Vehicle |
| **BHP** | Brake Horse Power | **min** | Minimum |
| **C&R** | Command and Reconnaissance | **MG** | Machine Gun |
| **CET** | Combat Engineer Tractor | **MLRS** | Multiple Launch Rocket System |
| **CEV** | Combat Engineer Vehicle | **mm** | Millimetre |
| **CFV** | Cavalry Fighting Vehicle | **MVEE** | Military Vehicles and Engineering |
| **CRR** | Carro de Reconhecimento Sobre | | Establishment |
| | Rodas | **NATO** | North Atlantic Treaty Organisation |
| **CTRA** | Carro de Transporte Sobre Rodas | **NBC** | Nuclear, Biological, Chemical |
| | Anfíbio | **RAP** | Rocket Assisted Projectile |
| **CVR(T)** | Combat Vehicle Reconnaissance | **ROF** | Rate of Fire or Royal Ordnance |
| | (Tracked) | | Factory |
| **CVR(W)** | Combat Vehicle Reconnaissance | **rpm** | Revolutions per minute or Rounds per |
| | (Wheeled) | | minute |
| **DCA** | Défense Contre Avions | **SAM** | Surface-to-air-Missile |
| **DIVADS** | Division Air Defense System | **SPG** | Self-Propelled Gun |
| **EBR** | Engine Blindé de Reconnaissance | **SPH** | Self-Propelled Howitzer |
| **EMD** | Electronic Marcel Dassault | **SPRR** | Self-Propelled Recoilless Rifle |
| **ERC** | Engine Reconnaissance Canon | **TAM** | Tanque Argentino Mediano |
| **FCS** | Fire Control System | **USMC** | United States Marine Corps |
| **FRG** | Federal Republic of Germany | **VAB** | Véhicule de l'Avant Blindé |
| **FVRDE** | Fighting Vehicles Research & | **VCI** | Véhicule de Combat Infanterie *or* |
| | Development Establishment (now the | | Vehicule Combat Infanteria |
| | Military Vehicles and Engineering | **VCR** | Véhicule de Combat à Roues |
| | Establishment) | **VDAA** | Véhicule d'Auto-Defence |
| **FVS** | Fighting Vehicle System | | Antiaérienne |
| **G/clearance** | Ground Clearance | **V/obstacle** | Vertical Obstacle |
| **GCT** | Grande Cadence de Tir | **WAPC** | Wheeled Armoured Personnel Carrier |
| **GMC** | General Motors Corporation | **WFSV** | Wheeled Fire Support Vehicle |
| **G/pressure** | Ground Pressure | **WMSV** | Wheeled Maintenance and Support |
| **GPO** | Gun Position Officer | | Vehicle |
| **HE** | High Explosive | **w/o** | Without |
| **HEAT** | High Explosive Anti-Tank | | |

# Introduction

Since the third edition of *Armoured Fighting Vehicles of the World* was published in 1977, there have been many new vehicles developed as well as further improvements to existing vehicles to extend their useful lives.

In the United States the latest version of the M60 series, the M60A3 is now in service in significant numbers and many older M60A1s are now being upgraded to M60A3 standard. First production M1 MBTs (previously designated the XM1) were handed over to the US Army early in 1980 and a second source will come into use when production of the M60A3 is completed late in 1982 at Detroit. The US Army has a requirement for some 7,058 by the end of fiscal year 1987. To operate with the M1 MBT as part of the combined arms team, FMC have developed the M2 Infantry Fighting Vehicle and the M3 Cavalry Fighting Vehicle, with first deliveries of the former taking place in May 1982. In the next two years the Army should also take delivery of its first of 618 40mm DIVAD SP AA gun systems which will replace the clear weather and range limited 20mm M163.

The cancellation of the Iranian order for 125 Shir 1(FV4030/2) and 1,225 Shir 2 (FV4030/3) MBTs by the new Iranian Government late in 1979 left the ROF Leeds with little work for the next five years. In mid-1980 the British Government announced that the MBT-80 had been cancelled not only due to rising costs but also because the in service date was slipping to the late 1980s. Following this decision an order was placed for some 240 Challenger MBTs with first deliveries expected in 1984/85. To replace the FV432 APC, between 1,800 and 2,000 GKN Sankey MCV-80s have been ordered for delivery from the mid-1980s but unlike more recent MICVs such as the American M2, Soviet BMP-1 and the upgraded West German Marder, there is no provision for the infantry to use their weapons from within the vehicle and no integral anti-tank system is provided.

Meanwhile in West Germany, production of 1,800 Leopard 2 MBTs for the West German Army is now well underway and all should be delivered by 1986, the Dutch Army has ordered 445 for delivery between 1982 and 1986. Production of the Marder MICV has been completed although the chassis remains in production for the Roland 2 SAM system. Delivery of 996 Transportpanzer (6×6) multi-role vehicles commenced in 1979.

France has yet to develop a second generation MBT such as the Leopard 2/M1 and is now upgrading its AMX-30s to AMX-30 B2 configuration to keep them effective through the 1980s. For the export market France has developed the AMX-32, the second prototype of which was shown in June 1982, this being armed with a 120mm gun and having increased armour protection. The AMX-10P MICV is now in service with the French and other armies as is the sophisticated AMX-10RC (6×6) vehicle which shares many common automotive components with the latter. France is also the first member of NATO to deploy a SP 155mm howitzer with an automatic loading system to enable a high rate of fire to be achieved. The West German/Italian/UK SP-70 is not now expected to enter service until the late 1980s.

The Soviet Union continues to deploy AFVs on a large scale and in 1980 built some 3,000 MBTs (2,500 T-72 and 500 T-64) and 5,500 other AFVs as well as SP AA guns and SP artillery systems. Well over 8,000 T-64/T-72s are now in service with the Warsaw Pact and the consensus of opinion is that the T-72 with its three-man crew and automatic loader is the equal of the West's Leopard 2 and M1 of which less than 300 were built by early 1981 with hardly any of the latter being deployed to Europe. A new MICV is now in service, provisionally called the BMP-80, and a replacement for the BTR-60 series, the BTR-70 is now also in service. New mobile SP AA gun systems and SP artillery systems are expected to be deployed in the near future.

In recent years many other countries have established a capability to design, develop and produce AFVs, especially armoured cars and APCs and this trend is expected to continue in future years.

This book contains data, brief development history, variants and a list of user countries of all tanks, reconnaissance vehicles, APCs (and IFV/MICV), SP guns (including AA missile systems likely to be found in the immediate battlefield area) at present in service or under development. This edition has been fully revised, almost all of the photographs have been replaced and over 50 new entries added. A list of vehicles phased out of service or whose development has been cancelled is given at the back of *Armoured Fighting Vehicles of the World*.

As usual, the author would like to take this opportunity of thanking the many governments, manufacturers and individuals from all over the world who have provided material for this book. In addition special thanks are due to Tony Cullen, Robert Forsyth, Terry Gander, Geoffry Tillotson and Arthur Volz for their most valuable assistance. A special word of thanks is also due to Simon Forty of Ian Allan for care in the production of this edition.

**Christopher F. Foss**

# Jagdpanzer SK105 Light Tank/Tank Destroyer   Austria

**Armament:** 1 × 105mm gun, elevation + 13°,
depression — 8° (44 rounds carried)
1 × 7.62mm coaxial MG (2,000 rounds carried)
2× 3 smoke dischargers
**Crew:** 3
**Length:** 7.763m (inc gun), 5.58m (excl gun)
**Width:** 2.50m
**Height:** 2.514m
**G/clearance:** 0.40m
**Weight:** 17,500kg (loaded)
**G/pressure:** 0.68kg/sq cm
**Engine:** Steyr Model 7FA 6-cylinder diesel,
developing 320hp at 2,300rpm
**Speed:** 65km/h (road)
**Range:** 520km
**Fuel:** 400 litres
**Fording:** 1.00m
**V/obstacle:** 0.80m
**Trench:** 2.41m
**Gradient:** 75%
**Armour:** 8mm-40mm

## Development
In 1965, Saurer, who were taken over by Steyr-
Daimler-Puch in 1970, started development of a
new tank destroyer to meet the requirements of the
Austrian Army. This used many automotive
components of the 4KH 7FA APC but had a new hull
with the engine, transmission and drive sprockets at
the rear instead of the front. The first prototype was

completed in 1967 with the second following in
1969. Five pre-production vehicles were completed
in 1971 and since then several hundred have been
built for the home and export markets.

The oscillating turret is an improved version of the
French FL-12 and is armed with a 105mm gun that
fires the same spin-stabilised ammunition as the
French AMX-30 MBT, including HE, HEAT and
smoke. Ammunition is fed to the gun by two revolver
type magazines each of which hold six rounds of
ammunition.

A laser rangefinder is mounted externally on the
turret roof at the rear and above this is an infra-red/
white light searchlight. Standard equipment includes
an NBC system and a heater.

## Variants
*Greif ARV:* Based on the hull of SK 105 but fitted
with a crane with a max lifting capacity of 6,500kg,
winch with a capacity of 20,000kg and a dozer/
stabilising blade at the front of the hull.
*Pioneer vehicle:* Called the Engineer Tank 4KH
7FA-PI and based on Greif hull, retains crane but is
not fitted with winch; it has a larger dozer blade for
increased dozing capability.
*Driver training tank:* Called the 4KH 7FA-FA,
basically SK 105 with turret replaced by a fully
enclosed cabin for instructor and additional drivers.
Any SK 105 can be converted for use in this role in
two hours.

## Employment
Argentina, Austria, Bolivia, Morocco and Tunisia.

*Jagdpanzer SK 105.*   Steyr-Daimler-Puch

# Steyr 4K 7FA APC

Austria

**Armament:** 1 × 12.7mm MG
**Crew:** 2 + 8
**Length:** 5.87m
**Width:** 2.5m
**Height:** 1.69m (w/o armament)
**G/clearance:** 0.42m
**Weight:** 14,800kg (loaded)
**G/pressure:** 0.55kg/sq cm
**Engine:** Steyr 7FA 6-cylinder diesel developing 320hp at 2,300rpm
**Speed:** 63.6km/h (road)
**Range:** 520km (road)
**Fuel:** 360 litres
**Fording:** 1m
**V/obstacle:** 0.8m
**Trench:** 2.1m
**Gradient:** 75%
**Armour:** 8mm-32mm (est)

## Development
The Steyr 4K 7FA is a further development of the Saurer 4K 4FA with the first prototype being completed in 1976 and first production vehicles following a year later. It has the same engine and transmission as the 4K 7FA Jagdpanzer SK 105 light tank/tank destroyer.

*Steyr 4K 7FA APC with 12.7mm M2 HB MG and LMG over troop compartment at rear.*
Steyr-Daimler-Puch

The basic model is designated the 4K 7FA G127 and is armed with a Browning 12.7mm M2HB MG with provision for mounting up to four MGs on pintle mounts over the rear troop compartment. Standard equipment includes passive night vision equipment and an NBC system.

### Variants
4K 7FA-FUE command vehicle; 4K 7FA/SAN ambulance; 4K 7FA-FLA 1/2.20 twin 20mm AA gun system (prototype built); 4K 7FA-GrW 81 81mm mortar carrier (project); 4K 7FA-GrW 120 120mm mortar carrier (project); Reconnaissance vehicle with 30mm Rarden cannon (under development); AA vehicle with twin 30mm cannon (prototype built).

### Employment
Austria, Morocco, Nigeria and Tunisia.

# Saurer 4K 4FA APC

Austria

**Data:** APC with 20mm turret
**Armament:** 1 × 20mm Oerlikon cannon
**Crew:** 2 + 8
**Length:** 5.40m
**Width:** 2.50m
**Height:** 2.17m (inc turret), 1.65m (hull top)
**G/clearance:** 0.42m
**Weight:** 15,000kg (loaded)
**G/pressure:** 0.52kg/sq cm
**Engine:** Steyr Model 4FA 6-cylinder diesel, developing 250hp at 2,400rpm
**Speed:** 65km/h (road)
**Range:** 370km
**Fuel:** 184 litres
**Fording:** 1.00m
**V/obstacle:** 0.80m
**Trench:** 2.20m
**Gradient:** 75%
**Armour:** 8mm-20mm

### Development
Development of an APC was started by Saurer in

1956, the first prototype was completed in 1958 this being the 3K 3H which was powered by a 3H 200hp Saurer diesel. This was followed by the 4K 3H in 1959 and the 4K 2P. First production vehicles, designated the 4K 4F, were completed in 1961. Later production models, which only had minor differences such as an improved engine, were the 4K 3FA and 4K 4FA. Production was completed in 1969 after some 450 vehicles had been built.

Further development by Steyr-Daimler-Puch, who took over Saurer in 1970, has resulted in the much improved 4K 7FA APC for which there is a separate entry.

**Variants**
The Austrian Army have two basic versions of the 4K 4FA, the 4K 4FA-G1 with a 12.7mm M2 Browning MG and the 4K 4FA-G2 with turret-mounted 20mm Oerlikon cannon. The 4K 4FA-G1 is provided with front and side armour; in addition the crew can mount a total of four MG42 7.62mm MGs on sockets around the top of the hull. The second model

*Saurer 4K 4FA-G2 with turret-mounted 20mm cannon.* Austrian Army

is fitted with an Oerlikon GAD-AOA turret armed with a 20mm 204 GK cannon with 100 ready rounds and a further 325 rounds in reserve. This cannon can be elevated from −12° to +70°, and turret has armour of 20mm.

Other versions include an ambulance (Sanitätspanzer San), multiple rocket launcher with 2 × 81mm launching system, 4K 3FA-FU1 (command vehicle), 4K 3FA-FUA (artillery command vehicle), 4K 3FA-FU/FLA (anti-aircraft command vehicle), 4K 3FA-FS2 (radio vehicle), 81mm mortar carrier (GrW1), 120mm mortar carrier (GrW2) (prototype only).

**Employment**
Used only by the Austrian Army.

# FN 4RM/62F Armoured Car
# Belgium

**Length:** Overall — 4.50m (MG version), 5.42m (gun version)
Hull — 4.50m
**Width:** 2.26m
**Height:** overall 2.37m (MG version), 2.52m (gun version)
**G/clearance:** 0.324m
**Weight loaded:** 8,800kg (MG version), 8,000kg (gun version)
**Crew:** 3
**Wheelbase:** 2.45m
**Track:** 1.62m
**Gradient:** 60%
**Armour:** 6.5mm-13mm

**Engine:** FN 652, 6-cylinder, in-line, OHV petrol engine developing 130hp at 3,500rpm
**Speed:** 110km/h (road)
**Range:** 550/600km
**Fuel:** 180 litres
**Fording:** 1.10m

**Development**
This armoured car was designed by Fabrique Nationale d'Armes de Guerre of Herstal, Belgium, and uses many components of the FN 4RM Ardennes truck. The first prototype was built in 1962, followed by the second prototype in 1965. Production was completed in 1971 and 62 were built, all being delivered to the Belgian Gendarmerie.

### Variants

*MG version:* This is armed with a 60mm mortar, 2 × 7.62mm machine guns and 12 smoke dischargers. The turret has a traverse of 360°, and the machine guns can be elevated from −10° to +55° and the mortar from −10° to +75°. Ammunition carried is: 46 mortar rounds, 4,830 MG rounds, 36 smoke grenades and 12 anti-personnel grenades.

*Gun version:* This is armed with a 90mm CATI gun, 1 × 7.62mm coaxial MG, 1 × 7.62mm AA MG and 12 smoke dischargers. The turret has a traverse of 360° and the gun has an elevation from −12° to +27°. Ammunition carried is: 40 rounds of 90mm, 3,680 MG rounds, 36 smoke grenades and 12 anti-personnel grenades.

*APC:* Only one of these was built.

### Employment

Belgian Gendarmerie.

*FN 4RM/62F AB armoured car with 60mm mortar and twin 7.62 MGs.* FN (Belgium)

# SIBMAS APC                                          Belgium

**Crew:** 2 + 14
**Length:** 7.32m
**Width:** 2.50m
**Height:** 2.24m (hull top), 2.77m (turret)
**G/clearance:** 0.4m
**Weight:** 14,500-16,500kg (loaded); 12,500kg (w/o armament)
**Track:** 2.07m
**Wheelbase:** 2.8m + 1.4m
**Engine:** MAN D 2566 MKF 6-cylinder turbo-charged diesel developing 320hp at 1,900rpm
**Speed:** 110km/h (road), 11.5km/h (water)
**Range:** 1,100km (road)
**Fuel:** 425 litres
**Fording:** Amphibious
**V/obstacle:** 0.6m
**Trench:** 1.2m
**Gradient:** 70%
**Side slope:** 40%

### Development

The SIBMAS (6 × 6) APC has been developed as a private venture by BN Constructions Ferroviaires et Métalliques with the first prototype being completed in 1977 and the second following in 1979. Development is now complete and the vehicle is ready for production. Wherever possible standard and proven MAN heavy truck components have been used in the construction of the vehicle.

The SIBMAS is fully amphibious being propelled in the water by two propellers at the rear of the hull and optional equipment includes night vision equipment, air conditioning system, NBC system, heater and a front mounted winch.

### Variants

In addition to being used as an APC with a two-man crew and carrying 14 men, the SIBMAS can be adopted for a wide range of other roles including ambulance, anti-tank (with HOT, MILAN and TOW ATGWs), cargo carrier, command vehicle, IS vehicle, mortar carrier, reconnaissance vehicle and recovery vehicle.

A wide range of armament installations can be fitted including Peak Engineering turret with 7.62mm or 12.7mm MGs, EMD twin 20mm AA turret, turret with Cockerill 90mm Mk III gun,

Hispano-Suiza Lynx 90 turret or a Serval 60/20 turret.

**Employment**
Development complete. Ready for production.

*SIBMAS APC with French Hispano-Suiza Lynx 90 turret.* SIBMAS

# BDX APC

Belgium

**Crew:** 2 + 10
**Length:** 5.05m
**Width:** 2.5m
**Height:** 2.84m (turret), 2.06m (hull top)
**G/clearance:** 0.4m
**Weight:** 10,700kg (loaded), 9,750kg (empty)
**Track:** 1.93m
**Wheelbase:** 3.003m
**Engine:** Chrysler V-8 water-cooled petrol developing 180bhp at 4,000rpm
**Speed:** 100km/h
**Range:** 500km-900km
**Fuel:** 248 litres
**Fording:** Amphibious
**V/obstacle:** 0.4m
**Gradient:** 60%
**Side slope:** 40%
**Armour:** 9.5mm-12.7mm

## Development

In 1976 the Engineering Division of Beherman Demoen obtained a licence to undertake production of the Irish Timoney (4 × 4) APC in Belgium. The Belgian Government ordered 123 BDX APCs, 43 for the Air Force and 80 for the Gendarmerie, all of

which were delivered by early 1981. Five have also been sold to Argentina.

The BDX can be used in a number of roles as well as an APC, including ambulance, command and reconnaissance and can be fitted with a wide range of armament installations including turret with 7.62mm or 12.7mm MGs, 20mm cannon or a 90mm Cockerill gun, or a Euromissile MCT turret with two MILAN ATGWs in the ready to launch position.

The vehicle is fully amphibious being propelled in the water by its wheels and optional equipment includes a front mounted dozer blade, winch, air conditioning system, heater and smoke dischargers.

## Variants

There are no variants apart from those mentioned above. Undergoing trials is a BDX with a General Motors Detroit Diesel Model 6V53 developing 180hp. Under development is the BDX Mk II which will have an improved hull and suspension and other detailed modifications.

## Employment

Belgium and Argentina.

*BDX APC with Peak Engineering turret for twin 7.62 MGs.* Beherman Demoen (Engineering Division)

# Cobra APC

Belgium

**Armament:** 1 × 12.7mm MG
2 × 101mm rocket launchers
2 × 7.62mm bow MGs
2 × 3 rifle grenade launchers
**Crew:** 3 + 9
**Length:** 4.2m
**Width:** 2.7m
**Height:** 1.65m (hull top)
**G/clearance:** 0.4m
**Weight:** 7,500kg (loaded)
**G/pressure:** 0.29kg/sq cm
**Engine:** V-6 diesel developing 143hp at 3,300rpm
**Speed:** 80km/h (road), 7km/h (water)
**Range:** 600km
**Fuel:** 260 litres
**Fording:** Amphibious
**V/obstacle:** 0.7m
**Trench:** 1.7m
**Gradient:** 60%

## Development

The Cobra APC has been developed as a private venture by the Ateliers de Constructions Electriques de Charleroi from 1977. By 1980 two prototypes had been built and tested but quantity production had yet to start.

The three-man crew consists of the main turret gunner/vehicle commander, and two drivers at the front, each of whom operates a bow mounted 7.62mm MG. The nine infantrymen enter and leave via a large door in the rear of the hull, there is no provision for the infantrymen to use their small arms from within the vehicle.

The Cobra is fully amphibious being propelled in the water by its tracks and optional equipment

includes passive night vision equipment and a NBC system.

An unusual feature of the Cobra is that the diesel engine provides power to an alternator which in turn provides power to a motor and reduction gear on each of the rear mounted sprockets.

## Employment

Trials. Not yet in production.

*Cobra APC.*
Ateliers de Constructions Electriques de Charleroi

# X1A2 Light Tank Brazil

**Armament:** 1 × 90mm gun, elevation +17°, depression −8° (66 rounds carried)
1 × 7.62mm coaxial MG (2,500 rounds)
1 × 12.7mm AA MG (750 rounds)
3 smoke dischargers either side of turret
**Crew:** 3
**Length:** 7.1m (gun forward), 6.5m (hull)
**Width:** 2.6m
**Height:** 2.45m (turret top)
**G/clearance:** 0.5m
**Weight:** 19,000kg (loaded)
**G/pressure:** 0.63kg/sq cm
**Engine:** Scania Model DS-11 6-cylinder water-cooled turbo-charged diesel developing 300hp at 2,200rpm
**Speed:** 55km/h (road)
**Range:** 600km
**Fuel:** 600 litres
**Fording:** 1.3m
**V/obstacle:** 0.7m
**Trench:** 2.1m
**Gradient:** 70%

*X1A2 light tank with Cockerill 90mm gun.
Ronaldo S. Olive*

wheel. This model was not placed in production but further development resulted in the X1A2 which is now in production for the Brazilian Army.

The X1A2 is a completely new vehicle rather than a modernisation of an existing vehicle as in the case of the X1A and X1A1 light tanks.

The three-man crew of the X1A2 consists of the tank commander/loader, gunner and driver. Prototypes were armed with a French 90mm D-921 gun but production vehicles have the Belgian Cockerill 90mm gun which is manufactured under licence in Brazil by ENGESA and is also installed in the ENGESA EE-9 Cascavel (6 × 6) armoured car.

Optional equipment includes a more advanced fire control system, active or passive night vision equipment and an air conditioning system.

## Development
After Bernardini rebuilt the American M3A1 Stuart light tank to the X1A configuration (see following entry), two prototypes of a further model called the X1A1 were built. This was essentially an X1A with the same engine and turret but with a longer hull with an additional volute spring suspension group, additional track return roller and a new tension

## Variants
There are no variants of the X1A2 at this time, but ARV and bridgelayer versions are under development.

## Employment
In service with Brazilian Army but also available for export.

12

# X1A1 Light Tank

Brazil

**Armament:** 1 × 90mm gun
1 × 7.62mm coaxial MG
1 × 12.7mm AA MG
2 × 3 smoke dischargers
**Crew:** 4
**Length:** 6.36m (gun forward), 5.3m (hull)
**Width:** 2.4m
**Height:** 2.45m (turret top)
**G/clearance:** 0.5m
**Weight:** 17,000kg
**G/pressure:** 0.55kg/sq cm
**Engine:** Scania 6-cylinder diesel developing 280hp
**Speed:** 60km/h
**Range:** 520km
**Fording:** 1.3m
**V/obstacle:** 0.8m
**Gradient:** 60%

## Development

Under the technical control of the Brazilian Army Research and Development Centre, the Bernardini Company of Sao Paulo rebuilt two old American supplied M3A1 Stuart light tanks. The extensive rebuild included new armour above the tracks, new turret with French D-921 F1 90mm gun, new fire control system, Scania diesel and a new volute suspension system.

The Brazilian Army then authorised Bernardini to rebuild 80 M3A1 Stuart light tanks to this new standard and these were called the X1A, weighed 15,000kg and had a max range of 450km.

Further development resulted in the X1A1 which is essentially an X1A with an additional track return roller, additional volute spring suspension group and a new track tension wheel either side. This model was not placed in production but is being offered for export by Bernardini. Further development resulted in the X1A2 (qv).

## Variants

*XLP-10 Bridgelayer:* Prototype of this bridgelayer was based on chassis X1A but production vehicles for Brazilian Army are based on X1A1 chassis. Carries bridge which will span gap of 10m and take a max load of 20 tonnes.
*XLF-40 Rocket Launcher:* Based on X1A1 chassis with three SS-60 surface-to-surface rockets.

## Employment

X1A light tank is in service with Brazilian Army; X1A1 is available for export.

*X1A light tank as used by the Brazilian Army.*
Bernardini

**Armament:** 1 × 105mm gun (37 rounds carried)
2 × 7.62mm MGs — coaxial and AA (optional)
2 × 2 smoke dischargers (optional)
**Crew:** 4
**Length:** 6.35m
**Width:** 2.60m
**Height:** 3.26m
**G/clearance:** 0.4m
**Weight:** 18,500kg (loaded)
**Track:** 2.1m
**Wheelbase:** 3.9m
**Engine:** Detroit Diesel model 6V53T 6-cylinder developing 300bhp at 2,800rpm
**Speed:** 90km/h (road)
**Range:** 750km
**Fuel:** 360 litres
**Fording:** 1m
**V/obstacle:** 0.6m
**Gradient:** 60%

## Development

The EE-17 Sucuri tank destroyer has been designed by ENGESA specifically for the export market but has not so far been placed in production. The four-man crew consists of the driver and radio operator, who are seated in the forward part of the hull and the commander and gunner who are seated in the turret at the rear of the hull.

The FL-12 is a French design and is fitted to a number of other AFVs including the French AMX-13

*ENGESA EE-17 Sucuri tank destroyer with 105mm gun in travelling lock.  ENGESA*

light tank and the Austrian Steyr SK105 tank destroyer. It is armed with a 105mm gun which is fed from two drum type magazines each of which holds six rounds of ammunition, once these have been expended one of the crew has to leave the vehicle to reload the magazines. The turret is of the oscillating type in which the main armament is fixed in the upper part of the turret which pivots on the lower part, this enables the weapon to be elevated from +12° 30′ to −8°.

Optional equipment includes a 7.62mm AA MG, two electrically operated smoke dischargers mounted either side of the turret, laser rangefinder on turret roof, night vision equipment for the commander and driver, infra-red/white light searchlight on turret so elevating with the main armament, central tyre pressure regulation system, air conditioning system, heater, fire detection and extinguishing system and engine start device for use in cold climates.

## Employment

Development complete. Ready for production.

# ENGESA EE-9 Cascavel Armoured Car          Brazil

**Armament:** 1 × 90mm gun, elevation +15°,
depression -8° (45 rounds carried)
2 ×7.62mm MGs — One coaxial and AA (optional)
— (2,400 rounds)
2 × 2 smoke dischargers
**Crew:** 3
**Length:** 6.22m (gun forwards), 5.19m (hull)
**Width:** 2.59m
**Height:** 2.36m (commander's cupola)
**G/clearance:** 0.375m (front axle)
**Weight:** 12,200kg (loaded), 11,800kg (empty)
**Track:** 2.1m
**Wheelbase:** 2.343m + 1.415m
**Engine:** Mercedes-Benz OM-352A 6-cylinder
water-cooled turbocharged diesel developing 190hp
at 2,800rpm
**Speed:** 100km/h
**Range:** 1,000km
**Fuel:** 360 litres
**Fording:** 1m
**V/obstacle:** 0.6m
**Gradient:** 60%
**Side slope:** 30%
**Armour:** 12mm (max)

## Development
The EE-9 armoured car was developed by ENGESA
to meet the requirements of the Brazilian Army with
the first prototypes being completed in 1970. A
pre-production batch of 10 vehicles was completed
in 1972/73 with first production vehicles being

*ENGESA EE-9 Cascavel armoured car with ENGESA
ET-90 turret, commander's cupola and laser
rangefinder.  ENGESA*

completed in 1974. The EE-9 shares many common
automotive components with the EE-11 Urutu APC
and in Brazilian Army service is called the Carro de
Reconhecimento Sobre Rodas (or CRR).

So far five models of the EE-9 Cascavel have been
built:
*Mark I* Armed with 37mm gun and used by Brazilian
Army only, most brought up to Mark III standard,
Marks 1, II and III all have Mercedes-Benz diesel
made in Brazil.
*Mark II* Fitted with French H-90 turret with 90mm
gun and automatic transmission, for export only, no
longer in production.
*Mark III* Currently in production has ENGESA
designed ET-90 turret with Brazilian manufactured
90mm gun, automatic transmission.
*Mark IV* Same turret as above but powered by a
General Motors Detroit Diesel 6V53 developing
212hp, automatic transmission and central tyre
pressure regulation system.
*Mark V* As Mark IV but fitted with standard
Mercedes-Benz diesel engine.

A wide range of optional equipment can be fitted
to the EE-9 including an automatic tyre pressure
regulation system, laser rangefinder, active or
passive night vision equipment, heater, automatic
fire extinguisher and a commander's cupola with a
7.62mm MG.

## Variants
There are no variants apart from those mentioned
above.

## Employment
In service with Bolivia, Brazil, Chile, Gabon, Iraq,
Libya.

# ENGESA EE-3 Jararaca Scout Car                Brazil

**Armament:** 1 x 12.7mm MG (see text)
**Crew:** 3
**Length:** 4.195m
**Width:** 2.13m
**Height:** 1.56m (w/o armament)
**G/clearance:** 0.315m
**Weight:** 5200kg (max)
**Track:** 1.71m
**Wheelbase:** 2.60m
**Engine:** Daimler-Benz OM-314 4-cylinder water-cooled diesel developing 120hp at 2,800rpm
**Speed:** 90km/h
**Range:** 750km
**Fuel:** 135 litres
**Fording:** 0.8m
**V/obstacle:** 0.50m
**Gradient:** 60%

**Development**
The ENGESA EE-3 Jararaca has been developed to meet the requirements of the Brazilian Army with the first prototype being completed in 1979 and first production vehicles following in 1980.

The hull of the Jararaca is similar to that used in the EE-9 Cascavel, EE-11 Urutu and EE-17 Sucuri members of the ENGESA family of wheeled AFVs. This consists of an outer layer of hard steel and an inner layer of softer steel roll-bonded and heat treated to give the maximum possible protection.

The EE-3 can be fitted with a wide range of armament installations including a 7.62mm or 12.7mm MG, 20mm cannon, 60mm breech-loaded mortar, 106mm M40 recoilless rifle or a MILAN ATGW.

Optional equipment includes passive night vision equipment, intercom system and various radio installations.

**Employment**
In service with undisclosed countries.

*ENGESA EE-3 Jararaca scout car without armament installed.* ENGESA

# ENGESA EE-11 Urutu APC                Brazil

**Armament:** See text below
**Crew:** 14
**Length:** 6m
**Width:** 2.6m
**Height:** 2.72m (top of MG mount): 2.09m (hull top)
**G/clearance:** 0.375m
**Weight:** 13,000kg (loaded), 11,000kg (empty)
**Track:** 2.1m
**Wheelbase:** 3.05m
**Engine:** Mercedes-Benz OM-352A 6-cylinder

water-cooled turbocharged diesel developing 190hp at 2,800rpm
**Speed:** 90km/h (road), 8km/h (water)
**Range:** 1,000km
**Fuel:** 380 litres
**Fording:** Amphibious
**V/obstacle:** 0.6m
**Gradient:** 60%
**Side slope:** 30%
**Armour:** 12mm (max)

## Development
The EE-11 Urutu APC was designed by ENGESA to meet the requirements of the Brazilian Army and Marines with the first prototype being completed in July 1970. Production commenced at the new ENGESA factory at Sao Jose dos Campos in 1974. The Brazilian Army call the EE-11 the Carro de Transporte Sobre Rodas Anfibio (or CTRA).

A wide range of armament installations can be fitted to the EE-11 including pintle and ring-mounted 7.62mm or 12.7mm MGs, turret-mounted MGs or a 20mm cannon, turret with a 60mm Brandt mortar, turret as fitted to the CVR(T) Scorpion, ENGESA ET-90 turret with ENGESA 90mm gun (as fitted to the EE-9 Cascavel armoured car), EMD turret with twin 20mm AA guns to name just a few.

A wide range of optional equipment can be fitted to the EE-11 including active or passive night vision equipment, automatic tyre pressure regulation system, 6,000kg front mounted winch, Detroit 6V53 diesel developing 212hp and a manual instead of automatic transmission. The hull is of all welded steel construction and provides the crew with complete protection from small arms fire, there are firing ports in the hull sides and rear. The driver and

*ENGESA EE-11 Urutu APC with 60mm breech-loaded Brandt mortar.* ENGESA

engine are at the front of the vehicle with the personnel compartment at the rear.

The basic model is fully amphibious being propelled in the water by its wheels. The Brazilian Marines required a model with better sea-keeping capabilities and a special model for them has been developed. This is provided with four snorkel type tubes on top of the hull and is propelled in the water by two propellers and also has electric bilge pumps.

## Variants
In addition to the armament installations mentioned above the following versions of the EE-11 have been built and are in service, ambulance (with raised roof), command/wireless vehicle and a workshop vehicle complete with tools and tow bars.

## Employment
In service with Bolivia, Brazil, Chile, Iraq, Libya and other countries.

# Armoured Vehicle General Purpose                Canada

After evaluating various vehicles to meet its requirements for an Armoured Vehicle General Purpose (AVGP), in 1977 the Canadian Armed Forces selected the Swiss designed MOWAG Piranha (6×6) to meet its requirements and a licence was obtained to enable the Diesel Division of General Motors Canada to undertake production of three versions of the vehicle. These became known as the Cougar 76mm Wheeled Fire Support Vehicle (WFSV) of which 189 were ordered, Grizzly Wheeled

Armoured Personnel Carrier (WAPC) of which 261 were ordered and the Husky Wheeled Maintenance and Recovery Vehicle (WMRV), 26 ordered.

The first production vehicles were handed over to the Canadian Armed Forces in February 1979 and final deliveries are expected to be made in late 1982. It should be noted that the production figures given above are the final ones, the original orders were significantly smaller than these.

The Canadian vehicles are powered by a Detroit

Diesel model 6V53T which develops 275hp, this being coupled to an Allison MT653 automatic transmission with five forward and one reverse gears. Standard equipment includes heaters for the engine and crew compartment and cold starting aids, some vehicles have a passive night driving periscope for the driver.

Full details of the Piranha range of vehicles are given under Switzerland.

*Cougar wheeled fire support vehicle (left) and Grizzly wheeled APC of the Canadian Armed Forces.* MOWAG

**Employment**
In service with the Canadian Armed Forces.

# Sexton SP Gun                                               Canada

**Armament:** 1 × 25pdr (88mm) gun elevation + 40°, depression − 9°, traverse 25° left and 15° right (112 cartridges carried — 87 HE and 18 AP projectiles) 2 × Bren LMGs with 1,500 rounds
**Crew:** 6
**Length:** 6.121m
**Width:** 2.717m
**Height:** 2.870m (inc canvas top), 2.438m (w/o canvas top)
**G/clearance:** 0.431m
**Weight:** 25,855kg
**G/pressure:** 0.81kg/sq cm
**Engine:** Continental R975-C1 petrol engine, 400hp at 2,400rpm *or* Continental R975-C4 petrol engine, 475hp at 2,400rpm
**Speed:** 40km/h (road)
**Range:** 290km (road)
**Fuel:** 682 litres
**Fording:** 0.914m
**V/obstacle:** 0.609m
**Trench:** 1.879m
**Gradient:** 60%
**Armour:** 13mm-25.4mm

**Development**
The Sexton, full designation 25 pounder self-propelled, tracked, was developed in Canada. The first prototype was built late in 1942, production commenced early in 1943 at the Montreal Locomotive Works. A total of 2,150 were built before production was completed late in 1945. The vehicle had an open roof although a cover was provided for use in bad weather. The Sexton served with the British Army until the 1950s.

**Variants**
The Sexton GPO — a Sexton without its armament — used as a Gun Position Officer vehicle. It has additional communications equipment as well as tables and seats.

**Employment**
The Sexton is still used by India and South Africa.

*Sexton SP gun of the South African Army.*
South African Army

# Type 59 MBT

China

### Development
Since the late 1950s China has been producing the Soviet T-54 MBT under the designation of the Type 59. First production models were not fitted with any infra-red equipment or a stabilisation system for the main armament. More recent production vehicles have a full range of night vision equipment and a laser rangefinder which is mounted externally and moves in elevation with the main armament.

### Employment
Albania, China, Congo, Kampuchea, North Korea, Pakistan, Sudan, Tanzania and Vietnam.

*Chinese Type 59 MBT on display in Australia.*
Paul Handel

# Type 62 Light Tank

## China

**Armament:** 1 × 85mm gun, elevation +18°, depression −5°
1 × 7.62mm coaxial MG
1 × 12.7mm AA MG
**Crew:** 4
**Length:** 8.27m (gun forward), 6.91m (hull)
**Width:** 3.25m
**Height:** 2.19m (turret roof)
**G/clearance:** 0.37m
**Weight:** 18,000kg (loaded)
**Armour:** 14mm
**Engine:** V-12 diesel developing 520hp at 2,000rpm
**Speed:** 50km/h (road), 9km/h (water)
**Range:** 300km
**Fuel:** 545 litres
**Fording:** Amphibious
**V/obstacle:** 1m
**Trench:** 2.8m
**Gradient:** 60%
(*Note*: Above data is provisional)

### Development
The Type 62 light tank has an all welded hull that is very similar in appearance to the Soviet PT-76 light amphibious tank but has a new turret which is virtually a scaled down version of that fitted to the Chinese Type 59 MBT. The engine installed in the Type 62 is the same as that installed in the Type 59 MBT.

The Type 62 is fully amphibious being propelled in the water by two water jets at the rear of the hull. Before entering the water a trim vane is erected at the front of the hull and the bilge pumps switched on. Some vehicles have been seen fitted with a 12.7mm Type 54 MG mounted on the turret roof for anti-aircraft defence, the Type 54 being the Soviet DShKM manufactured in China.

### Employment
China, Pakistan, Sudan, Tanzania and Vietnam.

*Type 62 light amphibious tank knocked out in Vietnam.*

# Type 63 Light Tank

## China

*Type 63 light tanks.*

**Armament:** 1 × 85mm gun, elevation +20°, depression −4° (47 rounds carried)
1 × 7.62mm coaxial MG (1,750 rounds)
1 × 12.7mm AA MG (1,250 rounds)
**Crew:** 4
**Length:** 7.90m (gun forward), 5.55m (hull)
**Width:** 2.86m
**Height:** 2.55m
**Weight:** 21,000kg
**G/pressure:** 0.71kg/sq cm
**Engine:** Diesel developing 380hp at 1,800rpm
**Speed:** 60km/h (road)
**Range:** 500km
**Fuel:** 730 litres
**Fording:** 1.30m
**V/obstacle:** 0.7m

**Trench:** 2.5m
**Gradient:** 60%
**Armour:** 14mm (max)
(*Note:* The above data is provisional)

**Development**
The Type 63 light tank is virtually a scaled down Type 59 MBT and its main armament is believed to be the same as that fitted to the Type 62 light tank. The Type 63 has no amphibious capability, no NBC system and has not been observed fitted with any type of night vision equipment.

**Employment**
Albania, Congo, China, North Korea, Mali, Sudan, Tanzania and Zaire.

# K-63 APC                                                    China

**Armament:** 1 × 12.7mm MG
**Crew:** 4 + 10
**Length:** 5.45m
**Width:** 2.96m
**Height:** 2.61m
**Weight:** 12,500kg
**Armour:** 10mm
**Engine:** 6-cylinder diesel developing 181hp at 1,300rpm
**Speed:** 50km/h (road), 5.7km/h (water)
**Range:** 400km
**Fuel:** 490 litres
**Fording:** Amphibious
**V/obstacle:** 0.9m
**Trench:** 2.1m
**Gradient:** 60%
(*Note:* The above data is provisional)

**Development**
The K-63 APC was developed in the 1960s and until the correct Chinese designation became known was

*K-63 APC undergoing trials in Australia.*
Paul Handel

called the M1967 or the M1970. It is possible that the K-63 uses some components of the Type 62 light amphibious tank.

The vehicle has a four-man crew consisting of commander, radio operator, driver and 12.7mm machine gunner. The K-63 is fully amphibious being propelled in the water by its tracks; before entering the water a trim vane is erected at the front of the vehicle. A single firing port is provided in either side of the hull, but as far as it is known it does not have a NBC system or any night vision equipment.

**Variants**
It is probable that anti-tank, command and mortar versions of the K-63 exist but the only two known versions are a 122mm SP gun and a multiple rocket launcher. The former is the basic chassis adopted to take the Type 54 howitzer which is the older Soviet M1938 built in China while the latter is a K-63 with the 107mm (12-round) Type 63 multiple rocket system mounted on the roof.

**Employment**
Albania, China, North Korea, Sudan, Tanzania, Vietnam and Zaire.

# Type 63 SP AA Gun                                    China

**Armament:** 2 × 37mm guns, elevation +85°,
depression −5°
**Length:** 6.432m (guns forward)
**Height:** 2.955m (turret top), 3.268m (inc AA sight)
(Other data is similar to T-34/85 tank)

**Development**
The Type 63 SP AA gun is essentially a T-34/85 tank
with its turret removed and replaced by a new turret

*Type 63 SP AA gun on display in the United States.*
Christopher F. Foss

armed with twin 37mm guns identical to those used
in the towed system. Turret traverse and gun
elevation is manual and each gun has a cyclic rate of
fire of 160/180 rounds/min but practical rate of fire
is 80rounds/min. Effective vertical AA range is
8,000m and the following types of fixed ammunition
can be fired: API-T with a m/v of 880m/sec; HEI-T
with a m/v of 880m/sec; HVAP with a m/v of
960m/sec.

**Employment**
China and Vietnam.

# Type 56 APC                                          China

China uses the Soviet-supplied BTR-152 (6 × 6)
APC under the designation of the Type 56 APC. It is
possible that this has also been manufactured in

China as quantities of this vehicle have been
supplied to a number of other countries by China
including Kampuchea, Tanzania and Vietnam.

# Type 55 APC                                          China

China uses the Soviet-supplied BTR-40 (4 × 4) APC
under the designation of the Type 55 APC. It is
probable that this vehicle has also been

manufactured in China as quantities of this vehicle
have been supplied to a number of other countries by
China including Kampuchea, Tanzania and Vietnam.

# AFV Production                    Czechoslovakia

From the 1960s Czechoslovakia produced the Soviet-designed T-55 MBT for both the home and export markets but this has recently been phased out in favour of the Soviet-designed T-72 MBT. In addition to producing the OT-62 APC, which is essentially an improved version of the Soviet BTR-50PK, Czechoslovakia has also manufactured vehicles to meet its own specific requirements including the OT-64 (8 × 8) APC, M53/59 twin 30mm SP AA gun and the more recent 152mm (8 × 8) SP gun/howitzer. Unconfirmed reports have indicated that Czechoslovakia may be producing the Soviet BMP-1 MICV and the 122mm M1974 SP howitzer.

# OT-64 APC                         Czechoslovakia

**Data:** OT-64C(1)
**Armament:** 1 × 14.5mm MG, elevation +29.5°, depression −6° (500 rounds carried)
1 × 7.62mm coaxial MG (2,000 rounds)
**Crew:** 2 + 15
**Length:** 7.44m
**Width:** 2.55m
**Height:** 2.71m (inc turret)
**G/clearance:** 0.46m
**Weight:** 14,500kg
**Armour:** 10mm
**Track:** 1.86m
**Wheelbase:** 1.3m + 2.15m + 1.3m
**Engine:** Tatra T-928-18, V-8 diesel developing 180hp at 2,000rpm
**Speed:** 94.4km/h (road), 9km/h (water)
**Range:** 710km
**Fuel:** 320 litres
**Fording:** Amphibious
**V/obstacle:** 0.50m
**Trench:** 2.00m
**Gradient:** 60%

## Development
The OT-64 was developed from 1959 to meet the requirements of Czechoslovakia and Poland and is used by these countries in place of the Soviet BTR-60 (8 × 8) APC.

Standard equipment on all vehicles includes a central tyre pressure regulation system, powered

*OT-64C (1) with roof hatches open.*

steering on the front four wheels, overpressure NBC system and a front mounted winch.

All members of the family are fully amphibious being propelled in the water by two propellers at the rear of the hull. Before entering the water a trim vane is erected at the front of the hull and the bilge pumps switched on.

## Variants
*OT-64A (SKOT):* Original member of series. Czechoslovak versions are unarmed while Polish models have a 7.62mm MG. Some have been seen fitted with 'Sagger' ATGWs over rear troop compartment.

*OT-64B (SKOT-2):* Has plinth with 7.62mm or 12.7mm MG fitted with shield to give front and side protection to gunner. Only used by Poland and probably interim model pending delivery of turrets.

*OT-64C (1) (SKOT-2A):* Fitted with same turret as Soviet BRDM-2 (4 × 4) reconnaissance vehicle and BTR-60PB (8 × 8) APC.

*OT-64C (2) (SKOT-2AP):* Only used by Poland and is similar to OT-62C (1) except that it has a new turret with a curved top which allows the 14.5mm and 7.62mm machine guns to be elevated to a max of +89.5° so enabling them to be used in the AA role. The turret is also fitted to the OT-62C tracked APC. Some vehicles have been observed with a 'Sagger' ATGW mounted either side of the turret.

*OT-64 Command Vehicle:* Two versions are in service, designated R-2 and R-3, these have additional communications equipment and aerials fitted.

*OT-64 Recovery Vehicle:* Officially called the Armoured Repair and Maintenance Vehicle SKOT-WPT and fitted with a light crane.

**Employment**
Czechoslovakia, India, Iraq, Libya, Morocco, Poland, Sudan and Uganda.

# OT-62 APC

Czechoslovakia

**Data:** OT-62B
**Armament:** 1 × 82mm recoilless gun T-21 (outside turret)
1 × 7.62mm MG M59 (inside turret)
**Crew:** 2 + 18
**Length:** 7.08m
**Width:** 3.14m
**Height:** 2.23m (inc turret), 2.038m (w/o turret)
**G/clearance:** 0.364m
**Weight:** 15,000kg
**G/pressure:** 0.53kg/sq cm
**Engine:** Model PV-6, 6-cylinder, in-line diesel developing 300hp at 1,800rpm
**Speed:** 58.4km/h (road), 11km/h (water)
**Range:** 460km
**Fording:** Amphibious
**V/obstacle:** 1.10m
**Trench:** 2.80m
**Gradient:** 65%
**Armour:** 10mm-14mm

**Development**
The OT-62 is the Czechoslovak equivalent of the Soviet BTR-50PK APC and is almost identical to the BTR-50PU Model 2 command vehicle. Czech built vehicles can be distinguished from their Soviet counterparts as the latter have a distinct chamfer between the top and sides of their hulls.

The OT-62 has a more powerful engine than the

Soviet BTR-50 series which gives it a higher road and water speed, all models of the OT-62 have an NBC system. In the Polish Army the OT-62 is called the TOPAS.

**Variants**
*Model 1 (OT-62A):* This has two projecting bays (similar to the Soviet BTR-50PU Model 2), side doors in the troop compartment and two rectangular overhead hatches. No armament is fitted although an 82mm recoilless M59 may be carried and fired on the rear decking.
*Model 2 (OT-62B):* This is similar to the above model but in addition has a small turret on the right bay. This is armed with a 7.62mm M59 MG, a T-21 recoilless rifle can be mounted on the outside of the turret.
*Model 3 (OT-62C):* This model is fitted with the same turret that is fitted to the OT-64C(2), it is armed with a 14.5mm and a 7.62mm MG, turret has a traverse of 360°. The turret is mounted over the rear troop compartment, in the centre of the vehicle. This model has a crew of 3 + 12 and a height of 2.73m. Its Czech designation is TOPAS 2AP.

Other versions of the OT-62 include an ambulance, command vehicle and an armoured recovery vehicle called the WPT-TOPAS. This has a winch, crane, tools and welding equipment with a 7.62mm MG with a shield being mounted on the right bay.

**Employment**
Angola, Bulgaria, Czechoslovakia, Egypt, India, Iraq, Israel, Libya, Morocco, Poland and Sudan.

*OT-62 Model 3 of the Egyptian Army.*
Egyptian Army

*Basic OT-810 APC without armament.*

# OT-810 APC

Czechoslovakia

**Armament:** 1 × 7.62mm MG
**Crew:** 2 + 10
**Length:** 5.8m
**Width:** 2.1m
**Height:** 1.75m
**G/clearance:** 0.3m
**Weight:** 8,500kg
**Engine:** Tatra 928-3 V-8 6-cylinder diesel developing 120hp
**Speed:** 52.5km/h
**Range:** 520km
**Fuel:** 160 litres
**Fording:** 0.5m
**V/obstacle:** 0.255m
**Trench:** 1.98m
**Gradient:** 50%
**Armour:** 7mm-12mm

**Development**
With the German occupation of Czechoslovakia during World War 2 production of the Sd Kfz 251 half-track APC was undertaken at the Skoda Works in Pilsen. Production continued for a period after the war and many German vehicles were subsequently rebuilt with overhead armour protection and a new Tatra diesel engine. The OT-810 has no NBC system, no infra-red night vision equipment and no provision for deep fording.

**Variants**
Many OT-810s have been fitted with the 82mm M59A recoilless gun over the rear troop compartment, firing forwards.

**Employment**
Czechoslovakia.

# 152mm SP Gun-Howitzer

Czechoslovakia

*Czechoslovakian 152mm SP gun/howitzer from the front.*

**Armament:** 1 × 152mm gun/howitzer, elevation +60°, depression −3°
1 × 12.7mm AA MG
**Crew:** 6
**Length:** 10.40m (gun forward), 8.87m (hull)
**Width:** 2.722m (hull), 2.97m (turret)
**Height:** 2.03m (cab), 3.525m (AA MG)
**Weight:** 23,000kg
**Wheelbase:** 1.50m + 2.72m + 1.405m
**Engine:** Tatra 12-cylinder multi-fuel developing 320hp
**Speed:** 80km/h
**Range:** 1,000km
**Fuel:** 520 litres
**Fording:** 1.4m
**V/obstacle:** 0.6m
**Trench:** 1.6m
**Gradient:** 60%
(*Note:* above specification is provisional)

**Development**
During a parade held in Czechoslovakia late in 1980 a 152mm SP gun/howitzer based on a modified Tatra 813 (8 × 8) truck chassis was shown for the first time.

The fully armoured cab is at the front, fully enclosed turret in the centre and the engine at the rear. Before firing, hydraulic jacks are lowered to the ground, one each side, between the second and third axles and one at the rear.

The ordnance is a Czechoslovakian design and has a range of between 15,000 and 20,000m firing separate loading ammunition. A 12.7mm DShKM MG is mounted on the turret roof on the right side for local and AA defence.

Like the Tatra 813 the SP gun has a central tyre pressure regulation system and is assumed to have infra-red night vision equipment and a NBC system.

**Employment**
It is not known if this SP gun/howitzer is in service with the Czechoslovakian forces in quantity.

# M53/59 SP AA Vehicle

## Czechoslovakia

**Armament:** 2 × 30mm M53 cannon, elevation +85°, depression −10°, traverse 360°
**Crew:** 5
**Length:** 6.92m
**Width:** 2.35m
**Height:** 2.585m (w/o magazines), 2.95m (with magazines)
**G/clearance:** 0.40m
**Weight:** 10,300kg
**Track:** 1.87m (front), 1.755m (rear)
**Wheelbase:** 3.58m + 1.12m
**Engine:** Tatra T912-2 6-cylinder, in-line, water cooled diesel developing 110hp at 2,200rpm
**Speed:** 60km/h (road)
**Range:** 500km
**Fuel:** 120 litres
**Fording:** 0.80m
**V/obstacle:** 0.46m
**Trench:** 0.69m
**Gradient:** 60%
**Armour:** 10mm

**Development/Variants**
The M53/59 twin 30mm SP AA system is based on the Praga V3S 6 × 6 truck chassis. The guns have a vertical feed for loading whereas the towed version of these guns have a horizontal feed system. The guns have a cyclic rate of fire of 450/500 rounds/gun/min but the practical rate is 150 rounds/min. It fires HEI or API rounds, in clips of 10 (each magazine holds 50 rounds) these have an effective anti-aircraft range of 3,000m. The guns can be used both against ground and air targets.

The vehicle has a crew of five, the driver, the commander, who sits next to the driver and is provided with a transparent observation cupola on the right of the superstructure, gunner with the guns and two ammunition members. There is no provision for deep wading or radar control.

**Employment**
In service with Czechoslovakia, Libya and Yugoslavia.

*M53/59 with guns forward; the vertical magazines for the 30mm guns can be seen in this photograph.*

# Walid APC

Egypt

*Walid APC captured by Israel.* Kensuke Ebata

## Development

The Walid APC was developed in the 1960s by the NASR Automotive Plant at Helwan and is essentially a 4 × 4 Magirus Deutz chassis fitted with an armoured body.

In appearance the Walid is very similar to the Soviet BTR-40 (4 × 4) APC but the latter can be distinguished from the Egyptian vehicle by its vertical sides instead of the sloped sides to the troop compartment.

The infantry enter and leave the Walid by a door in the rear of the hull on which is mounted the spare wheel. The open topped troop compartment is provided with firing ports in the sides and rear. The vehicle has no NBC system, no night vision equipment and no amphibious capability.

## Employment

In service with Algeria, Burundi, Egypt, Israel, Sudan and Yemen Arab Republic (North).

# AMX-32 MBT

France

**Data:** First prototype
**Armament:** 1 × 105mm gun, elevation +20°, depression −8° (47 rounds carried)
1 × 20mm cannon coaxial with main armament (500 rounds)
1 × 7.62mm AA MG (2,050 rounds)
2 × 3 smoke dischargers
**Crew:** 4
**Length:** 9.48m (gun forward), 6.59m (hull)
**Width:** 3.24m
**Height:** 2.96m (cupola), 2.29m (turret roof)
**G/clearance:** 0.45m

**Weight:** 38,000kg (loaded), 36,000kg (empty)
**G/pressure:** 0.85kg/sq cm
**Engine:** Hispano-Suiza HS110 12-cylinder water-cooled supercharged multi-fuel developing 700hp at 2,400rpm
**Speed:** 65km/h
**Range:** 530km (road)
**Fording:** 1.3m (w/o preparation), 2.2m (with preparation), 4m (with snorkel)
**V/obstacle:** 0.93m
**Trench:** 2.9m
**Gradient:** 60%

*AMX-32 MBT.* GIAT

## Development
The AMX-32 MBT has been developed by the Atelier de Construction d'Issy-les-Moulineaux specifically for the export market with the first prototype being completed by 1979. The tank is based on the earlier AMX-30 MBT but has improvements in both armour protection and firepower.

Although the prototype of the AMX-32 was armed with the same 105mm gun as installed in the AMX-30, the second prototype is armed with a 120mm smooth bore gun that can fire French and German ammunition. Mounted coaxial with the main armament is a 20mm cannon which can be elevated to +40° enabling it to be used against low flying aircraft.

The AMX-32 has a new all welded turret with improved armour protection and increased armour protection is also provided over the frontal arc, side skirts provide some protection against attack by HEAT projectiles.

The COTAC fire control system of the AMX-32 is based on that installed in the AMX-10RC (6 × 6) reconnaissance vehicle and includes a laser rangefinder, LLLTV camera mounted coaxial with the main armament and screens for both the tank commander and gunner and a stabilised M527 periscopic sight for the tank commander.

The engine of the AMX-32 is the same as that installed in the AMX-30 but a new cooling system has been installed as well as the improved transmission also fitted to the AMX-30B2 MBT. The suspension has also been improved to give a better ride across rough country.

## Variants
There are no variants of the AMX-32 MBT.

## Employment
Prototypes. Not yet in production or service.

# AMX-30 MBT                                    France

**Armament:** 1 × 105mm gun, elevation +20°, depression −8° (50 rounds carried)
1 × 12.7mm MG or 20mm cannon coaxial with main armament, it can be elevated to +40° (1,050 rounds)
1 × 7.62mm MG on commander's cupola (2,050 rounds)
2 × 2 smoke grenade launchers
**Crew:** 4
**Length:** 9.48m (gun forward), 6.59m (hull only)
**Width:** 3.10m
**Height:** 2.86m (top of cupola)
2.29m (turret roof)
**G/clearance:** 0.45m
**Weight:** 36,000kg (loaded)
**G/pressure:** 0.77kg/sq cm

**Engine:** Hispano-Suiza HS-110, 12 cylinder multi-fuel, water cooled engine developing 720hp at 2,400rpm.
**Speed:** 65km/h
**Range:** 600km (road)
**Fuel:** 970 litres
**Fording:** 1.3m, 2.2m (with preparation), 4.00m (with snorkel)
**V/obstacle:** 0.93m
**Trench:** 2.90m
**Gradient:** 60%

## Development
In 1956, France, Germany and Italy decided to build a common tank. This idea did not work out and France decided to build the AMX-30. The first

*AMX-30 MBT.* GIAT

prototype AMX-30 was completed in 1960, being followed by the second prototype in 1961. These were followed by a further seven models in 1963 and pre-production tanks in 1965. In 1966 the tank entered production and the first French M47 units were re-equipped with AMX-30s in the summer of 1967.

The vehicle is fitted with infra-red driving and fighting equipment, it also has an NBC system and can be fitted with a snorkel. The 105mm gun can fire either HEAT (m/v 1,000m/sec), HE (m/v 700m/sec), smoke (m/v 696m/sec), illuminating (m/v 290m/sec) and the new APFSDS with a m/v of 1,525m/sec.

### Variants

|  | ARV | Bridgelayer | Roland |
|---|---|---|---|
| **Length:** (overall) | 7.53m | 11.40m | 6.65m |
| **Width:** (overall) | 3.15m | 3.95m | 3.10m |
| **Height:** (overall) | 2.65m | 4.29m | 3.02m |
| **Weight:** (loaded) | 38,000kg | 42,500kg | 33,000kg |
| **Crew:** | 4 | 3 | 3 |

*AMX-30 B2:* This is a development of the AMX-30 for the French Army and has the automatic COTAC integrated fire control system, laser rangefinder, LLLTV camera for engaging targets at night, new NBC system and clutch, combined steering and drive mechanism of the basic AMX-30 replaced by an hydraulic torque converter, an electro-hydraulically controlled gearbox with forward/reverse lever and five ratios and hydrostatic steering. In addition to new production vehicles for the French Army some existing AMX-30s will be brought up to this standard.

*AMX-30 Export Model:* This has no NBC system, no snorkel or infra-red equipment and a simple cupola.

*AMX-30S:* This model has been developed for use in hot climates; it is fitted with sandshields and its engine develops only 620hp at 2,400rpm; the gearbox has been modified. It is fitted with a CILAS/Sopelem day/night sight.

*AMX-30 Shahine:* This has a total of six Crotale missiles in the ready-to-launch position and is in service only with Saudi Arabia.

*AMX-30 AA tank.* Thomson-CSF

*French version of the Roland 2 SAM system mounted on an AMX-30 chassis.* Euromissile

*AMX-30 AA Tank:* This is simply an AMX-30 chassis with the turret of the AMX-13 AA tank. It is in service only with Saudi Arabia; there is a separate entry for this system at the end of the French section.

*AMX-30 155mm GCT:* For full details see separate entry.

*AMX-30 ACRA:* An AMX-30 tank was used to test the 142mm ACRA anti-tank system. In 1973 however the ACRA system was cancelled.

*AMX-30 Recovery Tank:* This is designed to carry out repairs in the field and to carry out this role it is fitted with a crane (can lift 15,000kg), main winch (35,000kg with 100m of cable), auxiliary winch (3,500kg and 120m of cable) and a dozer blade at the front. It is armed with a 7.62mm MG and smoke dischargers. This model is in service with the French Army and has been exported. An improved model is known as the AMX-30DI.

*AMX-30 Bridgelayer Tank:* This tank can lay a class 50 bridge across a 20m ditch. The bridge is 22m long, 3.1m wide (w/o widening panels) and 3.92m wide (with widening panels), when laid out. It is only in service with the French Army.

*AMX-30 Combat Engineer Tractor:* Under development for French Army as the replacement for the AMX-13 VCG in the late 1980s. Will be similar in appearance to ARV but based on AMX-30B2 chassis.

*AMX-30 Flail Tank:* Under development for the French Army and based on the AMX-30 MBT chassis, is fitted with a 7,000kg retractable frame with 12 heavy flails.

*AMX-30 Roland AA Tank:* This is now in production and has two Roland missiles in the ready-to-fire position, with a further eight in reserve. The first model to enter service with French Army was the clear weather Roland 1, this being followed by the all weather Roland 2 system.

*Pluton Weapon System:* This is an AMX-30 chassis fitted with a Pluton tactical nuclear missile with a range of 120km.

*AMX-30 Training Tank:* This is an AMX-30 on which the turret has been replaced by an observation cupola.

*AMX-30 with TSE 6000 Javelot:* This is a close-air defence system under development by Thomson-CSF.

*AMX-30 with Rapace radar:* An AMX-30 has been fitted with the EMD Rapace tank detection radar for trials purposes.

**Employment**

The AMX-30 is used by Chile, France, Greece, Iraq, Lebanon, Peru, Qatar, Saudi Arabia, Spain (manufactured under licence) and Venezuela.

AMX-30 AVLB in
travelling position.
GIAT

AMX-30 ARV.  GIAT

# AMX-13 Light Tank France

**Data:** AMX-13 with new 90mm gun
**Armament:** 1 × 90mm gun, elevation + 12.5°, depression −5.5° (32 rounds carried)
2 × 7.62mm MGs — coaxial and on commander's cupola (optional) — (3,600 rounds). Some AMX-13s have 7.5mm MGs
2 × 2 smoke dischargers.
**Crew:** 3
**Length:** 6.36m (with gun), 4.88 (w/o gun)
**Width:** 2.50m
**Height:** 2.30m (cupola)
**G/clearance:** 0.37m
**Weight:** 15,000kg (loaded), 13,000kg (empty)
**G/pressure:** 0.76kg/sq cm
**Engine:** SOFAM 8Gxb 8-cylinder water cooled, petrol engine developing 250hp at 3,200rpm (built by Renault)
**Speed:** 60km/h (road)
**Range:** 350km-400km (road)
**Fuel:** 480 litres
**Fording:** 0.60m
**V/obstacle:** 0.65m
**Trench:** 1.60m
**Gradient:** 60%
**Armour:** 10mm-40mm

## Development
The design of the AMX-13 started shortly after the end of World War 2 with AMX standing for the design centre (Atelier de Constructions d'Issy-les-Moulineaux) and 13 for the original requested weight. The first prototype was built in 1949 and deliveries to the French Army started in 1952. The AMX-13 was originally built by the Atelier de Construction Roanne but when this facility was tooled up for production of the AMX-30 MBT production of the whole AMX-13 family was transferred to Creusot-Loire. The AMX-13 tank chassis has been used for a whole range of AFVs, a few of which are described below, the rest later in the book.

## Variants
*AMX-13 Model 51:* This was the first model to enter service. It was armed with a 75mm gun in an FL-10 turret and a 7.5mm or 7.62mm MG and four smoke dischargers. 37 rounds of 75mm ammunition are

*AMX-13 bridgelayer in travelling order.*
E. C. P. Armées

AMX-13 light tank with SS-11 ATGWs.
E. C. P. Armées

carried, of these 12 rounds were in two revolver type magazines with six rounds each. This enabled the tank to fire 12 rounds very quickly. The drawback being that these magazines then had to be re-loaded again from outside the vehicle.

*AMX-13 with FL-11 turret:* This was designed in the mid-1950s for use in Algeria. It is armed with a short 75mm gun in an FL-11 turret.

*AMX-13 Model 58 with FL-12 turret:* This was designed specifically for the export market and is armed with a 105mm gun that fires HEAT projectiles with a muzzle velocity of 800m/sec and HE projectiles with a muzzle velocity of 700m/sec, the former will penetrate 360mm of armour. A total of 32 rounds of 105mm ammunition is carried.

*AMX-13 with 90mm gun:* This is the current production model and is armed with a 90mm gun whose barrel is fitted with a two-piece thermal sleeve. The gun fires the following types of fin-stabilised ammunition: HE, HEAT (m/v 950m/sec and will penetrate 320mm of armour at an incidence of 0°), smoke and canister. This and other AMX-13 light tanks can now be fitted with passive night vision equipment and a laser rangefinder.
Undergoing trials is an AMX-13 light tank with diesel engine.

*AMX-13 Model 51 with SS-11 missiles:* This retains its gun armament but also has four SS-11 ATGW,

these are mounted two either side of the gun. The missiles have an effective range of 3,000m. This system is in service with the French Army.

*AMX-13 with HOT ATGW:* This version was developed to prototype stage but has not been adopted by French Army.

*AMX Armoured Recovery Vehicle (Char de Dépannage Model 55):* This has spades at the rear, 15tonne capacity winch, an auxiliary winch, 5tonne A frame, lighting equipment and tools. The French ARVs are armed with a 7.5 or 7.62mm MG, the Netherlands ARVs have six smoke dischargers and a 7.62mm MG. Basic data is similar to the AMX-13 except: Crew: 3; Width: 2.60m; Length: 5.515m; Weight: 15,300kg; Height: 2.682m.

*AMX-13 Bridgelayer:* Called Poseur de Pont by the French. It is a modified AMX-13 chassis fitted with a scissors bridge. When opened out this is 7.15m in length and can take tanks up to class 25, two of these bridges used together can take class 50 tanks. Basic data is similar to the AMX-13 except: Weight: 19,700kg (with bridge); Length: 7.75m (with bridge); Width: 3.35 (with bridge); Height: 4.30m (with bridge).

*AMX-13 Training Tank:* This is an AMX tank without its turret and used for driver training.

**Employment**
Algeria, Argentina, Chile, Djibouti, Dominican Republic, Ecuador, France, El Salvador, India, Indonesia, Ivory Coast, Morocco, Netherlands, Nepal, Peru, Saudi Arabia, Singapore, Tunisia and Venezuela.

# AMX-10RC Reconnaissance Vehicle     France

**Armament:** 1 × 105mm gun (38 rounds carried)
1 × 7.62mm coaxial MG (4,000 rounds)
2 × 2 smoke dischargers
**Crew:** 4
**Length:** 9.13m (gun forward), 6.35m (hull)
**Width:** 2.86m
**Height:** 2.68m (overall)
**G/clearance:** 0.3m (adjustable)
**Weight:** 15,800kg (loaded)
**Track:** 2.425m
**Wheelbase:** 1.55m + 1.55m
**Engine:** Hispano-Suiza HS-115 8-cylinder
supercharged diesel developing 280hp at 3,000rpm
**Speed:** 85km/h (road), 7km/h (water)
**Range:** 800km
**Fording:** Amphibious
**V/obstacle:** 0.7m
**Trench:** 1.15m
**Gradient:** 60%

## Development
Design of the AMX-10RC commenced at the AMX in 1970 with the first of three prototypes being completed in 1971. First production AMX-10RCs were delivered to the French Army in 1979 as the replacement for the Panhard EBR heavy armoured car.

The AMX-10RC has an aluminium hull and turret and uses many automotive components of the AMX-10P MICV.

The 105mm gun has an elevation of +20° and a depression of −8°, turret traverse being a full 360°. It fires a fin-stabilised HEAT-T round with a m/v of 1,120m/sec or a HE round with a m/v of 800m/sec. The fire control system includes a laser rangefinder and a passive night TV system, the latter having been developed by Thomson-CSF especially for the vehicle.

The vehicle is fully amphibious being propelled in the water by two water jets, one each side of the hull. A NBC system is also provided as is a passive night periscope for the driver. The AMX-10RC is fitted with a hydropneumatic suspension system which allows the driver to adjust the ground clearance from 0.2 to 0.6m to suit the type of ground being crossed.

## Variants
A prototype of a 6 × 6 wheeled APC called the AMX-10R was shown in 1971 but this has not been put into production. A tracked version of the AMX-10RC has also been built, this is called the AMX-10C, and weighs 14,500kg, but so far has not entered production.

## Employment
In service with France and Morocco, on order for one other undisclosed country.

*AMX-10RC 6×6 reconnaissance vehicle.* GIAT

34

# EBR 75 Heavy Armoured Car France

**Armament:** See below
**Length:** 6.15m (o/a FL-11 turret); 5.56m (vehicle only)
**Width:** 2.42m
**Height:** 2.32m (FL-11 on 8 wheels), 2.24m (FL-11 on 4 wheels)
**G/clearance:** 0.41m (on 8 wheels), 0.33m (on 4 wheels)
**Weight:** 13,500kg (loaded FL-11)
**Track:** 1.74m
**G/pressure:** 0.75kg/sq cm (on 8 wheels)
**Engine:** Panhard 12-cylinder petrol engine, developing 200hp at 3,700rpm
**Crew:** 4
**Speed:** 105km/h (road)
**Range:** 650km
**Fuel:** 380litres
**Fording:** 1.20m
**V/obstacle:** 0.40m
**Trench:** 2.00m
**Gradient:** 60%
**Armour:** 10mm-40mm

## Development
In 1937 Panhard started to design an 8 × 8 armoured car for the French Army. A prototype was completed in December 1939 and the vehicle was given the Panhard No Model 201. The vehicle, together with its drawings, was lost during the war. Development work started again after the war and the first postwar prototype was completed in July 1948. This had an FL-11 turret and was called the EBR 75 (Engin Blindé Reconnaissance), its Panhard Designation being Model 212. The vehicle entered production in August 1950 and production was completed in 1960 by which time 1,200 had been built. The EBR has a number of unusual features. It has a crew of four which consists of a commander, gunner and two drivers (one at the front and one at the rear). All eight wheels are powered and when crossing rough country its centre four wheels, which have steel treads, can be lowered into position. All of

*EBR 75 with FL-11 turret mounting a 90mm gun. Panhard*

the turrets used, the FL-10 and FL-11, are of the oscillating type. In the French Army, the EBR 75 is now being slowly replaced by the AMX-10 RC (6 × 6) vehicle.

## Variants
*EBR 75 with FL-11 turret:* Has a 75mm gun, elevation + 15°, depression −10°, with 56 rounds of ammunition. This was the first model to enter service. A 7.5mm MG is mounted coaxial with the main armament and both drivers have a fixed 7.5mm MG that fires forwards, although this is not normally fitted.
*EBR 75 with FL-10 turret:* This has the same turret as that fitted to the AMX-13 light tank. As far as is known none of this model, which weighed 15,200kg compared to the standard EBR with FL-11 turret which weighs 13,500kg, remain in service.
*EBR 75 with 90mm gun in FL-11 turret:* This is the latest version and mounts a 90mm gun that fires fin-stabilised ammunition, all earlier versions have been refitted with this new gun.
*EBR AA Vehicle:* One of these was built in 1952. It consisted of an EBR chassis on which was mounted a turret armed with 2 × 30mm cannon.
*EBR ETT APC:* This had the Panhard No Model 238, the first vehicle was built in 1957 and a total of 30 were built. There were two models — one had a single large MG turret and the other had two small turrets, one at each end of the vehicle. Some vehicles had their metal centre wheels replaced by conventional wheels with tyres. This is used by Portugal.

## Employment
Used by France, Mauritania, Morocco, Portugal and Tunisia.

# Renault VBC-90 Armoured Car

France

**Armament:** 1 × 90mm gun, elevation +15°, depression −8° (47 rounds carried)
2 × 7.62mm MG — coaxial and AA (optional) — (4,000 rounds)
2 smoke dischargers either side of turret
**Crew:** 3
**Length:** 8.152m (gun forward), 5.495m (hull)
**Width:** 2.49m
**Height:** 2.55m (turret top)
**Weight:** 12,800kg
**Track:** 2.035m
**Wheelbase:** 1.5m + 1.5m
**Engine:** MAN D.2356 HM 72 in-line air-cooled diesel developing 235hp at 2,200rpm
**Speed:** 92km/h
**Range:** 1,000km
**Fording:** 1.2m
**V/obstacle:** 0.6m
**Trench:** 1m
**Gradient:** 60%

*Renault VBC-90 (6×6) armoured car.*
Renault Vehicules Industriels

## Development/Variants

The Renault VBC-90 has been developed specifically for the export market by Renault Vehicles Industriels and was shown for the first time in 1979. It shares many common components with the Renault VAB (4 × 4 and 6 × 6) series of APC, including the engine, transmission and suspension but has a new all welded hull with the engine at the rear.

The vehicle has a GIAT-developed TS90 turret which is also fitted to the Panhard ERC 90 F4 Sagie (6 × 6) armoured car and to the AMX-10 PAC 90 fire support vehicle. This has a rifled gun that fires fin-stabilised canister, HE, HEAT and smoke projectiles with an APFSDS projectile being developed.

A wide range of optional equipment can be fitted including a 7.62mm AA MG, laser rangefinder, passive night vision equipment, power-assisted traverse, NBC system and a front-mounted winch.

## Employment

In service with United Arab Emirates and at least one other country. On order for French Gendarmerie.

# Panhard ERC 90 F4 Sagie Armoured Car

France

**Armament:** 1 × 90mm gun, elevation +15°, depression −8° (20 rounds carried)
2 × 7.62mm MGs — coaxial and AA (optional) — (2,000 rounds)
2 smoke dischargers either side of turret
**Crew:** 3
**Length:** 7.785m (gun forward), 5.21m (hull)
**Width:** 2.495m
**Height:** 2.24m (overall), 1.188m (hull top)
**Weight:** 7,800kg (loaded)
**Track:** 2.155m

**Wheelbase:** 1.63m + 1.22m
**Engine:** Peugeot V-6 petrol developing 140hp at 5,250rpm
**Speed:** 110km/h (road), 4.5km/h (water, propelled by wheels), 9.5km/h (water, propelled by waterjets)
**Range:** 950km
**Fording:** 1.2m (amphibious optional)
**V/obstacle:** 1m
**Trench:** 1m
**Gradient:** 60%
**Armour:** 8mm-12mm

### Development
The ERC (Engine Reconnaissance Cannon) has been developed for the export market by Panhard. First prototypes were completed in 1977 with the first production vehicles following in 1979. The range shares many common components such as engine, transmission and suspension, with the VCR range of 6 × 6 APCs also developed by Panhard.

All vehicles have 6 × 6 drive with steering on front wheels, when travelling on roads the centre wheels are raised clear of the ground. Two amphibious models are available, one being propelled by its wheels when afloat and the other being propelled by two waterjets.

The ERC 90 F4 Sagie has the same turret as that fitted to the Renault VBC-90 armoured car described in the previous entry.

### Variants
*ERC 90 Lynx:* Armed with turret-mounted 90mm

*Panhard ERC 90 F4 Sagie armoured car firing its 90mm gun.* Panhard

gun, 7.62mm coaxial MG and 7.62mm AA MG.
*ERC TG 120 Guepard:* Fitted with SAMM TG 120 turret armed with 20mm cannon and coaxial 7.62mm MG, prototype only.
*ERC 60-20 Serval:* Fitted with Hispano-Suiza 60-20 Serval turret with 60mm mortar, 20mm cannon and, as an option, a 7.62mm MG mounted coaxially on right side of turret towards rear.
*EMC 81mm Mortar Gun Carrier:* Fitted with large open topped turret armed with Hotchkiss-Brandt 81mm breech loaded mortar with 72 HE mortar bombs and six APFSDS mortar bombs being carried.

### Employment
Iraq, Ivory Coast and Niger. On order for French Army.

# Panhard AML/D Lynx 90 Armoured Car     France

**Armament:** 1 × 90mm gun, elevation +15°, depression −8° (21 rounds carried)
2 × 7.62mm MGs — coaxial and AA (2,000 rounds)
2 smoke dischargers either side of turret
**Crew:** 3
**Length:** 5.439m (gun forward), 4.329m (hull)
**Width:** 2.495m
**Height:** 2.436m (turret top)
**Weight:** 6,200kg (loaded)
**Track:** 2.135m
**Wheelbase:** 2.59m
**Engine:** Mercedes-Benz OM 617A 5-cylinder supercharged diesel developing 115hp at 4,200rpm
**Speed:** 90km/h (road), 3.6km/h (water)

**Range:** 950km
**Fording:** Amphibious
**V/obstacle:** 1m
**Gradient:** 60%

### Development
The Panhard AML/D Lynx 90 armoured car is the successor to the AML and was shown for the first time in 1979, but has yet to enter production. Its main improvements over the earlier model can be summarised as greater operational range due to the replacement of the petrol engine by a diesel and an integral amphibious capability being propelled when afloat by its wheels.

The vehicle has an Hispano-Suiza Lynx 90 turret armed with a 90mm F1 gun that fires HEAT (m/v 640m/sec), HE (m/v 635m/sec), canister and smoke rounds. A 7.62mm MG is mounted coaxial with the main armament and a similar weapon is mounted on the turret for AA defence.

Optional equipment includes electro-hydraulic traverse for the turret, laser rangefinder, NBC system,

*Panhard AML/D Lynx 90 armoured car.* Panhard

passive night vision equipment and elevation of the main armament to +35°.

**Employment**
Prototype only. Not yet in production.

# Panhard AML Armoured Car France

**Data:** AML with H-90 turret
**Armament:** 1 × 90mm gun, elevation +15°, depression −8° (20 rounds carried)
2 × 7.62mm MGs — coaxial and AA (2,000 rounds)
2 smoke dischargers either side of turret
**Crew:** 3
**Length:** 5.11m (gun forward), 3.79m (hull)
**Width:** 1.97m
**Height:** 2.07m (overall)
**G/clearance:** 0.33m
**Weight:** 5,500kg (loaded)
**Track:** 1.62m
**Wheelbase:** 2.50m
**Engine:** Panhard Model 4 HD, 4-cylinder air-cooled petrol engine developing 90hp at 4,700rpm
**Speed:** 90km/h (road)
**Range:** 600km (road)

**Fuel:** 156 litres
**Fording:** 1.10m
**V/obstacle:** 0.30m
**Trench:** 0.80m (one channel), 3.10m (four channels)
**Gradient:** 60%
**Armour:** 8mm-12mm

**Development**
The AML (Automitrailleuse Légère, or light armoured car) was designed by Panhard to meet the requirements of the French Army with the first prototypes being completed in 1959 and first production vehicles following in 1961. Since then the vehicle has been exported in considerable numbers and production was also undertaken in South Africa by Sandock-Austral; the South Africans

call the vehicle the Eland. The AML can be fitted with a variety of night fighting and night driving equipment and is airportable by aircraft and helicopters (ie the SA 321 Super Frelon). The AML has been continuously developed over the last 20 years and a full list of variants is listed below. Many components of the AML are used in the Panhard M3, which is described later in the book. By 1981, 4,000 had been built.

**Variants**

*AML with HE 60-7 turret:* This is armed with a 60mm mortar HB 60 Hotchkiss Brandt with an elevation of +80°, depression −15°, this has a range of 300m-2,600m and 2 × 7.62mm MGs. These have an elevation of +60° and a depression of −15°. 53 rounds of 60mm and 3,800 rounds of 7.62mm ammunition are carried.

*AML with HE 60-20 turret:* This is armed with a 60mm breach-loaded mortar with an elevation of +80° and a depression of −15° and a 20mm M621 cannon. This has an elevation of +50° and a depression of −8°. 43 rounds of 60mm and 500 rounds of 20mm ammunition are carried. A 7.62mm AA MG is fitted to the roof of the vehicle and 1,000 rounds of 7.62mm ammunition are carried. This model is now out of production.

*AML with H-90 turret:* The 90mm gun fires the following types of fin-stabilised ammunition: HEAT (m/v 640m/sec), HE (m/v 635m/sec), smoke (m/v 750m/sec) and canister (m/v 640m/sec). The HEAT projectile will penetrate 320mm of armour at an incidence of 0° or 120mm of armour at an incidence of 65°.

*AML with H-90 turret and 90mm main gun. Panhard*

*AML with Lynx 90 turret:* This is the latest production model and has an Hispano-Suiza Lynx 90 turret which has the same armament as the above but the turret can be fitted with such options as passive night vision equipment and a laser rangefinder.

*AML with HS 30 turret:* Developed to prototype stage but not placed in production.

*AML with NA2 turret:* Developed to prototype stage but not placed in production.

*AML with HE 60-20 Serval turret:* AML with Hispano-Suiza HE 60-20 Serval turret with 60mm breech-loaded mortar, 20mm cannon (French M693 dual feed or Oerlikon KAD-B16) and a 7.62mm MG.

*AML with TG 120 turret:* SAMM turret with 20mm cannon (240 rounds) and 7.62mm MG, trials only, not in production.

*AML 81mm Mortar Gun Carrier:* AML with same turret as fitted to Panhard EMC 81 (6 × 6) mortar gun carrier.

*AML with HE 60-12 turret:* Same as HE 60-7 but has 12.7mm MG in place of twin 7.62mm MGs, former can be elevated from −15° to +60°.

*AML S 530 AA vehicle:* The prototype was completed in 1969 and the first production vehicle in 1971. It is a basic AML, fitted with a new turret designed by SAMM (Société d'Applications des Machines Motrices). This mounts 2 × 20mm M621 automatic cannon, with powered traverse and

39

*AML S530 AA vehicle with twin 20mm cannon.*
SAMM

elevation from +75° to −10°, traverse being 360°. Effective range is 1,300m and cyclic rate of fire is 740rpm/barrel. 600 rounds of 20mm ammunition are carried. In addition there are two smoke dischargers either side of the turret.

*Amphibious kit:* An amphibious kit has been developed that can be fitted to any of the AML series. This kit consists of thin steel sheets around the hull of the vehicle, these are filled with a self-

extinguishable non-spongy synthetic matter. A propeller kit is available, this gives the vehicle a speed of 6-7km/h in the water. Loaded weight of an AML 90 with the amphibious kit is 5,750kg.

**Employment**
The AML is used by Algeria, Angola, Burundi, Chad, Djibouti, Ecuador, El Salvador, France, Gabon, Iraq, Ireland, Ivory Coast, Kenya, Malaysia, Mauritania, Morocco, Nigeria, Portugal, Rwanda, Saudi Arabia, Senegal, Somalia, South Africa, Spain, Togo, Tunisia, United Arab Emirates, Upper Volta, Venezuela, Zaire and Zimbabwe (from South Africa).

# SOFRAMAG Fennec 5C Light Fighting Vehicle    France

**Armament:** See text
**Crew:** 3
**Length:** 3.68m
**Width:** 2.005m
**Height:** 1.51m (w/o armament)
**G/clearance:** 0.3m
**Weight:** 4,000kg (empty), 4,700kg (loaded)
**G/pressure:** 0.46kg/sq cm
**Engine:** Citroen CX 2400 4-cylinder in-line petrol developing 109hp at 5,000rpm
**Speed:** 80km/h
**Range:** 800km
**Fuel:** 225 litres
**Gradient:** 60%
**Side slope:** 30%

**Development/Variants**
The Lohr company (now SOFRAMAG) took over from Hotchkiss-Brandt the development of the VP 90 light tracked vehicle. This was subsequently redesigned and redesignated the VPX 110 and more recently this was changed again to the Fennec Type 5D. This model is unarmoured but two armoured models have been built, the VPX 110M (or Fennec 5C) with five road wheels each side, and the Fennec 6C with six road wheels each side. All have the same engine, transmission and other automotive components.

The basic model, the Fennec Type 5D, can be used for a wide range of roles including ambulance, AA (20mm), anti-tank (MILAN), cargo, command/radio, fire support (60mm breech loaded Brandt mortar) or towing a 120mm Brandt mortar.

SOFRAMAG Fennec 5C with Euromissile MILAN MCT turret with two MILAN ATGW in the ready-to-launch position. SOFRAMAG

The armoured Fennec Type 5C and 6C can be fitted with various turrets such as a Euromissile

MILAN MCT with two MILAN ATGWs in the ready-to-launch position or a HAKO turret with up to four HOT ATGWs in the ready-to-launch position.

**Employment**
Development complete, ready for production.

# AMX-10P Family MICV

France

**Armament:** 1 × 20mm cannon M693 and 1 × 7.62mm MG in a mount, traverse 360°, elevation +50°, depression −8°. 800 rounds of 20mm (of which 350 are ready for use) and 2,000 rounds of 7.62mm (of which 900 are ready for use) carried 4 smoke grenade launchers mounted on the rear of the vehicle
**Crew:** 3 + 8
**Length:** 5.778m
**Width:** 2.780m
**Height:** 2.57m (overall), 1.92m (hull top)
**G/clearance:** 0.45m
**Weight:** 14,200kg (loaded), 11,700kg (empty)

**G/pressure:** 0.53kg/sq cm
**Engine:** Hispano-Suiza HS 115-2, V-8 water-cooled diesel engine developing 280hp at 3,000rpm
**Speed:** 65km/h (road), 7km/h (water)
**Range:** 600km
**Fuel:** 410 litres
**Fording:** Amphibious
**V/obstacle:** 0.70m
**Trench:** 2.1m
**Gradient:** 60%

*AMX-10P MICV of French Army.* GIAT

*AMX-10 PAC 90 fire support vehicle.* GIAT

## Development

The AMX-10P was developed to meet the requirements of the French Army from 1965 by the Atelier de Construction d'Issy-les-Moulineaux with first production vehicles completed by the Atelier de Construction Roanne, who also built the AMX-30 MBT, in 1973. It is now replacing the AMX VCI tracked infantry combat vehicle which entered service in the 1950s.

The AMX-10P has an NBC system, full range of night vision equipment and is propelled in the water by two waterjets at the rear of the hull. Apart from two firing ports in the hydraulically operated ramp at the rear of the hull there is no provision for the infantrymen to fire their small arms from within the vehicle. The vehicle is also used to carry MILAN ATGW teams.

The AMX-10RC (6 × 6) wheeled vehicle shares many common automotive components with the tracked AMX-10P.

## Variants — tracked

*AMX-10TM:* This version is in production and tows the Hotchkiss-Brandt 120mm mortar, the vehicle has a crew of six and carries 56 mortar rounds.

*AMX-10PC:* This is a command vehicle and is in production. It has a crew of seven. The vehicle has been provided with an additional generator. Additional working space can be provided by erecting awnings at the rear and side of the vehicle.

*AMX-10P (RATAC):* This is the standard APC with the turret removed and replaced by the RATAC (Radar for Field Artillery Fire) is now in service with the French Army.

*AMX-10P (HOT):* This has its turret replaced by a new turret with a total of four HOT missiles in the ready-to-launch position, a further 14 missiles are carried inside the hull. A 7.62mm MG with 2,000 rounds of ammunition is also mounted in the turret. Crew is five men.

*AMX-10P (Training):* This has its turret removed and replaced by an observation cupola for the instructor and another trainee driver.

*AMX-10P (Ambulance):* This is a standard AMX-10P with armament removed and can carry a maximum of five casualties.

*AMX-10 ECH (Repair):* This was known as the AMX-10D and has a crew of five men. It has a Touchan 1 one-man turret which is armed with a 20mm cannon and a coaxial 7.62mm MG, the turret has manual traverse rather than powered traverse as has the standard AMX-10P.

*AMX-10RC:* For details of this family the reader is referred to the entry on the AMX-10RC 6 × 6 vehicle.

*AMX-10P (ACRA):* This project has been cancelled.

*AMX-10 PAC 90:* This fire support vehicle is the basic AMX-10P with turret replaced by a GIAT TS 90 two-man turret as mounted on the VBC-90 and Panhard ERC 90 F4 Sagie 6 × 6 armoured cars. It has been designed specifically for the export market.

*AMX-10 SAO Artillery Observation Vehicle:* This is used by the French Army and has its Toucan II turret replaced by a two-man turret armed with a 7.62mm MG, laser rangefinder and observation equipment. It has a five-man crew.

*AMX-10 SAT Artillery Survey Vehicle:* Based on AMX-10PC command vehicle but carries a gyro-stabilised theodolite, topographic survey equipment, distance measuring equipment and a vehicle navigation system.

*AMX-10P ATILA:* Two members of the AMX-10P are used in the ATILA automatic artillery fire-control system, AMX-10 VFA is used at regimental and battery level while the AMX-10 VLA is the artillery liaison vehicle.

## Employment

France, Greece, Indonesia (AMX-10, PAC-90), Saudi Arabia and Sudan, on order for Mexico.

# AMX VCI APC/ICV

**Armament:** 1 × 7.5mm or 7.62mm or 12.7mm MG
**Crew:** 3 + 10
**Length:** 5.7m
**Width:** 2.51m
**Height:** 2.41m (with turret), 2.10m (hull top)
**G/clearance:** 0.48m
**Weight:** 15,000kg (loaded), 12,500kg (empty)
**G/pressure:** 0.70kg/sq cm
**Engine:** SOFAM 8 Gbx 8-cylinder petrol engine
developing 250hp at 3,200rpm
**Speed:** 65km/h (road)
**Range:** 350/400km (road)
**Fuel:** 410 litres
**Fording:** 1m
**V/obstacle:** 0.65m
**Trench:** 1.60m
**Gradient:** 60%
**Armour:** 10mm-30mm

(*Note.* Above dimensions can vary according to date
built.)

## Development/Variants

The specification for the AMX APC was issued in
1954 and production commenced in 1957. It is
based on the AMX tank chassis which has been
lengthened and vehicles can be seen with three or
four return rollers. It was originally called the
AMX-VTP (Véhicule Transport de Personnel) or
TT.CH.Mle.56. (Transport de Troupe Chenillé Model
56) but it is now referred to as the AMX VCI
(Véhicule de Combat d'Infanterie). The MG can be
mounted in a turret (7.5mm or 7.62mm) or on a ring
mount (12.7mm mg). It can also be fitted with a
turret-mounted 20mm cannon. The infantry carried
can fire their weapons through firing ports in the
sides and rear of the vehicle. The vehicle has an NBC

system and can be fitted with infra-red driving lights.
A number of these vehicles were built in Belgium.
The vehicle has no amphibious capability.
*Command Vehicle:* This is known as the VTT/PC
(Poste de Commandement), and has been fitted with
additional radios, map boards and so on. It has a
crew of 4-9 men and is recognisable by its three
radio aerials.
*Ambulance:* Known as the VTT/TB (Transport de
Blesses), no armament is fitted. It has a crew of four
and can carry four seated and three stretcher
patients. Basic data is similar to the APC except that
its loaded weight is 13,500kg.
*Battery Command Vehicle:* This has been developed
for use with artillery, for example the 155mm SP gun
and is called the Véhicule de Commandement du Tir.
Equipment fitted includes additional radios, map
boards and fire control equipment. Data similar to
the APC except for its crew of seven.
*Mortar Vehicles:* These are called AMX-VTT/PM
(Porte Mortier) and there are two versions:
*81mm mortar* with an elevation of +43° to +80°,
traverse 40°, 128 rounds carried, crew of 6. Mortar
can also be fired away from the vehicle.
*120mm mortar* with an elevation of +45° to +77°,
traverse 46°, 60 rounds carried, crew of six. Mortar
can also be fired away from the vehicle.
*Pioneer Vehicle:* Known as the AMX-VCG (Véhicule
de Combat du Génie). This is fitted with a dozer
blade, winch. A frame, search-light and other
equipment. It has a crew of 9, armed with a 12.7mm
MG, weight 17,800kg, length 6.37m and height
3.46m.

*AMX VCI without armament towing an ammunition
trailer.* Creusot-Loire

AMX VCG fitted with dozer blade and A frame.
E. C. P. Armées

*Cargo Vehicle:* When used as a cargo vehicle the AMX VCI can carry 3,000kg of cargo.
*Missile Launcher Vehicle:* This is a standard AMX VCI fitted with two missile launchers at the rear, each launcher having two missiles. A total of 26 ENTAC missiles are carried and it has a crew of five.

Another version has two SS-11 missiles, one either side of the commander's cupola.
*Artillery Support Vehicle:* This is used to support the AMX 155mm SP gun and is called the VTT/VCA (Véhicule Chenillé d'Accompagnement). It has a crew of eight and carries 25 projectiles, 25 cartridge bags and 49 fuzes. It can also tow an ammunition trailer containing 30 projectiles, charges and fuzes.
*Roland AA Missile Vehicle:* This was a trials vehicle and mounted 2 Roland SAMs in the ready to fire position.
*TOW Launcher Vehicle:* DAF have fitted an AMX VCI of the Netherlands Army with a launcher system for the American TOW ATGW.
*Radar vehicle:* This is called the VTT/RATAC and is fitted with the RATAC (Radar de Tir pour Artillerie de Campagne) radar on the roof of the vehicle.

**Employment**
The AMX-VCI was originally manufactured by the Atelier de Construction Roanne (ARE) but when production of the AMX-30 started at the ARE production of the complete AMX-13 family, including the VCI, was transferred to Creusot-Loire at Châlon-sur-Saône. The AMX-VCI is in service with Argentina, Belgium, Ecuador, France, Indonesia, Italy, Netherlands, Venezuela and the United Arab Emirates.

# Renault VAB APC

# France

VAB (6×6) with Creusot-Loire TLi 127 turret armed with a 12.7mm and 7.62mm MGs.
Renault Vehicules Industriels

| Model: | 4 × 4 | 6 × 6 |
|---|---|---|
| Crew: | 2 + 10 | 2 + 10 |
| Length: | 5.98m | 5.98m |
| Width: | 2.49m | 2.49m |
| Height: | | |
| (w/o armament) | 2.06m | 2.06m |
| G/clearance: (hull) | 0.5m | 0.5m |
| Weight: (loaded) | 13,000kg | 14,200kg |
| (empty) | 11,000kg | 12,200kg |
| Track: | 2.05m | 2.05m |
| Wheelbase: | 3m | 1.5m + 1.5m |
| Engine: | MAN D 2356 HM 72 6-cylinder in-line water-cooled diesel developing 235hp at 2,200rpm | |
| Speed: (road) | 92km/h | 92km/h |
| (water) | 7km/h | 7km/h |
| Range: | 1,000km | 1,000km |
| Fuel: | 300 litres | 300 litres |
| Fording: | amphibious | amphibious |
| V/obstacle: | 0.6m | 0.6m |
| Trench: | not applicable | 1m |
| Gradient: | 60% | 60% |

## Development

To meet a French Army requirement for a front armoured vehicle (Véhicule de l'Avant Blinde) Creusot-Loire/Saviem and Panhard each built 4 × 4 and 6 × 6 prototypes which were tested between 1973 and 1974. In May 1974 the Creusot-Loire/Saviem 4 × 4 VAB was accepted for service and first production vehicles were delivered to the French Army in 1976. The 6 × 6 version is in production for export but will be eventually procured by the French Army who has a total requirement for between 4,000 and 5,000 VABs.

Saviem is now part of the Renault Group and supplies automotive components to Creusot-Loire at

Usine de Saint-Chamond who undertakes final assembly and delivery.

All VABs are fully amphibious being propelled in the water by two water-jets at the rear of the hull, before entering the water a trim vane is erected at the front of the vehicle, and are fitted with an NBC system. Optional equipment includes passive night vision equipment and a front-mounted winch.

The basic APC can be fitted with a wide range of armament installations including pintle or turret-mounted 7.62mm or 12.7mm MGs guns or a turret mounted 20mm cannon.

## Variants

Ambulance (unarmed), anti-tank one with the Euromissile UTM-800 turret and the other with the Euromissile Mephisto installation (both with four HOT ATGWs in the ready-to-launch position), command post, IS vehicle with hydraulically operated obstacle clearing blade at the front of the hull, mortar tractor towing a 120mm mortar and carrying 70 mortar bombs and a repair vehicle with tools, bench and welding equipment. There is a separate entry for the VBC-90 armoured car which uses automotive components of the VAB (6 × 6).

## Employment

France, Ivory Coast, Mauritius, Morocco and Qatar.

*VAB (4×4) with Creusot-Loire TLi 52A turret armed with a 7.62mm MG.* Renault Vehicules Industriels

# Berliet VXB-170 Multi-Role Vehicle France

*Berliet VXB with 7.62mm MG.* Berliet

**Armament:** See below
**Crew:** 1 + 11
**Length:** 5.99m
**Width:** 2.50m
**Height:** 2.05m (w/o turret)
**G/clearance:** 0.45m (transfer box)
**Weight:** 12,700kg (loaded), 9,800kg (empty)
**Engine:** Berliet V8 diesel, developing 170hp at 3,000rpm
**Speed:** 85km/h (road), 4km/h (water)
**Range:** 750km
**Fuel:** 220 litres
**Fording:** Amphibious
**Trench:** nil
**V/obstacle:** 0.3m
**Gradient:** 60%
**Armour:** 7mm (max)

## Development
This vehicle was originally known as the Berliet BL-12. The first of two prototypes was built in March 1968. One of these was tested by the French Army in 1969 and the other retained by Berliet. The first of five VXBs was built in May 1971 and tested by the French Gendarmerie. In 1973 a production order was given to Berliet for 50 vehicles for the French Gendarmerie; production commenced in 1973 at the Berliet factory at Bourg.

The VXB is a 4 × 4 vehicle and its hull is of all-welded construction. Firing ports are provided in the hull and the crew can enter and leave the vehicle by way of side, rear and roof hatches. It is fully amphibious being propelled in the water by its wheels.

A 3,500/4,500kg winch is fitted at the front. Optional extras were many and included heater, radios, NBC system, night driving equipment and a dozer blade.

## Variants
The VXB can be used for the following five basic roles: APC, load carrier, light combat vehicle, light reconnaissance vehicle and an anti-riot vehicle. Many types and combinations of armament could be fitted including the following: 90mm gun, 2 × 20mm cannon, 1 × 20mm cannon, 1 × 12.7mm MG, 2 × 7.62mm MGs, 2 single 7.62mm MGs, 81mm mortar, various anti-tank missile systems and anti-aircraft missile systems. The vehicle can also be used as a command vehicle or ambulance.

## Employment
Used by the French Gendarmerie, Gabon, Senegal, Tunisia. Production of the VXB-170 is now complete.

# Panhard VCR (6 × 6) APC                    France

**Armament:** 1 × 7.62mm, 12.7mm MG, or 1 × 20mm cannon, or 1 × 60mm breech-loaded mortar (front) and 1 × 7.62mm MG (rear) 2 smoke dischargers either side of hull (optional)
**Crew:** 3 + 9
**Length:** 4.565m
**Width:** 2.49m
**Height:** 2.03m (commander's position), 2.53m (inc armament)
**Weight:** 7,000kg
**Track:** 2.16m
**Wheelbase:** 1.425m + 1.425m
**Engine:** Peugeot V-6 petrol developing 140hp at 5,250rpm
**Speed:** 110km/h (road), 4.5km/h (water)
**Range:** 950km
**Fording:** Amphibious
**V/obstacle:** 1m
**Trench:** 1m
**Gradient:** 60%
**Armour:** 8mm-12mm

## Development
The VCR (Véhicule de Combat à Roues) has been developed for the export market by Panhard with the first prototypes completed in 1977 and first production vehicles following in 1979.

*Panhard VCR/TT with 20mm cannon (forward) and 7.62mm MG (rear).  Panhard*

The range shares many common components such as engine, transmission and suspension with the ERC range of 6 × 6 armoured cars also developed by Panhard. All vehicles have 6 × 6 drive with steering on the front wheels, when travelling on roads the centre wheels are raised clear of the road but still turn.

The basic APC is called the VCR/TT (Transport de Troupes) and carries nine troops in addition to the commander, gunner and driver. The main armament is normally positioned towards the front of the vehicle (roughly over the centre road wheels) with an optional 7.62mm machine gun at the rear. Infantry enter and leave the vehicle via a door in the rear and firing ports are provided in the sides and rear as well.

Optional equipment includes an air conditioning system, NBC system, infra-red or passive night vision equipment and a front mounted winch.

## Variants
*VCR/TH (Tourelle HOT):* Fitted with a Euromissile UTM 800 turret with four HOT ATGWs in the ready to launch position.
*VCR/IS (Intervention Sanitaire):* Unarmed ambulance model with a higher roof, has crew of three and can carry four stretcher or six sitting patients.
*VCR/PC (Poste de Commandement):* Command version of basic VCR/TT with additional communications equipment, mapboards and tables.

## Employment
In service with five countries including Iraq and UAE.

# Panhard VCR (4 × 4) APC

France

**Armament:** Depends on role
**Crew:** 2 + 10
**Length:** 4.565m
**Width:** 2.49m
**Height:** 2.03m (w/o armament)
**G/clearance:** 0.33m
**Weight:** 7,100-7,600kg (loaded)
**Track:** 2.16m
**Wheelbase:** 2.85m
**Engine:** Peugeot V-6 petrol developing 140hp at 5,250rpm
**Speed:** 100km/h (road)
7.2km/h (water)
**Range:** 950km
**Fording:** Amphibious
**V/obstacle:** 0.8m
**Gradient:** 60%
**Armour:** 8mm-12mm

## Development
The Panhard VCR (Vehicule de Combat à Roues) was developed as a private venture with first prototype being completed in 1979 and first production vehicles following in 1980. Some 95% of the automotive components of the VCR (4×4) are identical to those used in the VCR (6×6) APC described in an earlier entry.

Major differences between the two vehicles are that the VCR (4×4) has a different roof arrangement with two instead of three observation/firing hatches in each side of the hull.

*Panhard VCR (4×4) fitted with Euromissile Mephisto installation with launcher in elevated position.*
Simon Dunstan

A wide range of armament installations can be fitted including pintle-mounted 7.62mm or 12.7mm MGs, ring-mounted 20mm cannon, ring-mounted 60mm breech-loaded mortar or a Euromissile MILAN turret with two MILAN ATGWs in the ready-to-launch position. A 7.62mm MG on a rail mount can be mounted over the rear part of the troop compartment.

The VCR is fully amphibious being propelled in the water by two water jets positioned one on either side of the hull and can be fitted with a wide range of optional equipment including an air conditioning system, front mounted winch and passive night vision equipment.

## Variants
For trials purposes one of the prototypes of the VCR (4×4) has been fitted with the Euromissile Mephisto launcher with four HOT ATGWs in the ready-to-launch position with an additional eight missiles being carried in reserve.

## Employment
In service with undisclosed countries.

# Panhard M3 APC

France

**Armament:** See below, according to requirements
**Crew:** 2 + 10
**Length:** 4.45m
**Width:** 2.40m
**Height:** 2.48m (turret), 2.0m (w/o turret)
**G/clearance:** 0.35m
**Weight:** 6,100kg (loaded), 5,300kg (unloaded)
**Track:** 2.05m
**Wheelbase:** 2.70m
**Engine:** Panhard Model 4 HD, 4-cylinder, air cooled petrol engine developing 90hp at 4,700rpm
**Speed:** 100km/h (road), 4km/h (water)
**Range:** 600km (road)
**Fuel:** 165 litres
**Fording:** Amphibious
**V/obstacle:** 0.30m
**Trench:** 0.80m (with 1 channel)
**Gradient:** 60%
**Armour:** 8mm-12mm

## Development
The Panhard M3 armoured personnel carrier is based on components of the AML family, 95% of the components of the M3 are interchangeable with those of the AML. The prototype M3 was built in 1969 and the first production model in 1971. The hull of the M3 is of all welded construction. There are doors on either side of the vehicle and twin doors at the rear. A circular opening in the front part of the roof can be fitted with a variety of turrets or mounts. There is also a hatch on the rear part of the roof allowing use of a MG mounted on a rail. There are flaps in the sides of the vehicle and firing ports in the rear door. The M3 is fully amphibious without preparation; it is propelled in the water by its wheels.

## Variants
The basic vehicle can be used as an APC, load carrier, riot control vehicle, mortar carrier, radio vehicle or missile vehicle. A wide range of armament can be fitted, some of which is listed below:
Creusot-Loire STB rotary support shield with 7.62mm MG; Creusot-Loire CB rotating gun ring with 7.62mm MG; Creusot-Loire turret CAFL.38 with single 7.62mm MG; Creusot-Loire TLI.G turret with 7.62mm MG and 40mm smoke discharger; Creusot-Loire TL.2i turret with twin 7.62mm MGs; Creusot-Loire CB.127 gun ring shield with 12.7mm MGs; Creusot-Loire CB.20 gun ring shield armed with 20mm cannon; Creusot-Loire gun ring shield with 60mm Hotchkiss-Brandt mortar; Euromissile MCT turret with two MILAN ATGWs in ready-to-launch position; Toucan 1 turret with 20mm cannon and 7.62mm MG.
*M3 VPC Command Vehicle:* With communications equipment, additional batteries and mapboards.
*M3 VAT Repair Vehicle:* Crew of three, fitted with pulleyblock with struts and tackle, generator, cutting equipment and tools etc.
*M3 VTS Ambulance:* Unarmed with a crew of three, can carry six sitting wounded or four stretcher cases, or a combination.

*Panhard M3 with two single 7.62mm MGs.*
Panhard

**M3 VLA Engineer Vehicle:** Has a crew of six and is fitted with a hydraulically operated dozer blade at the front of the hull.

**Panhard M3 VDA:** This was shown for the first time at Satory in June 1973. It has been designed by Panhard in association with EMD, Galileo and Oerlikon. It is basically an M3 chassis with a turret mounting 2 × 20mm HS 820 SL guns with an elevation of +85° and a depression of −5°, these have power traverse and elevation. A total of 650 rounds of 20mm ammunition is carried. In addition there is a 7.62mm MG on the roof of the vehicle. It has a crew of three men. There are two stabilisers either side of the hull, which can be let down to provide a stable firing platform.

### Employment
Angola, Bahrain, Gabon, Iraq, Ireland, Ivory Coast, Kenya, Lebanon, Malaysia, Mauritania, Morocco, Niger, Portugal, Rwanda, Saudi Arabia, Senegal, Spain, Togo, United Arab Emirates, Upper Volta and Zaire.

*Panhard M3 VDA with hydraulic jacks lowered to provide a more stable firing platform.* Panhard

# Hotchkiss Carriers                                    France

Data similar to all vehicles: **Fording:** 1m, **V/obstacle:** 0.60m, **Trench:** 1.50m, **Gradient:** 60%, **Armour:** 8mm-15mm. All are powered by a Hotchkiss 6-cylinder, OHV, water-cooled petrol engine developing 164hp at 3,900rpm. In the table below:

**A**  Reconnaissance Vehicle SP.1A
**B**  Observation & Command Veh.SP.111
**C**  Mortar Carrier SP.1B
**D**  Armoured Ambulance SP.1V

### Development
These vehicles were developed from the earlier Hotchkiss TT6 series of carriers. They were built in France for the German Army, although some were also assembled in Germany. All of the above vehicles share the same engine, transmission, track and so on.

### Variants
*Reconnaissance Vehicle SP.1A:* This is armed with a turret-mounted Hispano-Suiza cannon with a 360° traverse, elevation is +75°, depression −10°.

500 rounds of 20mm ammunition are carried. This vehicle is designated SPz 11-2 in the German Army.
*Observation and Command Vehicle SP.111:* This is similar to the above vehicle but without the turret. It is armed with a 7.62mm MG and carries three radios. The vehicle is designated SPz 22.2 in the German Army.
*Mortar Carrier SP.1B:* This has an 81mm mortar firing through the roof, with an elevation of +45° to +90°, and a traverse of 30° left and 30° right, 50 rounds of mortar ammunition are carried. The vehicle also has a 7.62mm MG and 500 rounds of ammunition. It is designated SPz 51-2 by the German Army. Some have had their mortars removed and an AN/TPS-33 tactical radar system fitted. This model is called the SPz Radarpanzerkurz 1.
*Ambulance SP.1V:* This has a crew of three and can carry two stretchers and one sitting patient inside and a further two stretcher patients can be carried on the roof. No armament is fitted. It is designated SPz 2-2 in the German Army.

| | A | B | C | D |
|---|---|---|---|---|
| **Crew:** | 5 | 5 | 4/5 | 3/5 |
| **Length:** | 4.51m | 4.51m | 4.66m | 4.6m |
| **Width:** | 2.28m | 2.28m | 2.28m | 2.28m |
| **Height:** | 1.97m | 1.69m | 1.84m | 1.84m |
| **G/clearance:** | 0.35m | 0.35m | 0.35m | 0.35m |
| **Weight:** (loaded) | 8,200kg | 7,500kg | 8,200kg | 8,000kg |
| **G/pressure:** | 0.58kg/sq cm | 0.55kg/sq cm | 0.58kg/sq cm | 0.57kg/sq cm |
| **Speed:** (road) | 58km/h | 58km/h | 58km/h | 58km/h |
| **Range:** | 390km | 400km | 320km | 350km |
| **Fuel:** | 330 litres | 345 litres | 375 litres | 295 litres |
| **Armament:** | 20mm | 7.62mm | 7.62mm | unarmed |

*Experimental Models:* Many experimental models were developed to the prototype stage including: 120mm mortar carrier, 90mm tank destroyer, enclosed cargo carrier, armoured personnel carrier and various rocket models.

**Employment**
In use in limited numbers with West German Army.

*Hotchkiss carrier of the German Army.* Hotchkiss

# 155mm GCT SP Gun

France

**Armament:** 1 × 155 gun, elevation +66°, depression −4°, traverse 360° (42 rounds carried) 1 × 7.62mm or 12.7mm AA MG, elevation +45°, depression −10°, traverse 360° (2,050 rounds) 2 smoke dischargers mounted either side of turret
**Crew:** 4
**Length:** 10.234m (gun forward), 9.50m (gun rear), 6.485m (hull only)
**Width:** 3.150m (turret), 3.115m (over hull)
**Height:** 3.30m
**Weight:** 42,000kg (loaded), 38,000kg (empty)
**G/clearance:** 0.43m
**Engine:** Hispano-Suiza HS-110, 12-cylinder multi-fuel water-cooled engine developing 720hp at 2,200rpm. This is built in France by Renault
**Speed:** 60km/h (road)
**Range:** 450km (road)
**Fuel:** 970 litres
**Fording:** 2.10m
**V/obstacle:** 0.93m
**Trench:** 1.9m
**Gradient:** 60%

**Development**
The 155mm GCT (Grande Cadence de Tir) SP gun was developed from 1969 to replace the 105mm and 155mm SP guns and howitzers at present in service with the French Army. The first prototype was completed in 1972 and following trials with 10 pre-production vehicles it was accepted for service with the French Army in 1979, although first deliveries were made to Saudi Arabia in 1977.

The GCT is based on a modified AMX-30 MBT chassis. The 155mm gun is mounted in a fully enclosed turret which can be traversed through a full 360°. Turret traverse and gun elevation is hydraulic. The breech block is of the vertical wedge type and is also hydraulically operated.

An automatic loading system enables eight rounds to be fired per minute until the ammunition supply is exhausted. A typical ammunition load would consist of 36 HE and six smoke projectiles, 42 projectiles and 42 cartridge cases are carried in the turret rear. Max range with a TA 68 projectile is 23,500m or 30,500m with a Brandt RAP.

Standard equipment includes a NBC system and night equipment of the passive type.

**Variants**
A German Leopard 1 chassis has also been fitted with the same turret and, according to the GIAT, other MBTs could be fitted with this turret.

**Employment**
France, Sudan and Saudi Arabia.

*The GCT 155mm SP gun.* GIAT

# 155mm Mk F3 SP Gun

France

**Armament:** 1 × 155mm howitzer, 33 calibre barrel
**Crew:** 2 (on weapon)
**Length:** 6.22m (gun forward), 4.88m (chassis only)
**Width:** 2.72m
**Height:** 2.10m (travelling)
**G/clearance:** 0.47m
**Weight:** 17,400kg (loaded)
**G/pressure:** 0.80kg/sq cm
**Engine:** SOFAM 8Gxb 8-cylinder water-cooled petrol engine developing 250hp at 3,200rpm
**Speed:** 65km/h (road)
**Range:** 300km (road)
**Fuel:** 450 litres
**Fording:** 0.65m
**V/obstacle:** 0.60m
**Trench:** 1.50m
**Gradient:** 50%
**Armour:** 10mm-40mm

### Development/Variants

The system was developed in the 1960s with the ordnance being developed by the Atelier de Construction de Tarbes, chassis by Atelier de Construction Roanne and system integration by Etablissement d'Etudes et de Fabrications d'Armament de Bourges. Production is by Creusot Loire.

This weapon consists of a modified AMX chassis on which has been mounted an OB 155-50-BF weapon. The chassis has five road wheels, three return rollers and the driving sprocket at the front; there is no idler at the rear. There are two spades at the rear of the chassis, which are lowered for firing and anchored in the ground by reversing the vehicle. Elevation limits are 0° to +67°, traverse being 20° left and 30° right (elevation 0° to +50°) and 16° left and 30° right (elevation 50° to 67°). When travelling the gun is located 8° to the right.

It can fire HE Mk 56 projectiles to a range of 20,000m, Brandt RAPs to a range of 25,300m or American M107 HE projectiles to a range of 18,000m, as well as illuminating and smoke projectiles.

The weapon is supported in action by an AMX-13 VCI. This carries the rest of the crew of eight men and also carries 25 shells, 25 cartridges and 39 fuzes. In addition this vehicle can tow the ARE 2T F2 ammunition trailer with a further 30 shells and 30 cartridge bags. Another AMX VCI acts as a battery command post and controls four guns.

### Employment

Argentina, Chile, Ecuador, France, Kuwait, Morocco, United Arab Emirates and Venezuela.


# 105mm SP Howitzers

France

**Data:** Model A (fixed)
**Armament:** 1 × 105mm howitzer (56 rounds carried)
2 × 7.5mm or 7.62mm MGs (2,000 rounds)
**Crew:** 5
**Length:** 6.40m
**Width:** 2.65m
**Height:** 2.70m
**G/clearance:** 0.275-0.32m
**Weight:** 16,500kg (loaded)

**G/pressure:** 0.80kg/sq cm
**Engine:** SOFAM 8Gxb 8-cylinder water-cooled petrol engine developing 250hp at 3,200rpm
**Speed:** 60km/h (road)
**Range:** 350km (road)
**Fuel:** 415 litres

*105mm Model A SP howitzers of the French Army.*
MoD (UK)

**Fording:** 0.80m
**V/obstacle:** 0.65m
**Trench:** 1.90m
**Gradient:** 60%
**Armour:** 10mm-20mm

### Development/Variants

*Self-Propelled Howitzer Mk 61:* This was the first model built and is also known as the Model A or Obusier de 105 Model 1950 sur Affût Automoteur by the French. It entered service with the French Army in 1952. It consists of an OB-105-61-AU weapon on a modified AMX chassis. The 105mm howitzer has an elevation of +70° and a depression of −4°, traverse being 20° left and 20° right. It has a max range of 15,000m using the Mk 63 French ammunition, projectile weight being 16kg and m/v 220/670m/sec. Of the 56 rounds carried six are anti-tank rounds. Two MGs are carried, one inside the vehicle and another on top of the vehicle. The latter MG can be either on a pintle mount or in a cupola.
*Self-Propelled Howitzer (turret):* This had a 105mm turret-mounted howitzer but was not placed in production.

### Employment

France (23 calibre barrel), Morocco, Netherlands (30 calibre barrel).

# AMX-13 DCA AA Gun System                        France

**Armament:** 2 × 30mm Hispano-Suiza HSS 831A guns, elevation +85°, depression −8°, traverse 360° (600 rounds carried, 300 rounds/barrel)
2 × 2 smoke dischargers either side of turret
**Crew:** 3
**Length:** 5.373m
**Width:** 2.50m
**Height:** 3.8m (radar up), 3m (radar down)
**G/clearance:** 0.37m
**Weight:** 17,200kg (loaded)
**G/pressure:** 0.86kg/sq cm
**Engine:** SOFAM 8Gxb 8-cylinder water-cooled petrol engine developing 250hp at 3,200rpm
**Speed:** 60km/h (road)
**Range:** 300km (road)
**Fuel:** 415 litres
**Fording:** 0.60m
**V/obstacle:** 0.65m
**Trench:** 1.70m
**Gradient:** 60%
**Armour:** 10mm-20mm

### Development

Development of the AMX-13 DCA (Défense Contre Avions) started in 1960, the first prototype with radar being completed in 1964. A total of 60 vehicles was built for the French Army between 1968 and 1969. A later version of the turret installed on the AMX-13 DCA is fitted to the AMX-30 DCA which was built specifically for Saudi Arabia.

The system consists of an AMX-13 type chassis fitted with a cast turret armed with 2 × 30mm cannon. These cannon have a rate of fire of 600 rounds/min/barrel and an effective range of 3,000m. The guns can fire either single, 5, or 15-round bursts, or continuous fire. The turret has a max traverse speed of 80° a second and cannon 45° a second in elevation.

Mounted on the rear of the turret is RD 515 Oeil Noir 1 (Black Eye) radar system. This scans through 360° and can pick up targets at a range of 12km and an altitude of 3,000m. Sight corrections are controlled by an electric servo-motor and determined by an analogue computer. In addition two periscope sights are provided for use against ground targets.

The system was developed by DTAT, SAMM (turret), Hispano-Suiza (guns) and Thomson-CSF (radar).

### Employment

In service with the French Army.

*AMX-13 DCA with radar retracted.*   Thomson-CSF

# Crotale Low Altitude SAM System

France

|  | Acquisition Vehicle | Launch Vehicle |
|---|---|---|
| **Crew:** | 3 | 3 |
| **Length:** | 6.33m | 6.22m |
| **Width:** | 2.65m | 2.65m |
| **Height:** (reduced) | 2.04m | 2.04m |
| **G/clearance:** (deployed) | 0.156m-0.656m | 0.156m-0.656m |
| (travelling) | 0.45m | 0.45m |
| **Weight:** | 12,500kg | 14,500kg |
| **Wheelbase:** | 3.6m | 3.6m |
| **Speed:** (max road) | 70km/h | 70km/h |
| **Range:** (max) | 500km | 500km |
| **Fording:** | 0.68m | 0.68m |
| **Gradient:** | 40% | 40% |
| **V/obstacle:** | 0.3m | 0.3m |
| **Armour:** | 3mm-5mm | 3mm-5mm |

*Crotale acquisition unit deployed with jacks in lowered position.* Thomson-CSF

*Crotale firing unit launching a Crotale missile.* Thomson-CSF

## Development

The Crotale system was originally developed to meet the requirements of South Africa and three batteries were delivered between 1970 and 1973. Thomson-CSF is prime contractor for the complete system with Engins Matra being responsible for the missile.

The Crotale system has an all weather capability and takes only five minutes to bring into action once it has stopped, a typical battery consists of one acquisition unit and three firing units. The acquisition unit carries out target surveillance, identification and designation and has a Thomson-CSF E/F band radar with a range of 18km.

Once the target has been detected and confirmed as hostile it is allocated to one of the firing units which has four missiles in the ready to launch position. The firing unit also has an I/J band command transmitter, infra-red gathering system, integrated TV tracking mode as a back up, optical tracking device, digital computer, operating console and a digital data link. The radar can track one target and two missiles simultaneously. Once the four missiles have been launched another four can be quickly loaded. The missile has a range of 500-8,500m and an effective altitude of 3,000m.

## Variants

There is a separate entry for the Shahine low altitude SAM system which has been developed from 1975 to meet the requirements of Saudi Arabia and mounted on a modified AMX-30 chassis.

For close range defence Thomson-CSF have fitted the Crotale 4 × 4 chassis with a turret armed with twin 20mm guns, but this has not yet been placed in production.

## Employment

Egypt, France, Libya, Morocco, Pakistan, Saudi Arabia (and Shahine), South Africa, United Arab Emirates and two other unnamed countries.

# Shahine Low Altitude SAM System

France

## Development

In 1975 Thomson-CSF were awarded a contract by Saudi Arabia for the design, development and production of a low-level, mobile all weather SAM system called the Shahine. This is essentially a further development of the Crotale but the system is based on the tracked AMX-30 chassis instead of a 4 × 4 wheeled vehicle as in the case of the Crotale. First systems were delivered to Saudi Arabia in 1980.

A typical battery consists of one acquisition unit with four firing units with each of the latter having six missiles in the ready to launch position instead of four as in the case of Crotale.

The acquisition unit has a pulse doppler surveillance radar with a digital receiver for MTI function and a automatic information processing and threat evaluation system that allows 40 targets to be registered in the computer and 18 targets to be handled simultaneously.

The firing unit has a triple-channel fire control radar which can simultaneously guide two missiles to the target. The radar has a digital receiver and a circularly polarised antenna and tracks the missile and sends out the guidance commands. The missile, which has a range of about 10,000m, is acquired during the initial part of the flight via an infra-red receiver. In the event of jamming a TV system can be used.

In the original Crotale system, the unit had to stop and deploy before it was fully operational but Shahine can become operational at once as both the acquisition and firing units are fitted with an automatic data transmission and reciprocal location microwave system (L.LIV).

## Employment

In service only with Saudi Arabia.

*Shahine firing unit with six missiles in ready-to-launch position.* Christopher F. Foss

# Véhicule d'Auto Défense Antiaérienne      France

Following the cancellation of the VADAR (Véhicule Autonome de Défense Antiaérienne Rapprochée) which was being developed to meet the requirements of the French Army by GIAT, Thomson CSF, SAMM and Electronique Marcel Dassault, a new system is being developed called the VDAA, Véhicule d'Auto-Défense Antiaérienne. This will consist of a 4 × 4 or 6 × 6 version of the Renault Vehicules Industrials VAB armoured vehicle fitted with the Electronique Marcel Dassault turret model TA-20 which is currently in production for installation on other vehicles such as the Panhard M3 (4 × 4) APC, the latter version, which is already in service with two countries, is called the M3 VDA and is covered in the entry for the M3 in this section.

# Leopard 3 MBT      FGR

The West German Army has a requirement for a new MBT to replace its current fleet of 2,437 Leopard 1 MBTs in the 1990s. France has a similar requirement to replace its 1,000 AMX-30 MBTs in the same period. As this edition of *Armoured Fighting Vehicles of the World* went to press no final decision had been taken as to the possible collaboration between France and the FGR. Although the FGR has developed and placed in production a second generation MBT, the Leopard 2, France has yet to develop a tank of this type.

This new tank is often called the Napoleon or Leopard 3. Instead of starting from scratch again a number of people believe that the current Leopard 2 chassis could form the basis for a new MBT with perhaps a new type of armament system, possibly an externally mounted 120mm smooth bore gun.

# Leopard 2 MBT      FRG

**Armament:** 1 × 120mm gun, elevation +20°, depression −9° (42 rounds carried)
2 × 7.62 MGs — coaxial and AA on loader's or commander's hatch (2,000 rounds)
8 smoke dischargers either side of turret
**Crew:** 4
**Length:** 9.613m (gun forward) 7.4m (hull)
**Width:** 3.7m
**Height:** 2.46m (turret roof), 2.79m (commander's sight)

**G/clearance:** 0.55m (front), 0.50m (rear)
**Weight:** 55,000kg (loaded), 53,000kg (empty)
**G/pressure:** 0.83kg/sq cm
**Engine:** MTU MB 873 12-cylinder multi-fuel, exhaust turbocharged developing 1,500hp at 2,600rpm

*Leopard 2 MBT showing turret bustle.*
Krauss-Maffei

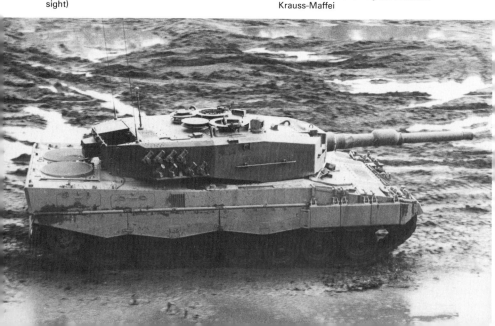

**Speed:** 72km/h (road)
**Range:** 550km (road)
**Fuel:** 1,200 litres
**Fording:** 0.80m (w/o preparation), 2.35m (with preparation), 4m (with snorkel)
**V/obstacle:** 1.1m
**Trench:** 3m
**Gradient:** 60%

## Development

Following the cancellation of MBT-70 in 1970 the FRG went ahead to develop a new MBT which eventually became known as the Leopard 2. Prime contractor for this was Krauss-Maffei of Munich who built 16 chassis and 17 turrets. These had the same power-pack as the MBT-70 and were armed with a Rheinmetall developed 105mm or 120mm smooth bore gun, but had different secondary armament and various types of fire control systems; two were fitted with a hydropneumatic suspension system instead of the advanced torsion bar type that was adopted for production vehicles.

To meet the requirements of the US, Krauss-Maffei designed a new version armed with a 105mm rifled tank gun and fitted with a new fire control system and numerous other improvements learned as a result of the Middle East war of 1973. This model was known as the Leopard 2(AV) but was not adopted by the United States Army.

In 1977 the West German Army ordered 1,800 Leopard 2, 990 to be built by Krauss-Maffei of Munich and 810 by MaK of Kiel. First production

tanks were delivered late in 1979 and final deliveries are expected to be made in 1986. In 1979 the Netherlands ordered 445 Leopard 2s for delivery between 1982 and 1986.

The Leopard 2 is armed with a 120mm smooth bore gun that fires APFSDS-T and HEAT-MP-T rounds that have a combustible cartridge case. The 120mm gun is expected to be fitted in American M1 MBTs produced from 1984/85, these will be designated the M1A1.

The main armament is fully stabilised and the commander has a roof mounted periscope that enables him to lay and fire the main armament. The fire control system includes a laser rangefinder and a computer. A full range of night vision equipment of the passive type is fitted as is a NBC system.

The armour of the Leopard 2 is believed to be a combination of Chobham and spaced armour that provides a high degree of protection against all battlefield weapons, especially ATGWs.

## Variants

There are no variants of the Leopard 2 at this time but it is anticipated that ARV and engineer versions will eventually be built. For trials purposes a Leopard 2 has been fitted with the gas turbine installed in the American M1 MBT, but this was not adopted by the FRG.

## Employment

In service with the FRG. On order for Netherlands.

# Leopard 1 MBT                                    FRG

**Armament:** 1 × 105mm L7A3 gun, elevation +20°, depression −9° (stabilised) (60 rounds carried)
2 × 7.62mm MGs — coaxial and AA (5,500 rounds)
4 smoke dischargers either side of turret
**Crew:** 4
**Length:** 9.54m (gun forward), 7.09m (hull only)
**Width:** 3.25m (3.40m with skirts)
**Height:** 2.61m (commander's periscope)
**G/clearance:** 0.44m
**Weight:** 40,000kg (loaded), 38,700kg (empty)
**G/pressure:** 0.90kg/sq cm
**Engine:** MTU MB 838 Ca.M500, 10-cylinder, multi-fuel engine developing 830hp at 2,200rpm
**Speed:** 65km/h (road)
**Range:** 600km (road), 450km (cross-country)
**Fuel:** 955 litres
**Fording:** 2.25m, 4.00m (with snorkel)
**V/obstacle:** 1.15m
**Trench:** 3.00m
**Gradient:** 60%
**Armour:** 10mm-70mm (estimate)

## Development

The development of the Leopard can be traced back as far as 1956 when France, Germany and Italy formulated requirements for a standard tank. In the end France built the AMX-30, Germany the

Leopard 1 and Italy the M60A1 (only to purchase the Leopard in 1970). Two teams, A and B, each built four prototype tanks. A decision was then taken to concentrate on the team A design and a further 26 prototype tanks were built. These were followed by 50 pre-production tanks. In July 1963 Krauss-Maffei of Munich were nominated as prime contractor for production of the Leopard 1 MBT while MaK of Kiel produced the specialised versions (ARV, AEV and bridgelayer). Although MaK has also produced a number of Leopard 1 MBTs. The first production Leopard 1 was completed in September 1965.

There are the following models of the basic tank: Leopard 1A1 (series 1 through to 4), Leopard 1A1A1 (with a number of modifications including additional turret armour); the Australian, Belgian and Canadian Leopard 1s have a SABCA fire control system incorporating a laser rangefinder; Leopard 1A2, Leopard 1A3 with a new turret of welded construction and numerous other modifications (5th production batch, 110 built) and the Leopard 1A4 (6th production batch, 250 built), the Leopard 1A4 is similar to the A3 but has an integrated fire control system and a fully automatic gearbox. The Leopard 1 has a NBC system and a full range of night fighting and night driving aids, in addition it can be fitted with a snorkel for deep wading.

## Variants

*Armoured Recovery Vehicle:* This is basically a Leopard 1 chassis fitted with a superstructure, dozer blade, winch with 90m of cable and a max capacity of 35,000kg, and a crane with a traverse of 270° and a max lifting capacity of 20,000kg. The German Army only has a product improved version whose crane has increased lifting capacity. Armament consists of a 7.62mm AA MG and a 7.62mm bow MG, and smoke dischargers. Data is similar to the Leopard MBT except: **Length:** 7.57m (travelling); **Width:** 3.25m; **Height:** 2.7m (inc AA MG); **G/clearance:** 0.44m; **G/pressure:** 0.83kg/sq cm; **Weight:** 39,200kg (loaded); **Range:** 850km (road); **Fuel:** 1,410 litres; **Fording:** 2.10m.

*Armoured Pioneer Vehicle:* This is very similar to the armoured recovery vehicle but it has an earth boring tool and the dozer blade can be fitted with excavating teeth. Data is similar to the ARV except that it has a loaded weight of 40,200kg.

*GPM Engineer Vehicle:* Prototypes built by Krupp MaK and EWK for clearing river crossing points. Not yet in service.

*AA Vehicle:* Separate entry for Gepard SPAAG.

*Bridgelayer:* Two models of this were built in 1969. These were known as the Model A and Model B. The production version is the Model B and this entered service in 1973 with the German Army. It has a loaded weight of 45,300kg and its bridge is 22m long when in position. Other data is similar to the MBT except: **Crew:** 2; **Length:** 11.82m (with bridge), 10.56m (w/o bridge); **Width:** 4.00m (with bridge); **Height:** 3.57m (with bridge), 2.56m (w/o bridge); **G/pressure:** 0.97kg/sq cm; **Bridge capacity:** 50,000kg.

*Training Tank:* This is simply a Leopard 1 MBT with its turret removed and a cab fitted. It is used for training drivers. Loaded weight is about 40,000kg.

*Self-Propelled Gun:* Leopard 1 chassis fitted with the turret mounting a 155mm gun as fitted to the AMX-30 155mm GCT SP gun. Trials only.

## Employment

Australia (also ARV, bridgelayer), Belgium (also ARV, AEV, training), Canada (also ARV, bridgelayer), Denmark, FRG (also ARV, AEV, bridgelayer, training), Greece, Italy (also ARV, AEV), Netherlands (also ARV, AEV, bridgelayer, training), Norway (also ARV), Turkey.

*Leopard IA3 (left) and Leopard IA2.* Krauss-Maffei

*Leopard ARV of the Australian Army.* Paul Handel

*Leopard Biber bridgelayer laying its bridge in position.* Krauss-Maffei

# TAM Tank                                    FRG

**Armament:** 1 × 105mm gun, elevation +18°, depression −7° (50 rounds carried)
2 × 7.62mm MGs — coaxial and AA (6,000 rounds)
4 smoke dischargers either side of turret
**Crew:** 4
**Length:** 8.23m (gun forward), 6.775m (hull)
**Width:** 3.25m
**Height:** 2.42m (turret top)
**G/clearance:** 0.44m
**Weight:** 30,500kg
**G/pressure:** 0.79kg/sq cm
**Engine:** Supercharged MTU V-6 diesel developing 710hp at 2,200rpm
**Speed:** 75km/h
**Range:** 550km, 900km with long range fuel tanks
**Fuel:** 650 litres
**Fording:** 1.4m, 2.25m (with preparation), 4m (with snorkel)
**V/obstacle:** 1m
**Trench:** 2.5m
**Gradient:** 60%

## Development
The TAM (Tanque Argentino Mediado) was developed from 1974 by Thyssen Henschel to meet the requirements of Argentina who has a requirement for at least 200 vehicles. The first of three prototypes was completed in 1976 with the remaining two vehicles following in 1977. Production of the vehicle is now underway in Argentina but many components are still being supplied by Thyssen Henschel from West Germany.
    The TAM is based on a modified Marder MICV

chassis but with a more powerful engine and a new all welded turret armed with a stabilised 105mm rifled tank gun. Optional equipment includes two long range fuel tanks at the rear of the hull, snorkel for deep fording and passive night vision equipment.

## Variants
*VCTP:* Thyssen Henschel has also developed an infantry fighting vehicle for Argentina called the Vehiculo de Combate y Transporte de Personal, this is similar to the Marder but has a new two man turret armed with a 20mm cannon and 7.62mm MG. Argentina has a requirement for 300 VCTPs.
*TAM-4:* As a private venture Thyssen Henschel has developed to the prototype stage the TAM-4 which has a different powerpack and a more advanced fire control system.
*Dragon:* This twin 30mm SP AA system is a joint development between Thyssen Henschel (chassis) and Thomson-CSF of France (turret) and was shown in 1979. It has not yet been placed in production.
*155mm SP:* Project only.
*57mm SP AA gun:* Fitted with Bofors 57mm gun, project only.
*57mm Support tank:* Armed with 57mm Bofors gun, prototype only.

## Employment
The TAM is in service with Argentina.

*TAM tank armed with 105mm gun and fitted with long range fuel tanks.* Thyssen-Henschel

# Spähpanzer Luchs Reconnaissance Vehicle   FRG

**Armament:** 1 × 20mm Rh.202 cannon, elevation +80°, depression −15°, traverse 360° (500 rounds)
1 × 7.62mm MG3 AA MG (800 rounds)
2 × 4 smoke dischargers each side of turret
**Crew:** 4
**Length:** 7.743m
**Width:** 2.98m
**Height:** 2.905m (MG rail), 2.125m (hull top)
**G/clearance:** 0.44m (hull)
**Weight:** 19,500kg (loaded)
**Track:** 2.54m
**Wheelbase:** 1.4m + 2.365m + 1.4m
**Engine:** Daimler Benz Model OM 403 VA
10-cylinder multi-fuel engine developing 390hp at 2,500rpm
**Speed:** 90km/h (road), 9km/h (water)
**Range:** 800km
**Fuel:** 500 litres
**Fording:** Amphibious
**V/obstacle:** 0.6m
**Trench:** 1.9m
**Gradient:** 60%

## Development
In 1964 the German Army laid the foundations for a new range of vehicles which were to have included an 8 × 8 reconnaissance vehicle, 4 × 4 and 6 × 6 armoured load carriers and a whole range of 4 × 4, 6 × 6 and 8 × 8 trucks, all of these would share many common components. Prototypes of the 8 × 8 reconnaissance vehicle (Spähpanzer 2) were built by Daimler-Benz and a consortium of companies known as the Joint Project Office. The production contract was awarded to Rheinstahl (now Thyssen-Henschel) in December 1973, and the first production vehicle was completed in May 1975, and the last of 408 vehicles were completed early in 1978.

The vehicle is fully amphibious being propelled in the water by two propellers at the rear of the hull. An NBC system is fitted as is a full range of night vision equipment. The vehicle has full 8 × 8 drive and can also be driven backwards at max speed. The crew of four consists of front driver, commander and gunner in the turret, and rear driver/radio operator.

## Variants
Oerlikon has proposed that the Luchs could be fitted with their 35mm turret model GDD-B. It has also been proposed that the chassis could be used as the basis for a highly mobile version of the Euromissile Roland SAM system.

## Employment
In service with the German Army.

*The Spähpanzer Luchs 8×8 reconnaissance vehicle.* West German Army

# Wiesel Airportable Vehicle   FRG

**Armament:** Depends on role
**Crew:** 3
**Length:** 3.26m
**Width:** 1.82m
**Height:** 1.84m
**G/clearance:** 0.3m
**Weight:** 2,600kg
**G/pressure:** 0.35kg/sq cm
**Engine:** Audi water-cooled petrol developing 100hp

**Speed:** 85km/h
**Range:** 200km
**Fuel:** 80 litres
**V/obstacle:** 0.4m
**Trench:** 1.5m
**Gradient:** 60%
*Note:* Weight and height depends on armament fitted.

## Development/Variants

The Wiesel airportable light armoured vehicle has been developed by Porsche to meet the requirements of the German airborne units but owing to budgetry problems has not yet been placed in production.

The Wiesel has so far been fitted with the following armament installations: 7.62mm or 12.7mm MG; Rheinmetall 20mm cannon; Hughes TOW ATGW system; Euromissile HAKO turret with two HOT ATGW in ready-to-launch position.

## Employment

Prototypes only. Not so far placed in production.

*Wiesel airportable armoured vehicle with Rheinmetall 20mm cannon.* Porsche

# APE Amphibious Engineer Reconnaissance Vehicle

FRG

**Armament:** 1 × 20mm cannon
6 smoke dischargers
**Crew:** 5
**Length:** 6.93m
**Width:** 3.08m
**Height:** 2.4m (hull top)
**G/clearance:** 0.485m (hull), 0.555m (axles)
**Weight:** 14,500kg (loaded)
**Wheelbase:** 3.5m
**Track:** 2.54m (front), 2.56m (rear)
**Engine:** Mercedes-Benz OM 403 V-8 water-cooled diesel developing 390hp at 2,500rpm
**Speed:** 83km/h (road), 12km/h (water)
**Range:** 800km (cross-country)
**Fording:** Amphibious
**Gradient:** 75%

## Development

The APE (*Amphibisches Pionier Erkundungsfahr-zeug*) has been developed by EWK to meet the requirements of the West German Army for an amphibious engineer reconnaissance vehicle. The first prototype was completed in 1977 but production has yet to start owing to budgetry problems.

Some 90% of the automotive components of the APE are identical to the Transportpanzer 1 multi-purpose 6 × 6 vehicle which entered service with the West German Army in 1979 and is manufactured by Thyssen Henschel.

The APE has low-pressure balloon tyres the pressure of which can be adjusted by the driver to suit the type of ground being crossed. When the vehicle is afloat its axles are hydraulically raised to reduce drag and so enable a higher water speed to be attained. The two propellers mounted at the rear of the hull can be turned through 360° giving the

APE excellent manoeuvrability when afloat. Standard equipment includes bilge pumps and an NBC system and a wide range of armament installations can be fitted including a Rheinmetall 20mm cannon or an Oerlikon turret with 35mm cannon.

## Variants

EWK have suggested that the vehicle can be adopted for a wide range of roles including ambulance, APC, anti-tank with various ATGW installations, artillery fire control vehicle, command vehicle, communications vehicle, IS vehicle, mortar carrier, NBC reconnaissance vehicle, reconnaissance vehicle, repair vehicle, or supply carrier.

## Employment

Prototypes only.

*APE amphibious engineer reconnaissance vehicle.* EWK

# HWK 10 Series
FRG

**Data:** HWK 11 APC
**Armament:** 1 × 7.62mm or 12.7mm MG
**Crew:** 2 + 10
**Length:** 5.05m
**Width:** 2.53m
**Height:** 1.585m (w/o MG)
**G/clearance:** 0.435m
**Weight:** 11,000kg (loaded), 9,000kg (empty)
**G/pressure:** 0.55kg/sq cm
**Engine:** Chrysler 361B, 8-cylinder petrol engine developing 211hp at 4,000rpm
**Speed:** 65km/h (road)
**Range:** 320km (road)
**Fuel:** 300 litres
**Fording:** 1.20m
**V/obstacle:** 0.68m
**Trench:** 2.00m
**Gradient:** 60%
**Armour:** 8mm-14.5mm

## Development
The HWK 10 series of light tracked vehicles were designed in the early 1960s as a private venture by Henschel-Werke (now Thyssen Henschel). The first prototypes of the HWK 11 were built in 1963 and these were followed by 40 production vehicles for export, in 1964. Only two HWK 13s were built. The

*HWK 11 APC.* Thyssen-Henschel

hull of the HWK 11 is of all-welded construction and is proof against 7.62mm ammunition. The driver and commander have individual hatches, the crew have overhead hatches enabling them to fire their weapons from within the vehicle and there are two large doors at the rear of the vehicle. The HWK 11 is not fitted with an NBC system and it can be fitted with infra-red driving lights. It is not amphibious, capable only of fording.

## Variants
*HWK 10:* Armed with 10 anti-tank guided missiles.
*HWK 11:* APC.
*HWK 12:* Anti-tank vehicle armed with a turret-mounted 90mm gun.
*HWK 13:* Reconnaissance vehicle armed with a turret-mounted 20mm cannon.
*HWK 14:* Mortar carrier with an 81mm or 120mm mortar.
*HWK 15:* Wireless, command or artillery fire control vehicle.
*HWK 16:* Ambulance, no armament fitted.
*HWK 13 with ATGW:* For trials purposes one of the prototypes of the HWK 13 reconnaissance vehicle has had its 20mm turret removed and replaced by a Euromissile HOT turret with two missiles in the ready-to-launch position.

## Employment
Used only by Mexico.

# Schützenpanzer Neu Marder MICV
FRG

**Armament:** 1 × 20mm Rh 202 cannon, elevation +65°, depression −17° (1,250 rounds carried)
2 × 7.62mm MG3 MGs — coaxial and at rear (5,000 rounds)

6 smoke dischargers on the turret
**Crew:** 4 + 6
**Length:** 6.79m
**Width:** 3.24m

**Height:** 2.95m (inc searchlight), 2.86m (turret top)
**G/clearance:** 0.45m
**Weight:** 28,200kg (loaded)
**G/pressure:** 0.80kg/sq cm
**Engine:** MTU MB 833 Ea-500, 6-cylinder diesel
developing 600hp at 2,200rpm
**Speed:** 75km/h (road)
**Range:** 520km (road)
**Fuel:** 652 litres
**Fording:** 1.50m, 2.50m (with kit)
**V/obstacle:** 1.00m
**Trench:** 2.50m
**Gradient:** 60%

*Roland 2 SAM system in a Marder chassis.*
*West German Army*

## Development
The requirements for a new infantry combat vehicle
for the German Army were drawn up in 1959. The
first contracts for the construction of prototype
vehicles were awarded in 1960 to Rheinstahl,
Henschel and MOWAG (Switzerland). These were
the first prototype series. They were followed by the
second prototype series in 1961/1963. In 1967 a
further 10 prototypes were built, these being known
as the third series. In October 1969 a contract was
awarded to Rheinstahl (now Thyssen Henschel) for
the production of 1926 vehicles, of which Atlas MaK
of Kiel would build 875 vehicles.

In 1974 Rheinstahl was awarded a contract for a
further 210 vehicles which were completed in 1975.
The chassis now remains in production only for the
Roland SAM missile system. It is fitted with an NBC
system and a full range of night driving and night
fighting equipment.

The crew is provided with roof hatches and there
is a single ramp at the rear of the vehicle. Either side
of the hull are two ball type mountings that allow the
crew to fire their weapons from inside the vehicle.
The two turrets can be used against both ground and
air targets.

All Marders, except command vehicles, are to be
fitted with the Euromissile MILAN ATGW system

which has a max range of 2,000m. Other
improvements planned include: increased firepower
due to a double feed belt for the 20mm cannon,
night capability, transverse transmission and
ammunition stowage in the hull. When modified
these will become the Marder A1A while 670
vehicles with the complete kit, including the passive
night sight, will be known as the Marder A1.

## Variants
*Roland SAM System:* The West German Army uses
the Marder chassis for the Euromissile Roland 2 all
weather system while France uses the AMX-30
chassis for the Roland 1 (clear weather) and Roland
2 (all weather) systems, the United States uses a
modified M109 chassis designated the XM975. Two
missiles are carried in the ready to launch position
with a further eight rounds in reserve. The Roland
can engage aircraft flying at a maximum altitude of
5,000m and at a max range of 6,500m. First
production systems were delivered to the German
Army in 1978. Brazil also has four systems on a
Marder chassis.

*Trials models:* These have included an air defence
radar carrier, a 120mm mortar carrier and various
armament installations including a stabilised turret.
The chassis has also been proposed as the basis for
the British Aerospace Rapier SAM system.

*TAM Tank:* The Marder MICV is the basis of the
TAM Tank which is also used for the VCTP APC and
the Dragon twin 30mm SP AA gun system. There is
a separate entry for TAM earlier in the West German
section.

## Employment
Marder is used only by the West German Army.

63

# Transportpanzer 1 Multi-Purpose Armoured Vehicle

**Armament:** 1 × 7.62mm MG, elevation +40°, depression −15°
6 smoke dischargers
**Crew:** 2 + 10
**Length:** 6.76m
**Width:** 2.98m
**Height:** 2.3m (w/o MG)
**G/clearance:** 0.406m (hull), 0.506m (axles)
**Weight:** 17,000kg (loaded), 14,000kg (empty)
**Track:** 2.54m (front), 2.56m (rear)
**Wheelbase:** 1.75m + 2.05m
**Engine:** Mercedes-Benz Model OM 402A V-8 water-cooled diesel developing 320hp at 2,500rpm
**Speed:** 105km/h (road), 10.5km/h (water)
**Range:** 800km (road)
**Fuel:** 430 litres
**Fording:** Amphibious
**Trench:** 2.75m
**Gradient:** 70%

## Development
In the 1960s the West German Army laid the foundations for a complete family of wheeled armoured vehicles and high mobility cross-country trucks. The former included an 8 × 8 reconnaissance vehicle which was eventually placed in production as the Luchs and 4 × 4 and 6 × 6 amphibious multi-purpose vehicles. The latter was standardised as the Transportpanzer 1 (or Fuchs) and the first of 996 were handed over to the West Germany Army by Thyssen Henschel late in 1979.

In the West German Army the Transportpanzer 1 will be used for the following roles: armoured radar equipment vehicle (with Rasit radar), armoured command and radio vehicle, armoured engineer vehicle, armoured NBC defence and reconnaissance vehicle, armoured electronic warfare set carrier and armoured supply carrier.

All members of the family, with the exception of the electronic warfare carrier, are fully amphibious being propelled in the water by two propellers at the rear of the hull, and all have an NBC system.

## Variants
GLS, a subsidiary of Krauss-Maffei, has a licence for the sale and production of the Transportpanzer outside of West Germany and the vehicle has already been tested in Malaysia and the Philippines. It can be fitted with a wide range of armament installations including 7.62mm or 12.7mm MGs or a turret with 20mm or 25mm cannon or a 76mm or 90mm gun. Other roles that the vehicle could undertake include ambulance, anti-tank (with HOT, MILAN or TOW ATGWs), cargo, command, maintenance vehicle and recovery vehicle. In 1981 GLS built an 8 × 8 version of the Transportpanzer which has been tested in the Netherlands.

## Employment
In service with the West German Army.

*Transportpanzer 1 with 20mm Rheinmetall Rh202 cannon.* Daimler-Benz

# Schützenpanzer SPz 12-3 APC FRG

**Armament:** 1 × 20mm Hispano-Suiza 820 gun, elevation +75°, depression −10° (2,000 rounds carried)
1 × 7.62mm MG (optional)
2 × 4 smoke grenade launchers
**Crew:** 3 + 5
**Length:** 6.31m (inc gun), 5.56m (hull only)
**Width:** 2.54m
**Height:** 1.85m (inc turret), 1.63m (w/o turret)
**G/clearance:** 0.40m
**Weight:** 14,600kg (loaded)
**G/pressure:** 0.75kg/sq cm
**Engine:** Rolls-Royce B81 Mk 80F, 8-cylinder petrol engine developing 220hp at 4,000rpm
**Speed:** 58km/h (road)
**Range:** 270km
**Fuel:** 340 litres
**Fording:** 0.70m
**V/obstacle:** 0.60m
**Trench:** 1.60m
**Gradient:** 60%
**Armour:** 8mm-30mm

## Development
The SPz 12-3 (or Hispano-Suiza 30) was originally developed as a private venture by Hispano-Suiza of Switzerland. The chassis started off as an AA vehicle. For a number of reasons production of the vehicle was undertaken from 1958 to 1962 in England (by Leyland Motors) and Germany (Henschel and Hanomag). All models have a British built engine, the 20mm cannon was made in Germany by Rheinmetall. The SPz 12-3 does not have an NBC system, the vehicle is however fitted with infra-red

*HS-30 APC from rear.* West German Army

driving lights. In 1971 there were still over 1,800 of these vehicles in service. Hispano-Suiza projects included a 90mm tank destroyer, light tank with a 90mm gun, various AA vehicles and a rocket launcher vehicle. Variants used by the German Army are listed below.

## Variants
*SPz 12-3 with 106mm Recoilless Rifle:* This is a standard SPz 12-3 fitted with the American M40A1 106mm recoilless rifle over the rear of the vehicle. It retains its 20mm gun turret. Weight is 14,300kg.
*SPz 52-3 Panzermörser:* This vehicle is armed with a French 120mm mortar firing through the roof of the vehicle. The turret has been removed and the only armament fitted is a 7.62mm MG which is provided with a shield.
*SPz 21-3 Funkpanzer:* This is a command and radio vehicle.
*SPz 81-3 Feuerleitpanzer:* This is an artillery fire control vehicle and can also be used as a command post.
*SPz 12-3 with TOW system:* In 1971 tests were started on an Spz 12-3 with its turret removed and a TOW ATGW system installed. Some have been fitted with the MILAN ATGW for trials.

## Employment
Used only by the German Army.

# Condor APC

**Armament:** 1 × 20mm cannon, elevation +60°, depression −6°
1 × 7.62mm coaxial MG (optional)
2 × 4 smoke dischargers (optional)
**Crew:** 3 + 9
**Length:** 6.06m
**Width:** 2.47m
**Height:** 2.79m (turret top), 2.10m (hull top)
**G/clearance:** 0.48m
**Weight:** 9,800kg (loaded), 7,340kg (empty)
**Track:** 1.85m
**Wheelbase:** 3.306m
**Engine:** Daimler Benz OM 352A 6-cylinder water-cooled diesel developing 168hp
**Speed:** 105km/h
**Range:** 500km (road)
**Fuel:** 160 litres
**Fording:** Amphibious
**V/obstacle:** 0.55m
**Gradient:** 70%

*Condor (4×4) APC with turret-mounted 20mm cannon.* Thyssen-Henschel

## Development

The Condor APC has been developed as a private venture by Thyssen Henschel specifically for the export market as a successor to their UR-416 (4 × 4) vehicle which has been exported in large numbers.

The infantry enter and leave the vehicle via three doors, one in each side of the hull and one at the rear, and four vision blocks each with a firing port enable some of the infantry to use their small arms from within the vehicle.

The Condor is fully amphibious being propelled in the water by its wheels and optional equipment includes propellers for a higher water speed, air conditioning system, intercom, night vision equipment, NBC system and a front-mounted winch.

## Variants

This basic model has a Rheinmetall TF20 one-man turret but a wide range of other types of armament can be fitted including turrets with MILAN or HOT ATGWs, and the vehicle can also be used as an ambulance, cargo carrier, command vehicle and internal security vehicle.

## Employment

Production. In service in Ecuador.

# UR-416 APC

**Armament:** 1 × 7.62mm MG, elevation +75°, depression −10°
**Crew:** 2 + 8
**Length:** 4.99m
**Width:** 2.30m
**Height:** 2.225m (hull top)
**G/clearance:** 0.44m (differential)
**Weight:** 7,600kg (loaded), 5,700kg (empty)
**Track:** 1.78m
**Engine:** DB OM-352, 6-cylinder, water-cooled, in-line, diesel developing 120hp at 2,800rpm
**Speed:** 85km/h (road)
**Range:** 700km (road)
**Fuel:** 150 litres
**Fording:** 1.40m
**V/obstacle:** 0.55m
**Trench:** nil
**Gradient:** 70%
**Armour:** 9mm
**Wheelbase:** 2.90m

## Development

The UR-416 has been designed by Rheinstahl (now Thyssen Henschel) primarily for internal security duties and border patrols. The first prototype was completed in 1965 and series production commenced in 1969. The chassis used is that of the famous Daimler-Benz Unimog; this is a 4 × 4 (cross country) or 4 × 2 (road vehicle). The hull is of all welded construction and doors are provided in the sides and rear of the vehicle, in addition there are hatches in the roof and firing ports are provided at the sides and rear of the vehicle. The hull can be easily separated from the chassis for maintenance

*UR-416 APC armed with turret-mounted Rh202 20mm cannon. Thyssen-Henschel*

purposes. Optional extras include radios, various types of tyres and a winch.

## Variants

The following versions of the basic armoured personnel carrier have been developed by Rheinstahl:

*Ambulance:* Carrying eight sitting, or four stretcher, or four sitting and two stretcher patients.
*Command:* Crew of four with various radios, mapboards etc.
*Scout Car:* Various versions armed with: 1 × turret-mounted 7.62mm MG; 2 × turret-mounted 7.62mm MGs; 1 × turret-mounted cannon (two versions); 1 × turret-mounted 90mm recoilless rifle; 1 × turret-mounted 20mm Rh.202 cannon.
*Missile:* Two versions: Cobra anti-tank missile vehicle and TOW anti-tank missile vehicle.
*Maintenance:* Has a jib at the front, welding equipment, benches and tools.
*Police:* Three types of police vehicle have been designed: one fitted with obstacle clearing blade at the front; one fitted with observation Cupola Model I; and one fitted with observation Cupola Model II.

## Employment

Over 500 UR-416s have been built. Known users include Ecuador, El Salvador, Ethiopia, the FRG, Greece, Morocco, Netherlands, Peru, Togo, Turkey, Venezuela, Zimbabwe. Producion is now undertaken by Thyssen Maschinenbau.

# Jagdpanzer Kanone JPz 4-5 SP Anti-Tank Gun FRG

**Armament:** 1 × 90mm gun, elevation + 15°, depression −8°, traverse 15° left and right (51 rounds carried)
2 × 7.62mm MGs — coaxial and AA (4,000 rounds)
8 smoke dischargers
**Crew:** 4
**Length:** 8.75m (inc gun), 6.238m (hull only)
**Width:** 2.98m
**Height:** 2.085m (w/o AA MG)
**G/clearance:** 0.45m (front), 0.44m (rear)
**Weight:** 25,700kg (loaded)
**G/pressure:** 0.75kg/sq cm (loaded)
**Engine:** Daimler-Benz, MB 837, 8-cylinder diesel developing 500hp at 2,000rpm
**Speed:** 70km/h (road)
**Range:** 400km (road)
**Fuel:** 470 litres
**Fording:** 1.40m, 2.10m (with kit)
**V/obstacle:** 0.75m
**Trench:** 2.00m
**Gradient:** 60%
**Armour:** 50mm (max)

### Development
This vehicle uses the same chassis as the Jagdpanzer Rakete. Design of the JPZ 4-5 started in the late 1950s and the first prototypes were built by Hanomag (1 RU 3/1, 1 RU 3/2), Henschel (1 HK 3/1, 1 HK 3/2) and MOWAG (HM 3), these were known as the first series. They were followed by the second series built by Hanomag and Henschel in 1962/63. Last came the third series from Hanomag (RU 331-333) and Henschel (RU 334-336). The vehicle

*Jagdpanzer Kanone: note 7.62mm MG on roof. Rheinmetall*

was then ordered in quantity. A total of 750 vehicles has been built for the German Army by Rheinstahl-Hanomag and Rheinstahl-Henschel, production ran from 1965 to 1967. In 1972 Belgium ordered 80 of these which were assembled in Belgium for the Belgian Army. The Belgian vehicles have modernised transmission and suspension system (using Marder components) and an improved fire control system which includes laser rangefinder, a Lyran launcher for launching flares has also been fitted.

An NBC system is fitted and infra-red driving and fighting lights can be fitted. The 90mm gun has an effective combat range of 2,000m and fires HEAT-T and HESH-T rounds; max stated rate of fire is 12 rounds/min. The gun is elevated and traversed by hand and a double baffle muzzle brake is fitted.

### Variants
The Jagdpanzer Rakete has the same hull. Other variants that have not reached production include a multiple rocket launcher system, an AA vehicle and a reconnaissance tank (Spähpanzer). Thyssen Henschel have suggested that the JPZ 4-5 could be refitted with a 105mm gun.

### Employment
Used by the Belgian and German armies.

# TM 170, TM 125 and TM 90 APCs

| | TM 170 | TM 125 | TM 90 |
|---|---|---|---|
| **Crew:** | 2 + 12 | 2 + 10 | 1 + 3 |
| **Length:** | 6.1m | 5.54m | 4.4m |
| **Width:** | 2.45m | 2.46m | 2.05m |
| **Height:** (w/o armament) | 2.2m | 2.015m | 1.85m |
| **G/clearance:** | 0.48m | 0.46m | not available |
| **Weight:** (loaded) | 9,500kg | 7,600kg | 4,200kg |
| (empty) | 7,000kg | 5,410kg | 3,400kg |
| **Track:** | 1.84m | 1.78m | 1.49m |
| **Wheelbase:** | 3.25m | 2.9m | 2.6m |
| **Engine:** | Daimler Benz diesel developing 168hp | Daimler Benz diesel developing 125hp | Diesel developing 90 or 142hp |
| **Speed:** (road) | 100km/h | 85km/h | 110km/h |
| (water) | 9km/h | 8km/h | not applicable |
| **Fuel:** | 175 litres | 175 litres | 105 litres |
| **Range:** | 670km | 700km | 600km |
| **Fording:** | Amphibious | Amphibious | not available |
| **Gradient:** | 80% | 80% | 70% |

## Development/Variants

The TM 170, TM 125 and TM 90 range of 4 × 4
vehicles has been developed as a private venture by
Thyssen Maschinenbau primarily for use in the
internal security role. First prototypes of all vehicles
were completed in 1978 and the TM 170 and TM
125 entered production the following year. The
largest two models in the series, the TM 170 and TM

125 are both based on a Mercedes Benz Unimog
chassis and are fully amphibious being propelled in
the water by their wheels. Both vehicles are provided
with firing ports and can be fitted with a wide range
of optional equipment including an auxiliary heater,
fire warning and extinguishing system, hydraulic
winch with a capacity of 5,000kg, NBC system and a
hydraulically operated obstacle clearing blade at the
front of the hull. It addition to being used as an
IS/APC they can also be used in the ambulance,
cargo and command roles.

## Employment

Production. In service with undisclosed countries.

*Thyssen Maschinenbau TM170 APC used in
command role with Plessey communications
equipment.   Plessey Co Ltd*

# Jagdpanzer Rakete RJPz-2 Missile-Armed Anti-Tank Vehicle

**Armament:** 1 × launcher for HOT ATGW (20 HOT carried)
2 × 7.62mm MGs — bow and AA (3,200 rounds carried)
8 smoke dischargers
**Crew:** 4
**Length:** 6.61m
**Width:** 3.12m
**Height:** 2.54m (inc missiles), 1.98m (hull top)
**G/clearance:** 0.45m (front), 0.44m (rear)
**Weight:** 23,000kg
**G/pressure:** 0.63kg/sq cm
**Engine:** Daimler Benz MB 837 8-cylinder water-cooled diesel developing 500hp at 2,000rpm
**Speed:** 70km/h
**Range:** 400km (road)
**Fuel:** 470 litres
**Fording:** 1.4m, 2.1m (with preparation)
**V/obstacle:** 0.75m
**Trench:** 2m
**Gradient:** 60%

## Development
Between 1967 and 1968 Hanomag and Henschel each built 185 Jagdpanzer Rakete (RJPZ-2) SP anti-tank vehicles for the West German Army. These have almost the same hull as the Jagdpanzer Kanone 90mm SP anti-tank gun but had two launchers for the French SS-11 ATGW for which 14 missiles were carried.

These are now being rebuilt with a single Euromissile K3S HOT ATGW system which has a single launcher for the 4,000m range HOT missile with a total of 20 missiles being carried in the hull. The first vehicle was handed over to the West German Army in 1978 and at least 316 of the 370 vehicles will be brought up to this standard. In addition, this vehicle, which is also called the Jaguar 1, has been fitted with additional armour to the front and sides of the hull.

## Variants
*Jaguar 2:* For trials purposes two vehicles have been fitted with the Hughes TOW ATGW system fitted with the AN/TAS-4 night sight, these are known as the Jaguar 2 and also have the additional armour protection.

## Employment
In service only with the West German Army.

*Jagdpanzer Rakete with HOT ATGW.* Euromissile

# Flakpanzer 1 Gepard SP AA Vehicle FRG

**Armament:** 2 × 35mm belt-fed Oerlikon cannon, elevation +85°, depression −10°, traverse 360° (620 AA and 40 AP rounds carried)
4 smoke dischargers mounted each side of the turret
**Crew:** 3
**Length:** 7.73m (guns forward)
**Width:** 3.25m
**Height:** 3.01m (radar retracted)
**Weight:** 47,300kg (loaded), 44,800 (empty)
**G/pressure:** 0.95kg/sq cm
**Engine:** MTU MB 838 Ca.M500, 10-cylinder multi-fuel engine developing 830hp at 2,200rpm. An auxiliary engine is also fitted
**Speed:** 65km/h (road)
**Range:** 550km (road), 400km (cross-country)
**Fuel:** 985 litres
**Fording:** 2.50m
**V/obstacle:** 1.15m
**Trench:** 2.00m
**Gradient:** 60%

## Development/Variants

The Gepard is an autonomous all weather anti-aircraft gun system for defence against low flying aircraft, and can be switched within seconds from an anti-aircraft to an anti-tank role.

The first prototype 5PZF-A was delivered in 1968 and tested the following year, the participating companies were: Oerlikon for the turret and armament, Contraves for the computer and integration, Siemens-Albis for the target tracking radar, Hollandse for the search radar and Krauss-

*CA 1 SP AA gun system as used by the Netherlands Army.* Oerlikon

Maffei for the chassis and power supply system. In 1969 a further four prototypes were ordered. These were designated 5PZF-B. At about the same time the Netherlands Army became interested in the vehicle and they ordered a model known as the 5PZF-C, these differ only in their make and type of radar system. After successful trials 12 pre-production 5PZF-Bs were ordered by Germany in 1970 followed by an order from the Netherlands for five 5PZF-Cs. The 5PZF-B has a search radar developed by Siemens and a tracking radar developed by Siemens-Albis whilst the 5PFZ-C has an integrated search and tracking radar by Hollandse. Both of these systems have radars with a range of 15km approx. If required the search antenna can be folded down behind the turret and the tracking antenna can be turned towards the turret in an armoured position. The 35mm Oerlikon KDA cannon have a cyclic rate of fire of 550 rounds/min/barrel and each cannon has 310 rounds of AA and 20 rounds of armour-piercing ammunition for ready use. A typical burst, when used in the anti-aircraft role, is 20 to 40 rounds, with engagement range between 3,000 and 4,000m.

## Employment

Production completed late in 1980. In service with Belgium, FGR and the Netherlands.

# Wildcat SP AA Vehicle

FGR

**Armament:** 2 × 30mm Mauser MK 30-F cannon, elevation +85°, depression −5°, turret traverse 360° (520 rounds carried)
**Crew:** 3
**Length:** 6.88m
**Width:** 2.98m
**Height:** 2.74m (radar lowered)
**G/clearance:** 0.4m
**Weight:** 17,500kg (loaded)
**Engine:** Daimler-Benz 8-cylinder exhaust turbocharged diesel developing 320hp at 2,500rpm
**Speed:** 105km/h
**Range:** 800km
**Fuel:** 430 litres
**Gradient:** 60%

## Development

The Wildcat twin 30mm SP AA gun system has been developed as a private venture by a consortium consisting of Daimler-Benz (automotive components) Hollandse Signaalapparaten (optronic tracker), Mauser (armament) and Siemens (search radar), with Krauss-Maffei being prime contractor and responsible for system integration. The vehicle, which was shown for the first time at the 1981 Paris Air Show, uses many automotive components of the Transportpanzer 1 (6 × 6) vehicle already in service with the West German Army.

Five versions of the Wildcat have been proposed with the first prototype being a V3 model, major differences between the models are listed below:

|  | V1 | V2 | V3 | V4 | V5 |
|---|---|---|---|---|---|
| **IFF:** | visual | visual/or via data link | integrated | integrated | integrated |
| **Weather:** | fair | fair | fair | light haze | all-weather |
| **Time:** | day | day | day | day/night | day/night |
| **Target detection:** | optical | optical or via data link on PPI | radar/ optical | radar/ optical | radar/ optical |
| **Target tracking:** | manual/ automatic | automatic | automatic | automatic | automatic |

## Variants

There are no variants apart from the different versions mentioned above although the turret is also suitable for installation on other chassis, both tracked and wheeled.

## Employment

Trials.

*V3 prototype of the Wildcat twin 30mm SPAAG.*

# SK-1 Armoured Car

**Armament:** 1 × 7.92mm MG34
**Crew:** 5
**Length:** 4.00m
**Width:** 2.00m
**Height:** 2.80m
**G/clearance:** 0.28m
**Weight:** 5,400kg (loaded)
**Engine:** Model 30K, 4-cylinder, in-line, petrol engine developing 55hp at 2,800rpm
**Speed:** 80km/h (road)
**Range:** 350km
**Fording:** 0.54m
**V/obstacle:** 0.40m
**Track:** 1.5m (front), 1.45m (rear)
**Wheelbase:** 3.77m
**Armour:** 8mm

The SK-1 armoured car is based on the chassis of the Robur Garant 30K (4 × 4) truck and entered service with the East German security units in 1954. It has not been employed by the East German Army.

The SK-2 is an armoured water cannon based on the chassis of the G 5 (6 × 6) 3,500kg truck. East Germany has also developed specialised versions of the T-34 and T-54/T-55 tanks for use in the recovery role as well as an armoured repair vehicle based on the chassis of the SU-76 SP gun.

*SK-1 armoured cars without armament installed.*

# FUG Amphibious Scout Car

**Armament:** 1 × 7.62mm MG (1,250 rounds carried)
**Crew:** 2 + 4
**Length:** 5.79m
**Width:** 2.5m
**Height:** 1.91m (hull top), 2.25m (with turret, OT-65A)
**G/clearance:** 0.34m
**Weight:** 7,000kg
**Track:** 1.9m
**Wheelbase:** 3.2m
**Engine:** Csepel D.414.44 4-cylinder in-line water-cooled diesel developing 100hp at 2,300rpm
**Speed:** 87km/h (road), 9km/h (water)
**Range:** 600km (road)
**Fuel:** 200 litres
**Fording:** Amphibious
**V/obstacle:** 0.4m
**Trench:** 1.2m
**Gradient:** 60%
**Armour:** 13mm (max)

## Development

The FUG entered service with the Hungarian Army in 1964 and with the Czechoslovakian and Polish Armies in 1966 and has, in the past, been called the FUG-63. The vehicle carries out the same role as the Soviet BRDM-1 but has its engine at the rear instead of the front.

The vehicle is fully amphibious being propelled in the water by two water jets at the rear of the hull, before entering the water a trim vane is erected at the front and the bilge pumps switched on.

All vehicles have two powered belly wheels on

73

either side, these are lowered when crossing rough country or when crossing ditches. Standard equipment includes infra-red driving lights and a central tyre pressure regulation system. The FUG is not fitted with a winch.

**Variants**
*Ambulance:* With stretchers being loaded through the roof hatches.
*Radiological-chemical reconnaissance vehicle:* Used to mark lane lines through contaminated areas. Mounted at the rear of the hull are two racks that dispense marking pennants into the ground.
*OT-65A:* Czechoslovakian modification with turret of OT-62B APC mounted on the roof. This is armed with a 7.62mm MG with an elevation of +20° and a depression of −10°; mounted externally on the turret is a 82mm T-21 Tarasnice recoilless gun.
*FUG-70:* This was a designation given to a new vehicle first seen in 1970 but it is now known that this in fact was an APC. There is a separate entry for this vehicle which is now known to be called the PSzH-IV.

**Employment**
Czechoslovakia, Hungary and Poland.

*FUG amphibious scout car without armament fitted.*

# PSzH-IV APC

# Hungary

**Armament:** 1 × 14.5mm MG, elevation +30°, depression −5° (500 rounds carried)
1 × 7.62mm coaxial MG (2,000 rounds)
**Crew:** 3 + 6
**Length:** 5.70m
**Width:** 2.50m
**Height:** 2.30m
**G/clearance:** 0.42m
**Weight:** 7,500kg
**Wheelbase:** 3.3m

**Engine:** Csepel D.414.44 4-cylinder in-line water-cooled diesel developing 100hp at 2,300rpm
**Speed:** 80km/h (road), 9km/h (water)
**Range:** 500km (road)
**Fuel:** 200 litres
**Fording:** Amphibious
**V/obstacle:** 0.4m
**Trench:** 0.6m (with channel)
**Gradient:** 60%
**Armour:** 14mm (max)

*PSzH-IV APC.*

## Development

Following the development of the FUG amphibious scout car Hungary developed an APC. This was incorrectly identified as the FUG-66 and then the FUG-70 in the West. It is now known that its correct designation is the PSzH-IV and it is in fact an APC and not a reconnaissance vehicle. It is sometimes called the FUG D-944.

The vehicle is fully amphibious being propelled in the water by two water jets at the rear of the hull, before entering the water a trim vane is erected at the front of the hull and the bilge pumps are switched on.

The main difference between the PSzH-IV and the FUG is that the former has a turret but not fitted with belly wheels as a door is provided in each side of the hull. All vehicles have a central tyre pressure regulation system, infra-red night vision equipment and a NBC system.

## Variants

Ambulance, Command vehicle with turret, Command vehicle without turret, NBC reconnaissance vehicle.

## Employment

GDR and Hungary.

# AFV Production                                      India

Since 1965 the Indian Tank Plant at Avadi has been producing the Vijayanta MBT, which was designed to meet the requirements of the Indian Army by Vickers Limited of Elswick, England, and by early 1981 it is estimated that some 1,200 tanks have been completed with production continuing. Future production tanks are to be fitted with the British Marconi Radar Systems SFCS 600 fire control system, a contract for this being announced early in 1981. Following trials with two vehicles, India ordered a quantity of Soviet T-72 MBTs but it is not known if India intends to produce this under licence in the future. India has also been given presentations of the British Vickers Valiant and the Royal Ordnance Factories FV4030/2 and FV4030/3 MBTs. It is also reported that India is developing a new APC to supplement its existing fleet of BTR-50, BTR-152, OT-62 and OT-64 APCs.

# 155mm SP-70                                International

Currently undergoing trials are prototypes of the 155mm SP-70 SP howitzer. This is a joint project between FRG, Italy and the UK for a new rapid fire system to replace the current M109 from the late 1980s. FRG is the project leader and is responsible for the development of the ordnance, the main powerpack and the chassis which is based on the Leopard 1 MBT; Italy is responsible for the cradle, recoil system, elevating and balancing gear, the auxiliary power unit and the fuel system and the United Kingdom is responsible for the turret including ammunition handling and sighting system.

The first of 12 prototypes was completed in 1976 and when accepted for service production will be undertaken in all three countries, in Italy by OTO-Melara and in the UK by Royal Ordnance Factory Nottingham.

The SP-70 will feature a high rate of fire and fire HE projectiles to a max range of 24,000m as well as RAPs to a max range of 30,000m; other types of ammunition can also be fired including smoke, illuminating and the Martin Marietta Cannon Launched Guided Projectile.

## Employment

Trials. Not yet in production or service.

*One of the prototypes of the International SP-70.*
Rheinmetall

# AFV Production

## Ireland

From 1972 Technology Investments designed the Timoney 4 × 4 APC with the first prototypes being completed the following year. In 1976 the Belgian company of Beherman Domoen obtained a licence to undertake production of the Timoney APC in Belgium both for the Belgian Government and for export. Full details of the Timoney APC, called the BDX by Beherman Domoen, are given in the Belgian section.

More recently Technology Investments have delivered five pre-production Timoney APCs to the Irish Army who have a requirement for between 100 and 200 vehicles of this type. Technology Investments are also designing a 6× 6 version of this APC as well as a 6 × 6 armoured car and a 13,000kg light tank.

# Merkava MBT

## Israel

**Armament:** 105mm gun, elevation +20°, depression −8° (65+ rounds carried) 3×7.62mm MG (1 coaxial, 2 AA) (3,000 approx rounds carried) Smoke dischargers and 60mm roof-mounted mortar
**Crew:** 4
**Length:** 8.63m (gun forward), 7.45m (hull)
**Width:** 3.7m
**Height:** 2.64m (turret roof)
**G/clearance:** 0.5m
**Weight:** 56,000kg
**Engine:** Continental AVDS-1790-5A V-12 diesel developing 900hp at 2,400rpm
**Speed:** 46km/h
**Range:** 500km
**Fuel:** 1,200 litres (estimate)
**Fording:** 1m
**V/obstacle:** 1m
**Trench:** 3m
**Gradient:** 60%

### Development
The Merkava MBT was developed from the late 1960s by the Israeli Ordnance Corps under the direction of General Tal and was revealed for the first time in 1977 with first production tanks being delivered in 1979.

The layout of the Merkava is unusual with the engine and transmission at the front and the fighting compartment with its small cross section turret at the rear. Doors in the rear of the hull allow ammunition to be quickly replenished. The Merkava normally carries about 65 rounds of 105mm ammunition (including APFSDS) but this can be increased to 85 rounds at least. As an alternative to the increased ammunition load six infantrymen or battlefield casualties.

Standard equipment includes night vision equipment, fire control system incorporating a laser rangefinder, fire detection and suppression system and a NBC system.

### Variants
Under development is the Merkava Mark 2· with hydropneumatic suspension while the Mark 3 with a larger calibre gun and more powerful engine is projected for the mid-1980s.

### Employment
In service with Israel.

*Merkava Mark 1 MBT.*

# RAM V-1 Light Armoured Reconnaissance Vehicle

Israel

**Armament:** See below
**Crew:** 2 + 4
**Length:** 5.02m
**Width:** 2.03m
**Height:** 1.59m (loaded), 1.71m (unloaded)
**G/clearance:** 0.31m
**Weight:** 4,100kg (unloaded)
**Track:** 1.726m
**Wheelbase:** 3.4m
**Engine:** Deutz F6L-912 air-cooled diesel developing 115hp
**Speed:** 95km/h
**Range:** 850km (road)
**Fuel:** 120 litres
**Fording:** 0.75m
**Gradient:** 65%
**Side slope:** 30%

## Development

The RAM V-1 has been designed by RAMTA Structures and Systems, a subsidiary of Israel Aircraft Industries as the successor to the early RBY Mark 1. In appearance the RAM V-1 is almost identical to the earlier vehicle but is powered by a diesel engine for increased operating range, has

*RAM V-1 light armoured reconnaissance vehicle with overhead protection; photo taken from the rear.* RAMPTA Structures and Systems

larger tyres and wheels giving a higher ground clearance and an automatic instead of a manual gear box.

In the light combat configuration it carries six men, commander, driver and four infantrymen, and is armed with three 7.62mm MGs, six rifles, one 52mm mortar plus grenades, flares and ammunition.

## Variants

AA (twin 20mm cannon), anti-tank, attack, company/brigade command vehicle, light combat, long range surveillance, medical evacuation, multiple rocket launcher and strike. There is also an armoured version of the RAM V-1 with overhead protection.

## Employment

Development was completed in 1980.

# RBY Mk 1 Armoured Reconnaissance Vehicle

Israel

*RBY Mk 1 armed with 7.62mm MGs.*
RAMPTA Structures and Systems

**Armament:** See text below
**Crew:** 2 + 6
**Length:** 5.023m
**Width:** 2.03m
**Height:** 1.66m (w/o armament)
**G/clearance:** 0.48m (hull), 0.375m (transfer case)
**Weight:** 3,600kg (empty)
**Track:** 1.665m
**Wheelbase:** 3.4m
**Engine:** Dodge Model 225.2, 6-cylinder water cooled petrol engine developing 120hp
**Speed:** 100km/h (road)
**Range:** 550km (road), 400km (cross country)
**Fuel:** 140 litres
**Fording:** 0.75m
**Gradient:** 60%
**Armour:** 10mm (max)

## Development

The RBY Mk 1 light armoured reconnaissance vehicle has been designed and produced by RAMTA Structures and Systems, a subsidiary of Israel Aircraft Industries and was announced in 1975. It has now been succeeded in production by the RAM V-1 light armoured reconnaissance vehicle which is very similar in appearance but is powered by a diesel instead of a petrol engine for increased operational range. The driver and commander are seated at the front of the vehicle whilst the six passengers are seated to the rear, three down each side of the hull. There is no overhead protection for the crew and passengers' compartment in the RBY Mk 1. It does not have a NBC system and has no amphibious capabilities. The vehicle can be carried internally by the Sikorsky CH-53 helicopter which is used by the Israeli Air Force.

## Variants

The basic vehicle is normally armed with up to four 7.62mm or 12.7mm MGs on individual mounts around the top of the hull. Other variants include an anti-tank model with a single 106mm M40 recoilless rifle which is made in Israel by Israel Military Industries and an AA vehicle with two 20mm rapid fire cannon. If required a winch with a capacity of 2,722kg can be mounted at the front of the hull.

## Employment

Israel and Guatemala.

78

# Modified AFVs

Israel has been modifying and adapting AFVs to its own requirements for many years. Below is a resumé of some of these modifications.

## Centurion MBT
These have been rebuilt by the Israeli Ordnance Corps and now have the 105mm L7 series rifled tank gun, Teledyne Continental AVDS-1790-2A diesel, Allison CD-850-6 automatic transmission and a new cooling system plus many other minor modifications and are designated the Upgraded Centurion by the Israeli Army. The tank has a max road speed of 43km/h and twice the operational range of the Centurion Mark 5 on which it is based.

## M1 Super Sherman
100 were delivered from France in the 1950s armed with 76.2mm guns, all have now been converted to other specialised roles.

## M50 Mark 1 and M50 Mark 2 Shermans
Sherman with French 75mm CN-75-50 gun mounted in a new cast turret (Mark 1), later fitted with Cummins 460hp diesel, wider tracks and HVSS suspension (Mark 2).

## M50 Sherman
Sherman with 460hp Cummins diesel, HVSS suspension, wider tracks, modified steering, transmission and exhaust, infra-red/white light searchlight mounted over main armament, two smoke dischargers mounted either side of turret. Has French modified CN-105-F1 gun designated the D1504 which fires non-rotating HEAT, HE, smoke and practice rounds. Also fitted with new French SAMM CH 23-1 hydraulic turret/gun control system.

## Specialised versions
These include an armoured ambulance, mine clearing vehicle, artillery observation vehicle (with hydraulic observation system), armoured command vehicle and various engineer and mine clearing versions.

## M48
Israel has received M48A1, M48A2 and M48A2Cs from the United States and Germany. The following modifications have been carried out which bring the vehicle up to M60 standards: 105mm gun fitted, Continental diesel engine, wider tracks and an Xenon searchlight. Some M48s have a smaller commander's cupola and an open 12.7mm machine gun.

## T-54 and T-55
Israel has rebuilt many captured Soviet T-54 and T-55 tanks. These are called TI-67 and are not liked by the Israelis. The modifications have included the fitting of an American diesel engine, the 100mm gun has been replaced by a 105mm British gun, a 12.7mm AA MG has replaced the Soviet one, a fire control system has been installed as has a new electrical system and air-conditioning.

## 160mm Self-Propelled Mortar Carrier
This is an M7 or M4 Sherman chassis on which has been mounted a 160mm Soltam mortar. When in action the sides and front of the vehicle can be folded horizontal thus providing space for the crew of

*Sherman fitted with dozer blade for use in forward combat areas.* Israeli Army

4-7 men to load the weapon. The mortar has a max range of 9,600m and is breech loaded. A high rate of fire can be achieved. A 12.7mm AA MG is fitted.

**Half-Tracks**
The Israeli Army has adapted many M2 and M3 half-tracks for various roles including ambulances, command vehicles, ammunition vehicles, load carriers and engineer vehicles. Other versions include:
*Missile:* This had four SS-11 ATGW mounted in the ready-to-fire position, it is no longer in service.
*Anti-Aircraft:* This is armed with 2 × 20mm cannon.
*Mortar:* This is armed with a Soltam 120mm mortar which has a range of 400m-6,500m. Over 30 rounds

*Israeli half-track with 120mm Soltam mortar firing forwards.* Soltam

of ammunition are carried. The mortar can also be moved from the vehicle for firing.
*Anti-Tank:* Armed with a 106mm recoilless rifle.
*Anti-Tank:* Armed with a 90mm Mecar gun, it is doubtful if any of these remain in service.

**Soviet and Egyptian APCs**
The Israeli Army have adapted BTR-40, BTR-50, BTR-152 and the Egyptian Walid APCs to their own requirements. These wheeled vehicles are used in the internal security role.

# 155mm L-33 SP Gun/Howitzer Israel

**Armament:** 1 × 155mm howitzer
1 × 7.62mm AA MG
**Crew:** 8
**Length:** 8.47m (with armament), 6.47m (hull)

*L-33 SP gun/howitzer.* Israeli Army

**Width:** 3.45m
**Height:** 3.45m
**G/clearance:** 0.43m
**Weight:** 41,500kg
**G/pressure:** 0.84kg/sq cm
**Engine:** Cummins VT 8-460-B1, diesel developing 460hp at 2,600rpm
**Speed:** 36km/h
**Range:** 260km
**Fuel:** 640 litres
**Fording:** 0.9m
**V/obstacle:** 0.91m
**Trench:** 2.3m
**Gradient:** 60%
**Armour:** 64mm (max)

### Development
The L-33 has been in service with the Israeli Army since 1973 and was used for the first time operationally in the 1973 Middle East conflict. It consists of a Sherman chassis (with horizontal volute suspension) on which has been mounted a Soltam M-68 155mm gun howitzer with armour protection. This weapon has an elevation of +52° and a depression of −3°, total traverse being 30° left and 30° right. It fires a projectile weighing 43.7kg with a m/v of 725 m/sec to a max range of 21,000m. A total of 60 rounds of ammunition are carried, of these 16 are ready for immediate use. The ammunition consists of the projectile, cartridge and the charge. An automatic compressed air rammer is mounted on the cradle and this can be used at all angles of elevation. A 7.62mm MG with a traverse of 360° is mounted on the right side of the roof, this can be used against both ground and air targets.

### Employment
In service with the Israeli Army.

# 155mm M-50 SP Howitzer                                    Israel

*155mm M-50 SP howitzer.* Israeli Army

This was developed in the late 1950s and entered service in 1963 and consists of a Sherman tank chassis with its engine moved to the front right and a French 155mm Model 50 howitzer mounted at the rear of the hull. The howitzer, which was originally a towed model, fires an HE projectile weighing 43kg to a max range of 17,000m.

Sherman chassis with both horizontal and vertical volute suspension systems were used for these conversions.

### Employment
In service only with the Israeli Army

# Soltam 155mm SP Gun/Howitzer
Israel

As a private venture Soltam Limited have designed a turret fitted with a 155mm gun/howitzer that has for trials purposes been fitted to a modified Centurion MBT chassis, although it can also be fitted to other types of chassis such as the M48 or M60. The

*Soltam 155mm SP gun/howitzer on Centurion chassis.* Soltam

ordnance has an elevation of +65° and a depression of −3° and is fitted with a fume extractor, single baffle muzzle brake and a travelling lock. It fires an HE projectile (weight 43.7kg) to a max range of 20,000m, a total of 44 projectiles are carried with 16 of these ready for immediate use. A pneumatic rammer enables the ordnance to be loaded at all angles of elevation. The prototype has a 33 calibre barrel but a 39 calibre barrel is also available, this having a range of 23,500m.

# AFV Production
Italy

Although Italy did contribute to the technical requirements that resulted in the development of the West German Leopard 1 and French AMX-30 MBTs in the mid-1950s the country decided to adopt the American M60A1. 200 of these were built under licence by OTO-Melara with a further 100 being supplied direct from Chrysler in the United States.

In 1970 Italy placed an order for 800 Leopard 1 MBTs, 200 of which were supplied from Krauss-Maffei of West Germany, with the remaining 600 being produced under licence by a consortium headed by OTO-Melara. Italy also ordered 69

Leopard 1 ARVs and 12 AEVs which were built by MaK. The first Italian built Leopard 1 was completed in 1974 and the last of the original order was completed in 1978. A further order was then placed by the Italian Government for 120 Leopard 1s, the last of which were complete in 1981/82. From late 1981 OTO-Melara built 160 specialised versions of the Leopard 1 including ARVs, AEVs and bridgelayers.

There is a separate entry for the OF-40 MBT which has been developed by OTO-Melara and FIAT specifically for the export market.

# OF-40 MBT

Italy

**Armament:** 1 × 105mm gun, elevation +20°, depression −9° (61 rounds carried)
2 × 7.62mm MGs — coaxial and AA (5,500 rounds)
4 smoke dischargers either side of turret
**Crew:** 4
**Length:** 9.222m (gun forward), 6.893m (hull)
**Width:** 3.51m (with skirts)
**Height:** 2.68m (commander's sight)
**G/clearance:** 0.44m
**Weight:** 43,000kg (loaded), 40,000kg (empty)
**G/pressure:** 0.86kg/sq cm
**Engine:** 90° V-10 supercharged multi-fuel developing 830hp at 2,200rpm
**Speed:** 60km/h
**Range:** 600km (road)
**Fuel:** 1,000 litres
**Fording:** 1.2m (w/o preparation), 2.25m (with preparation)
**V/obstacle:** 1.15m
**Trench:** 3m
**Gradient:** 60%

### Development
The OF-40 MBT has been developed from 1977 as a private venture for export with OTO-Melara being responsible for the hull, chassis and armament and FIAT responsible for the power-pack. First prototype

was completed in 1980 with production tanks following in 1981.

The hull and turret is of all welded steel armour construction with the OTO-Melara developed 105mm rifled tank gun being provided with a thermal sleeve and a fume extractor. The gun fires standard NATO fixed ammunition including APDS (m/v 1,470m/sec), HEAT 1,170m/sec) and HESH (730m/sec). The fire control system includes a computer and a laser rangefinder and the commander has a stabilised roof mounted SFIM 580-B sight which enables him to lay and fire the main armament.

Standard equipment includes a fire extinguishing system, hull escape hatch and an NBC system. Optional equipment includes a snorkel which enables the tank to ford to a depth of 4m and passive night vision equipment.

### Variants
The chassis of the OF-40 MBT with a new powerpack is used as the basis for the Palmaria 155mm SP howitzer.

*OF-40 MBT announced early in 1981.* OTO-Melara

# FIAT/OTO-Melara Type 6616 Armoured Car

Italy

**Armament:** 1 × 20mm Rh.202 cannon with an elevation of +35° and a depression of −5° (400 rounds carried)
1 × 7.62mm coaxial MG (1,000 rounds)
2 × 3 smoke dischargers either side of turret
**Crew:** 3
**Length:** 5.37m
**Width:** 2.5m
**Height:** 2.035m (top of turret)
**G/clearance:** 0.37m
**Weight:** 7,400kg (loaded), 6,900kg (empty)

**Track:** 1.96m
**Wheelbase:** 2.75m
**Engine:** Model 8062.24 super-charged in-line diesel developing 160hp at 3,200rpm
**Speed:** 100km/h (road), 5km/h (water)
**Range:** 700km
**Fuel:** 150 litres
**Fording:** Amphibious
**V/obstacle:** 0.45m
**Gradient:** 60%
**Armour:** 5-8mm

**Development**
The Type 6616 armoured car is a joint development between OTO-Melara and FIAT with the former being responsible for the turret and the latter for the hull and final assembly. The first prototype was completed in 1972 and the first production order was for the Italian Carabinieri who ordered 50 vehicles. It has a hull of all welded steel construction with the fighting compartment at the front of the hull and the engine, transmission and fuel at the rear. The commander and the gunner are both seated in the turret which has full powered traverse through 360°. If required a TOW/MILAN anti-tank missile system can be mounted on the turret roof. The 6616 is fully amphibious being propelled in the water by its wheels. Optional equipment includes an NBC system, air conditioning system, fire extinguishing system, passive night vision equipment and a front

*FIAT/OTO-Melara Type 6616 armoured car.*
*OTO-Melara*

mounted winch with a max capacity of 4,500kg and 40m of cable.

**Variants**
There are no variants of the 6616 armoured car although it does use a number of automotive components of the Type 6614 APC. For trials purposes the FIAT/OTO-Melara Type 6616 armoured car has been fitted with a turret mounted Cockerill 90mm gun.

**Employment**
Italian Carabinieri, Somalia and other undisclosed countries.

# VCC-80 Infantry Fighting Vehicle  Italy

OTO-Melara is currently building three prototypes of an Infantry Fighting Vehicle for the Italian Army under the designation of the VCC-80 (Veicolo Corazzato de Combattimento). Major sub-contractors to OTO-Melara are FIAT and Lancia.

The VCC-80 will weigh between 16 and 18 tonnes, be powered by a 500hp diesel, have a maximum road speed of 70km/h, road range of 600km, climb a vertical obstacle of 0.85m, a slope of 60%, a side slope of 40% and cross a trench 2.5m wide.

The vehicle will have a three-man crew, commander, gunner and driver, and be able to carry seven fully equipped infantrymen. Main armament will consist of an Oerlikon 25mm KBA-B cannon and a coaxial 7.62mm MG mounted in a two-man

stabilised turret. Mounted on the right side of the turret will be a twin launcher for the Euromissile MILAN ATGW system.

Standard equipment will include a NBC system and a full range of passive night vision equipment. It will also be fully amphibious being propelled in the water by its tracks at a speed of 4km/h. It is anticipated that a complete family of vehicles will be built on the same chassis as the VCC-80 including ambulance, command post, mortar carrier, pioneer vehicle, signals vehicle and a tank destroyer.

**Employment**
Under development for the Italian Army. Expected to enter service in 1988.

# Infantry Armoured Fighting Vehicle                    Italy

**Armament:** 1 × 12.7mm MG at front (1,050 rounds carried)
1 × 7.62mm MG at rear (1,000 rounds)
**Crew:** 2 + 7
**Length:** 5.041m
**Width:** 2.684m (overall), 2.54m (tracks)
**Height:** 2.552m (over 12.7mm MG), 1.828m (hull top)
**G/clearance:** 0.406m
**Weight:** 11,600kg (loaded)
**G/pressure:** 0.57kg/sq cm
**Engine:** GMC Model 6V53 6-cylinder water-cooled diesel developing 215bhp at 2,800 rpm
**Speed:** 64.4km/h (road), 5km/h (water)
**Range:** 550km
**Fuel capacity:** 360 litres
**Fording:** Amphibious
**V/obstacle:** 0.61m
**Trench:** 1.68m
**Gradient:** 60%
**Armour:** Aluminium/steel

## Development
In the 1960s OTO-Melara obtained a licence to manufacture the American FMC M113 APC in Italy for the Italian Army and about 3,000 vehicles were produced until production was phased out in favour of the diesel engined M113A1. Some 500 of the latter were built as well as quantities of the M106 120mm mortar carrier (the original American model having a 107mm mortar), M577 command vehicles and M548 tracked carriers.

*Infantry Armoured Fighting Vehicle.* OTO-Melara

The Infantry Armoured Fighting Vehicle (IAFV) has been developed to meet the requirements of the Italian Army for a vehicle with increased protection and firepower when compared to the basic M113 APC.

The vehicle is essentially an M113A1 with an additional layer of steel armour added to the basic aluminium armoured hull for increased ballistic protection. The sides of the upper part of the troop compartment at the rear of the hull are sloped and five of the infantrymen can fire their rifles as each is provided with a firing port above which is a vision block, two are in each side of the hull and one in the rear. To provide more room in the troop compartment the fuel tanks are now mounted externally either side of the power operated ramp. The 12.7mm M2 HB MG is mounted on the right side, to the rear of the engine compartment with the 7.62mm MG mounted in the centre of the hull roof at the rear. Both machine gunners are provided with side and rear armour protection.

The IAFV is fully amphibious being propelled in the water by its tracks and is fitted with infra-red night vision equipment but does not have an NBC system.

## Variants
For trials purposes an IAFV was fitted with a remote controlled 20mm cannon but this never progressed past the prototype stage.

## Employment
In service with the Italian Army, where it is called the Veicolo Corazzato de Combattimento — 1 (VCC-1) or, more commonly, the Camilo.

# FIAT/OTO-Melara Type 6614 APC     Italy

**Armament:** 1 × 12.7mm MG
**Crew:** 1 + 10
**Length:** 5.86m
**Width:** 2.5m
**Height:** 1.75m (w/o armament)
**G/clearance:** 0.37m (axles)
**Weight:** 8,500kg (loaded)
**Track:** 1.96m
**Wheelbase:** 2.9m
**Engine:** Model 8062.24 supercharged liquid-cooled in-line diesel developing 160hp at 3,200rpm
**Speed:** 100km/h (road), 3.5km/h (water)
**Range:** 700km
**Fuel:** 142 litres
**V/obstacle:** 0.4m
**Gradient:** 60%
**Armour:** 6-8mm

### Development
The Type 6614 APC is a joint development between FIAT and OTO-Melara with the latter being responsible for the hull and the former being responsible for the automotive components and final assembly. It shares many common components with the FIAT/OTO-Melara Type 6616 armoured car.

In addition to being used as an APC the Type 6614 can also be used as a ambulance, cargo carrier, command vehicle, internal security vehicle, reconnaissance vehicle and a mortar carrier. Various types of armament installation can be fitted including a pintle-mounted 12.7mm M2HB MG or a turret with twin 7.62mm MGs. For trials purposes one vehicle has been fitted with a SNIA Viscosa FIROS 6 48-round 51mm multiple rocket launcher. It has a hull of all welded steel construction which gives the crew protection from small arms fire. There is a single door in each side of the hull and a large ramp in the hull rear, firing ports are provided in the hull sides and rear. The vehicle is fully amphibious being propelled in the water by its wheels. Run-flat tyres are fitted and the steering is power assisted. An NBC system can be installed as can night vision equipment.

### Variants
There are no variants apart from the versions mentioned above.

### Employment
Italy (Police), South Korea, Peru, Somalia and Tunisia.

*FIAT/OTO-Melara Type 6614 APC without armament installed.  OTO-Melara*

# OTO-Melara Palmaria 155mm SP Howitzer     Italy

**Armament:** 1 × 155mm howitzer, elevation +70°, depression −5° (30 projectiles and charges carried) 1 × 7.62mm AA MG
**Crew:** 5
**Length:** 11.474m (gun forward), 7.4m (hull)
**Width:** 2.35m
**Height:** 2.874m (w/o AA machine gun)

**G/clearance:** 0.4m
**Weight:** 46,000kg (loaded), 43,000kg (empty)
**Engine:** 8-cylinder multi-fuel developing 750hp
**Speed:** 60km/h
**Range:** 400km
**Gradient:** 60%

## Development

The Palmaria 155mm SP howitzer has been developed from 1977 by OTO-Melara specifically for the export market. The first prototype was completed in 1981 and the company has already an order for 200 vehicles with first deliveries scheduled for 1982.

The chassis of the Palmaria is similar to the OF-40 MBT but it has an eight cylinder engine instead of a 10-cylinder model. The turret is of all welded aluminium construction and is positioned in the centre of the hull.

The 155mm howitzer has a screw breech, fume extractor and a double baffle muzzle brake and can be delivered with a manual or automatic loading system. With the latter one round can be fired every 15sec.

Max range with a Simmel-developed HE projectile is 24,000m, HE Base Bleed is 27,500m and HE RAP

*Artist's impression of the Palmaria 155mm SP howitzer.*

is 30,000m; in addition smoke and illuminating projectiles can be fired.

## Variants

There are no variants at this time although the chassis could be adopted for other applications, such as mounting a twin 35mm AA turret similar to that used for the Gepard SP AA gun.

## Employment

On order for an undisclosed country in the Middle East.

# Twin 25mm SP AA Gun                     Italy

In 1981 two prototypes of a twin 25mm SP AA gun designed to meet the requirements of the Italian Army were completed and delivered for operational trials. This system is basically a M113A1 APC chassis fitted with a two-man power-operated turret armed with two externally mounted Oerlikon 25mm KBA-C cannon with an elevation of +85° with 560 rounds of HE-I being carried for the AA role and 40 APDS-T for use in the anti-armour role. Effective range when being used in the AA role is 1,800m.

The clear weather fire control system includes a laser rangefinder, analogue computer and an IFF system. The system has a loaded weight of 15 tonnes and the three man crew consists of the commander, gunner and driver.

## Employment

If trials with the two prototypes are successful this system could enter service with the Italian Army as early as 1985.

# Type 74 MBT                              Japan

**Armament:** 1 × 105mm gun (51 rounds carried)
1 × 7.62mm coaxial MG (4,500 rounds)
1 × 12.7mm M2 AAMG (660 rounds)
1 ×3 smoke dischargers either side of turret
**Crew:** 4
**Length:** 9.41m (gun forward) 6.7m (hull)
**Width:** 3.18m

**Height:** 2.67m (normal)
**G/clearance:** 0.2-0.65m (variable)
**Weight:** 38,000kg (loaded), 36,300kg (empty)
**G/pressure:** 0.86kg/sq cm
**Engine:** Mitsubishi 10ZF Type 21 WT, 10-cylinder diesel, air-cooled, developing 750hp at 2,200rpm
**Speed:** 53km/h (road)

## Development/Variants

Design work on a new Japanese MBT commenced in 1962 with test rigs being completed between 1964 and 1967. The first two prototypes, called the STB-1, were completed in 1969 and had an automatic loader for the 105mm gun and a remote-controlled 12.7mm AA MG.

Further development resulted in the STB-3 which did away with both the automatic loader and the remote-controlled AA MG. The STB was subsequently standardised as the Type 74 MBT and production commenced at Mitsubishi Heavy Industries Sagamihara works in 1973.

The Type 74 has adjustable hydropneumatic suspension. This allows the height of the tank to be adjusted according to the tactical situation. Infra-red driving lights are fitted and an infra-red/white light searchlight is mounted to the left of the main gun. A Japanese-built laser range-finder and gun stabilisation system is installed as is an NBC system.

## Variants

The only variant is the Type 78 ARV which is very similar in appearance to the West German Leopard and French AMX-30 ARVs.

## Employment

In production for the JGSDF.

**Range:** 300km
**Fuel:** 950 litres
**Fording:** 1.00m, 2m (with preparation)
**V/obstacle:** 1.00m
**Trench:** 2.70m
**Gradient:** 60%

# Type 88 MBT                                              Japan

**Armament:** 1 × 120mm gun
1 × 7.62mm coaxial MG
1 × 12.7mm AA MG
Smoke dischargers
**Crew:** 4
**Length:** 7.5m (hull)
**Width:** 3.5m
**Height:** 2.4m
**Weight:** 43,000kg
**Engine:** Mitsubishi 8ZG turbocharged water-cooled diesel developing 1,500hp
**Speed:** 70km/h (road)
**Range:** 500km

## Development

Since 1976 the Technical Research Headquarters of the Japanese Self-Defence Agency has been working on a new MBT to succeed the current Type 74 MBT in production in the late 1980s. This has the development designation of the STC with prime contractors being Mitsubishi Heavy Industries for the chassis and automotive aspects, Japan Iron Works

for the 120mm gun, Mitsubishi Electric for the fire control system and Kyoto Ceramic Limited for the advanced multiple layer armour.

The 120mm smooth bore gun will fire fixed APFSDS and HEAT-FS projectiles but it is no expected that an automatic loader will be installed The fire control system will include a TV system laser rangefinder and a micro-computer. The tan will have a full range of passive night vision equipment and fitted with a NBC system.

It is expected that test vehicles will be completed by 1982 and that the STC will be standardised as the Type 88 MBT in 1988. The JGSDF has a requiremen for at least 600 Type 88 MBTs to replace its Type 6 MBTs.

## Variants

There are no variants at this time.

## Employment

Development. Not in production or service.

# Type 61 MBT

Japan

**Armament:** 1 × 90mm Type 61 gun
1 × 7.62mm M1919A4 coaxial MG
1 × 12.7mm M2 AA MG
**Crew:** 4
**Length:** 8.19m (gun foward), 6.30m (hull)
**Width:** 2.95m
**Height:** 3.16m (with AA MG), 2.49m (turret roof)
**G/clearance:** 0.40m
**Weight:** 35,000kg (loaded)
**G/pressure:** 0.95kg/sq cm
**Engine:** Mitsubishi Type 12 HM 21 WT, V-12,
turbo-charged air-cooled diesel developing 600hp at
2,100rpm
**Speed:** 45km/h (road)
**Range:** 200km (road)
**Fording:** 0.99m
**V/obstacle:** 0.685m
**Trench:** 2.489m
**Gradient:** 60%
**Armour:** 64mm

*Type 61 MBT.* K. Nogi

## Development

Design work on the Type 61 started in 1954 and it
was the first tank to be built in Japan since the end
of World War 2. The first prototypes were completed
in March 1957 and these were called the ST-A1 and
ST-A2. The ST-A1 had seven road wheels and four
return rollers and the ST-A2 had six road wheels and
three return rollers, both tanks were armed with a
90mm gun. After extensive trials a further series of
vehicles were built, these being called the ST-A3 and
ST-A4. These were completed in 1958/1959. In
April 1961 the tank was standardised as the Type 61
MBT and first production models were completed in
1962. Total production of the Type 61 amounted to
about 450 vehicles.

The Type 61 can be fitted with infra-red driving
and fighting equipment. It does not have an NBC
system and cannot be fitted with a snorkel.

## Variants

*Type 67 AVLB:* This is similar to the American AVLB
on the M48/M60 chassis. Weight 35,000kg, length
7.27m, width 3.50m, height 3.50m, crew three,
armament 1 × 7.62mm MG.
*Type 70 ARV:* This has a boom and a dozer blade.
Weight 35,000kg, length 8.40m, width 2.95m,
height 3.10m, armament 1 × 81mm mortar, 1 ×
7.62mm and 1 × 12.7mm MGs, crew four.
*Type 67 AEV:* Weight 35,000kg, length 7.46m,
width 3.21m, height 2.23m, armament 1 × 7.62mm
and 1 × 12.7mm machine guns, crew four.

## Employment

Used only by the JGSDF.

# New Family of Wheeled Vehicles

Japan

In the early 1970s Komatsu Seisaku-Jyo built a
prototype of a 4 × 4 reconnaissance vehicle to meet
the requirements of the JGSDF while Mitsubishi
Heavy Industries built a 6 × 6 prototype. Following
trials with these prototype vehicles it was decided to
concentrate on the 6 × 6 model with Mitsubishi
Heavy Industries building the reconnaissance vehicle
with Komatsu Seisaku-Jyo building the command
and communications vehicle but also being assisted
by Mitsubishi Heavy Industries.

The JGSDF has a requirement for about 50
reconnaissance vehicles armed with a 20mm cannon
and about 250 command and communications
vehicles armed with 12.7mm M2HB MG. It is
anticipated that first production reconnaissance
vehicles could be delivered in 1985 with first
command and reconnaissance vehicles being
delivered in 1983.

*One of the prototypes of the command and
communications vehicle armed with a 12.7mm
MG.* Kensuke Ebata

# Type 73 APC

Japan

**Armament:** 1 × 12.7mm roof-mounted MG, elevation +60°, depression −10°
1 × 7.62mm bow MG
2 × 3 smoke dischargers
**Crew:** 3 + 9
**Length:** 5.8m
**Width:** 2.8m
**Height:** 2.2m (with 12.7mm MG), 1.7m (hull top)
**G/clearance:** 0.4m
**Weight:** 13,300kg (loaded)
**Engine:** Mitsubishi model 4ZF 4-cylinder air-cooled diesel developing 300hp at 2,200rpm
**Speed:** 70km/h (road), 7km/h (water)
**Range:** 300km
**Fuel:** 450 litres
**Fording:** Amphibious
**V/obstacle:** 0.7m
**Trench:** 2m
**Gradient:** 60%

## Development
The development of a new full tracked APC to supplement the Type 60 commenced in 1963 and two prototypes were each built by Mitsubishi Heavy Industries (SUB-I-1 and SUB-I-2) and the Komatsu Manufacturing Co (SUB-II-1 and SUB-II-2). These

*Type 73 APC showing position of 12.7mm and 7.62mm MGs.* Kensuke Ebata

were tested in 1970 and in 1972 the SUB-I-2, with modifications, was standardised as the Type 73 APC. But production has been very slow owing to budgetry problems and by early 1981 just over 100 had been built.

The Type 73 APC has a hull of all welded aluminium construction and is fully amphibious with little preparation, being propelled in the water by its tracks. Two firing ports are provided in each side of the hull and in the rear and standard equipment includes an NBC system and infra-red night vision equipment.

## Variants
The only variant in service is the Type 75 SP ground-wind measurement vehicle used to calculate ballistic data for the Type 75 (30-round) multiple rocket launcher (*Artillery of the World,* 3rd edition page 121) which uses some components of the Type 73 APC as does the 105mm Type 74 SP howitzer.

## Employment
In service only with the JGSDF.


# Type SU60 APC

Japan

**Armament:** 1 × 12.7mm M2 MG, on roof
1 × 7.62mm M1919A4 bow MG
**Crew:** 4 + 6
**Length:** 4.85m
**Width:** 2.40m
**Height:** 2.31m (inc MG), 1.70m (w/o MG)
**G/clearance:** 0.40m
**Weight:** 11,800kg (loaded), 10,600kg (empty)
**Engine:** Mitsubishi 8 HA-21 WT, V-8 air-cooled

turbo-charged diesel developing 220hp at 2,400rpm
**Speed:** 45km/h
**Range:** 230km
**Fording:** 0.76m
**V/obstacle:** 0.60m
**Trench:** 1.82m
**Gradient:** 60%
**G/pressure:** 0.57kg/sq cm

## Development

Development of the SU APC started in 1956 and prototypes were built by two companies. Komatsu built the SU-1 and Mitsubishi built the SU-2. These prototypes were completed in 1957. The trials showed that the Mitsubishi vehicle was the better and after some re-design the vehicle was placed in production at the Maruko plant of Mitsubishi Heavy Industries. The first production vehicle was completed in 1960 and production continued until 1970 by which time over 400 had been built. The SU 60 does not have any amphibious capability, nor does it have an NBC system or any infra-red driving lights.

*Type SU60 APC.* Kensuke Ebata

## Variants

*81mm Mortar Carrier (SV):* Crew five, armed with an 81mm mortar in the rear of the vehicle. It retains its 12.7mm MG. A baseplate and stand are carried on the front of the vehicle enabling the mortar to be dismounted and fired away from the vehicle.

*107mm Mortar (4.2in) Carrier (SX):* Crew five and has a loaded weight of 12,900kg. The mortar is mounted in the rear of the vehicle and this model can easily be recognised as the rear of the hull is cut at an angle. The 12.7mm MG is retained. A baseplate and stand is carried on the front of the vehicle enabling the mortar to be fired away from the vehicle.

*Type 60 NBC detection vehicle:* Built in small numbers and fitted with soil sampling equipment at rear of hull.

*Type 60 dozer:* Two Type 60s have been fitted with a dozer blade at the front of the hull for clearing snow.

*105mm Howitzer (SY):* Did not progress beyond the prototype stage.

## Employment

Used only by the JGSDF.

# Type 60 106mm SP Recoilless Gun       Japan

**Armament:** 2 × 106mm recoilless rifles with 8 rounds of ammunition
1 × 12.7mm spotting MG
**Crew:** 3
**Length:** 4.30m
**Width:** 2.23m
**Height:** 1.59m
**G/clearance:** 0.35m
**Weight:** 8,000kg (loaded), 7,600kg (empty)
**G/pressure:** 0.67kg/sq cm
**Engine:** Komatsu 6T 120, 6-cylinder, air-cooled diesel developing 120hp at 2,400rpm
**Speed:** 45km/h (road)
**Range:** 130km (road)
**Fuel:** 77 litres
**Fording:** 1m
**V/obstacle:** 0.55m
**Trench:** 1.8m
**Gradient:** 60%
**Armour:** 12mm

## Development/Variants

Design of this vehicle started in 1954 and it was the first postwar Japanese armoured fighting vehicle. Prototypes were built by Komatsu (SS-1) and Mitsubishi (SS-2); these were completed at the end of 1955. The SS-1 had its engine at the front with its driving sprocket at the rear, the SS-2 having its engine at the rear and its driving sprocket at the

front. They both had different suspensions and were both armed with 2 × 105mm recoilless rifles. Following trials with the SS-1 and SS-2 prototypes, further prototypes were built under the designation of the SS-3 and SS-4. In 1960 the latter was accepted for service as the Type 60 SP 106mm Recoilless Gun.

Production was undertaken by Komatsu with the 106mm recoilless rifles being manufactured by the Japan Steel Works. Production was finally completed in 1979/80 with about 260 vehicles being built.

The first production model was called the model A, this was followed by the model B and in 1975 by the model C, the latter being powered by a commercial model SA4D105 four-cylinder diesel engine.

When in the lowered position the rifles have an elevation of +10° and a depression of −5°, traverse being 10° left and 10° right. When raised with their mount they have an elevation of +55° and a depression of −20°, traverse being 30° left and 30° right. The 106mm rifles can fire HE and anti-tank rounds, range being 1,100m.

The Type 60 does not have any infra-red driving lights nor does it have an NBC system.

## Employment

Used only by JGSDF.

# Type 75 155mm SP Howitzer
Japan

**Armament:** 1 × 155mm howitzer, elevation +65°, depression −5° (28 rounds carried)
1 × 12.7mm AA MG (1,000 rounds)
**Crew:** 6
**Length:** 7.79m (gun forward), 6.64m (hull)
**Width:** 3.09m
**Height:** 2.545m (turret roof)
**G/clearance:** 0.4m
**Weight:** 25,300kg (loaded)
**G/pressure:** 0.64kg/sq cm
**Engine:** Mitsubishi model 6ZF 6-cylinder air-cooled diesel developing 450hp at 2,200rpm
**Speed:** 47km/h
**Range:** 300km
**Fuel:** 650 litres
**Fording:** 1.3m
**V/obstacle:** 0.7m
**Trench:** 2.5m
**Gradient:** 60%

## Development
In 1969 the development of a 155mm SP howitzer to meet the requirements of the JGSDF commenced with Mitsubishi Heavy Industries being responsible

for the hull and Nihon Seiko Jyo/Japan Iron Works being responsible for the gun and turret.

The first prototypes were completed in 1971/72 and in October 1975 it was standardised as the Type 75 155mm SP howitzer.

The Type 75 is of all aluminium construction and is similar in appearance to the American 155mm M109 and Soviet 122mm M1974 and 152mm M1973 SP howitzers. Standard equipment includes a NBC system and infra-red night vision equipment.

The weapon fires a Japanese developed HE projectile to a maximum range of 19,000m or an American HE projectile to a range of 15,000m. Under development is a RAP which is expected to have a max range of 24,000m.

Two drum type magazines in the turret rear each hold nine projectiles and enable the weapon to fire 18 rounds in three minutes.

## Employment
In service with the JGSDF.

*Type 75 155mm SP howitzer.* K. Nogi

# Type 74 105mm SP Howitzer
Japan

**Armament:** 1 × 105mm howitzer
1 × 12.7mm AA MG
**Crew:** 5
**Length:** 5.9m
**Width:** 2.9m
**Height:** 2.39m
**G/clearance:** 0.4m
**Weight:** 16,500kg

**Engine:** Mitsubishi 4ZF air-cooled V-4 diesel developing 300hp at 2,200rpm
**Speed:** 50km/h
**Range:** 300km
**Fording:** 1.2m
**V/obstacle:** 0.61m
**Trench:** 2m
**Gradient:** 60%

*Type 74 105mm SP howitzer.* via Kensuke Ebata

## Development

In 1967 development of a 105mm SP howitzer commenced which would use the engine and transmission of the Type 73 APC. Komatsu Manufacturing Co were responsible for the hull and Japan Steel Works for the turret and the 105mm howitzer.

The first prototypes were completed in 1969/70 with the system being standardised as the Type 74 105mm SP Howitzer in 1974. Only 20 vehicles were built between 1975 and 1978 as a decision was taken to concentrate on the Type 75 155mm SP howitzer.

The Type 74 has an NBC system, infra-red night vision equipment and a flotation screen which is carried collapsed around the top of the hull. When erected the vehicle propels itself across water obstacles by its tracks.

## Variants

There are no variants of the Type 74.

## Employment

In service only with the JGSDF.

# AWX Twin 35mm SP AA Gun — Japan

Under development for the JGSDF is a twin 35mm SP AA gun system that has been given the development designation of the AWX. The prototype will be based on a Type 61 MBT chassis but it is anticipated that production vehicles will use the Type 74 MBT chassis. The twin 35mm cannon will be Swiss Oerlikon KDA cannon as installed in the Gepard SP AA used by Belgium, FRG and the Netherlands. Unconfirmed reports have stated that Japan has ordered a complete turret from Switzerland for use as the basis of the AWX. The JGSDF already uses the Oerlikon 35mm twin GDF-001 towed AA gun system, this being produced under licence in Japan.

# AFV Production — North Korea

It is known that North Korea has been producing Soviet-designed AFVs, including tanks and APCs, for some years, but the exact types are not known. AFVs known to be used by North Korea include PT-76, T-34/85, T-54/T-55, T-62, Type 59 and Type 63 tanks, BTR-40, BTR-50, BTR-60, BTR-152, K-63 and BMP MICV/APCs and SU-76 and SU-100 SP guns.

# AFV Production

# South Korea

The South Korean Army tank fleet consists of about 1,000 M47 and M48 tanks. Most of the latter are now being brought up to M48A5 standard with a 105mm M68 tank gun, improved fire control system, infra-red/white light over the main armament, electrically operated smoke dischargers either side of the turret and armoured track skirts hinged at the top to allow access to the suspension for maintenance purposes.

It is believed that Chrysler of the USA is designing a new tank to meet the requirements of South Korea, this is called the ROKIT (Republic of Korea Indigenous Tank) and is believed to weigh between 40 and 50 tonnes and armed with a 105mm M68 rifled tank gun.

South Korea is also manufacturing the Italian OTO-Melara/FIAT Type 6614 (4 × 4) APC under licence.

# YP-408 APC

# Netherlands

YP-408 PW-MT towing a 120mm Brandt mortar.
Dutch Army

**Armament:** 1 × 12.7mm MG, elevation +70°, depression −8°
2 × 3 barrelled smoke dischargers
**Crew:** 2 + 10
**Length:** 6.23m
**Width:** 2.40m
**Height:** 2.37m (inc MG gun), 1.80m (hull top)
**G/clearance:** 0.518m
**Weight:** 12,000kg (loaded), 9,500kg (empty)
**Track:** 2.054m (front)
**Wheelbase:** 1.275m + 2.145m (centre of first axle to centre of second axle, and centre of second axle to centre of rear tandem)
**Engine:** DAF DS 575, 6-cylinder, in-line, water-cooled, turbo-charged diesel developing 165hp at 2,400rpm
**Speed:** 80km/h (road)
**Range:** 500km (road), 400km (cross-country)
**Fuel:** 200 litres
**Fording:** 1.20m
**V/obstacle:** 0.70m
**Trench:** 1.20m
**Gradient:** 60%
**Armour:** 15mm (max)

## Development

The YP-408 was designed by Van Doorne's Automobielfabrieken (DAF) NV of Eindhoven. The first mock-up was completed in 1957 and the first prototype was completed in 1958. The prototypes were followed by a pre-production batch. The first production vehicle was completed in 1964 and the last in 1968, about 750 of all versions were built. The vehicle uses many components of the YA-328 artillery tractor.

The vehicle is an 8 × 6, the front two and rear four being powered, steering is hydraulically assisted and is on the front four wheels. The vehicle is not amphibious, capable only of fording. It does not have an NBC system although a heater is fitted, infra-red driving and fighting lights can be fitted. There is a total of six roof hatches; at the rear are two doors, these being provided with a firing port each.

The basic vehicle is designated PWI-S, which means Panzer Wagon Infanterie — Standard.

## Variants

*PWI-S (PC):* This is a platoon commander's vehicle and has a crew of nine and additional radios.
*PWCO:* This is a company and battalion commander's vehicle and has a crew of six men. It has map tables and additional batteries and a tent can be erected at the rear if required.

*PW-GWT:* This is an ambulance and does not have any armament. It has a crew of three and can carry two stretcher patients and four sitting patients.
*PW-V:* This is a freight carrier and can carry 1500kg of freight. It has a crew of two and does not have a radio. If required it can also be used as an ambulance.
*PW-MT:* This is a mortar-towing vehicle and tows the French Brandt 120mm mortar. A total of 50

rounds of ammunition is carried; it has a crew of seven.
*PWAT:* Basic vehicle with TOW ATGW system.
*PWRDR:* Basic vehicle with ZB298 ground surveillance radar.

**Employment**

Used by the Netherlands Army and Surinam.

# AFV Production Poland

Between 1951 and 1956 Poland produced the Soviet T-34/85 tank under licence for both the home and export markets. This was succeeded in production from 1956 by the T-54 and production of this, and the improved T-54M continued until 1964 when the T-55 was placed in production. Polish built T-55s are distinguishable from Soviet-built vehicles by having a large rectangular sheet metal stowage

box mounted on the left side of the turret. Production of the T-55 was completed in the late 1970s and from 1979 Poland started to produce the Soviet T-72 MBT with first production tanks being completed in 1980. Poland was also involved in the design of the Czechoslovak OT-64 (8 × 8) APC and it is possible that some components for production vehicles were made in Poland.

# Chaimite APC Portugal

**Armament:** See text
**Crew:** 11
**Length:** 5.606m
**Width:** 2.26m
**Height:** 2.26m (turret top), 1.84m (hull top)
**G/clearance:** 0.61m (hull), 0.41m (differential)
**Weight:** 7,300kg (loaded)
**Wheelbase:** 2.667m
**Engine:** V-8 petrol developing 210hp at 4,000rpm or V6 diesel
**Speed:** 99km/h (road), 7km/h (water)
**Range:** 804-965km (road, petrol engine model), 1,367-1,529km (road, diesel engine model)
**Fuel:** 300 litres
**Fording:** Amphibious
**V/obstacle:** 0.9m
**Gradient:** 65%
**Armour:** 6.35mm-9.35mm

*BRAVIA Chaimite V-200 APC without armament installed in turret. BRAVIA*

**Development**

The Chaimite range of vehicles was developed in the mid-1960s to meet the requirements of the Portuguese armed forces by BRAVIA of Lisbon. In appearance the Chaimite is very similar to the American Cadillac Gage Commando range of wheeled multi-purpose armoured vehicles which were already in volume production at the time of the development of the Chaimite.

The vehicle is fully amphibious being propelled in the water by its wheels. All models have a front mounted winch with a capacity of 4,530kg and optional equipment includes infra-red night vision equipment.

*V-200:* Fitted with BRAVIA turret with twin 7.62mm, twin 5.56mm or one 7.62mm and one 12.7mm MG.
*V-300:* Can be fitted with a variety of turrets including French SAMM S 530 with twin 20mm

cannon, French TA-20 with twin 20mm cannon, Oerlikon GAD-AOA turret with 20mm cannon or a BRAVIA turret with 20mm cannon, 7.62mm coaxial MG and 7.62mm AA MG.
*V-400:* Two-man turret fitted with 90mm Mecar gun, two-man French Lynx 90 turret with 90mm gun or turret with Bofors 90mm gun.
*V-500:* Command and communications vehicle.
*V-600:* 81mm or 120mm mortar carrier.
*V-700:* ATGW vehicle with HOT or Swingfire ATGWs.
*V-800:* Unarmed ambulance version.
*V-900:* Crash rescue vehicle.
*V-1000:* Riot control vehicle.

**Employment**

Lebanon, Libya, Peru, Philippines and Portugal.

# BRAVIA Commando Mk III APC          Portugal

**Armament:** See text
**Crew:** 3 + 5
**Length:** 4.975m
**Width:** 1.93m
**Height:** 2.42m (turret), 2.05m (hull top)
**G/clearance:** 0.21m
**Weight:** 4,855kg (loaded), 4,330kg (unloaded)
**Track:** 1.72m (front), 1.665m (rear)
**Wheelbase:** 3.03m

**Engine:** Perkins 4-cylinder diesel developing 81hp at 2,800rpm *or*
Dodge H225 6-cylinder petrol developing 150hp at 4,000rpm
**Speed:** 90km/h (diesel), 110km/h (petrol)
**Range:** 800km (diesel), 600km (petrol)
**Fuel:** 160 litres
**Gradient:** 70%
**Armour:** 6.35mm-7.94mm

*BRAVIA Commando Mk III APC.*  BRAVIA

### Development

Development[1] of the Commando Mark III APC commenced by BRAVIA in 1977 in response to a requirement issued by the Portuguese National Guard. First production vehicles were completed in 1978.

The Commando Mark III is very similar in appearance to the British Shorland armoured patrol vehicle and is based on the chassis of the BRAVIA Gazela (4 × 4) one tonne truck.

The basic vehicle is fitted with a BRAVIA designed turret armed with twin 7.62mm or one 7.62mm and one 12.7mm MGs, these have an elevation of +60° and a depression of −15°, with turret traverse through a full 360°. Firing ports with a vision block above are provided in both the sides and rear of the vehicle. The turret can also be fitted with a 60mm grenade launcher.

Optional equipment includes an air-conditioning system, run flat or sand tyres.

### Variants

The only variant is a model without a turret which therefore has an increased troop carrying capability.

### Employment

In service with the Portuguese National Guard.

# AFV Production          Romania

As far as it is known Romania has not so far undertaken production of any tanks although in 1979 a locally modified version of the Soviet supplied T-55 MBT was shown in public for the first time. The modifications have been extensive and include improved cooling for the engine, new suspension with six road wheels either side instead of the normal five, side skirts similar to those fitted to the British Centurion and Chieftain MBTs and a new 12.7mm AA MG with some ammunition boxes being stowed externally on the sides of the turret.

For some years, Romania has also been producing an improved version of the Soviet designed BTR-60PB under the designation of the TAB-72. In appearance this is very similar to the Soviet vehicle

but the turret is different and the 14.5mm and 7.62mm MGs can be elevated to +85° so enabling them to be used against low flying aircraft and helicopters.

The TAB-72 also has additional vision devices and is powered by twin V-6 petrol engines each developing 140hp (the Soviet BTR-60PB has two 90hp petrol engines). The more powerful engines of the TAB-72 give the vehicle a max road speed of 95km/h compared to the BTR-60PB. Like the Soviet vehicle, the TAB-72 is fully amphibious being propelled in the water by a single water jet at the rear of the hull. There is also an 82mm mortar carrying version of the TAB-72 which is not fitted with a turret.

In the 1960s South Africa obtained a licence from Panhard of France to produce the AML-60 and AML-90 armoured car. Production of these was undertaken by Sandock Austral Limited at Boksburg and it is believed that about 2,000 vehicles were produced by the time production was completed in the late 1970s. The South African's call the AML the Eland and reports have indicated that the AML-90 with 90mm gun gave a good account of itself during fighting in Angola against Soviet T-34/85 and T-54 tanks.

South Africa has also rebuilt many of its Centurion tanks and uses a wide variety of 6 × 4, 4 × 4 and 4 × 2 vehicles for IS operations, these have names such as Hippo and Rhino.

# Ratel 20 Infantry Fighting Vehicle

South Africa

**Armament:** 1 × 20mm cannon (500 rounds carried)
2 × 7.62mm MGs — coaxial and AA (500 rounds)
2 smoke dischargers either side of turret
**Crew:** 3 + 7
**Length:** 7.21m
**Width:** 2.7m
**Height:** 3.11m (overall), 2.30m (hull top)
**Weight:** 17,000kg (loaded), 15,000kg (unloaded)
**Track:** 2.08m
**Wheelbase:** 4.23m
**Engine:** 6-cylinder turbocharged diesel
**Speed:** 105km/h
**Fuel:** 480 litres
**Fording:** 1.2m
**V/obstacle:** 0.35m
**Trench:** 1.2m
**Gradient:** 70%

**Development**
The Ratel 20 (6 × 6) IFV has been designed by Sandock-Austral to meet the requirements of the South African Army for a vehicle to replace its Alvis Saracen (6 × 6) APCs which are now some 20 years old. It has been designed by Sandock-Austral of Boksburg who previously undertook production of the French Panhard AML (4 × 4) armoured car under the name of the Eland.

The three-man crew of the Ratel consists of the commander, gunner and driver. Main armament consists of a French 20mm F2 (M693 cannon) dual feed cannon that fires both AP and HE projectiles and has a cyclic rate of fire of 740rpm. A 7.62mm MG is mounted coaxial with the main armament and a similar weapon can be mounted on the turret roof for AA defence.

The engine compartment is at the rear of the Ratel on the right side and the troop compartment is provided with side and rear doors, roof hatches and both firing ports and vision blocks. A 7.62mm MG can be mounted over the rear part of the troop compartment if required.

The Ratel has no amphibious capability and is not believed to be fitted with an NBC system or any type of night vision equipment.

**Variants**
There are no known variants of the Ratel 20.

**Employment**
The only known user is South Africa.

*Ratel 20 IFV.* Simon Dunstan

# AFV Production

Since the early 1970s Spain has been building the French AMX-30 under licence and it is estimated that by early 1982 some 400 vehicles will have been completed for the Spain Army and Foreign Legion. As far as it is known the Spanish tanks are identical to the French models with the exception of the commander's AA MG which is a 7.92mm MG42. Prime contractor in Spain is the Alcalá de Guadaira factory of Empressa Nacional Santa Barbara (ENSB).

The Spanish Army has significant numbers of M47 and M48 tanks which were supplied by the USA in the 1950s and 1960s. Most of the former have now been rebuilt by Chrysler Spain with their original powerpacks having been replaced by the same powerpack as installed in the M48A3/M60 series, as well as improvements to the tanks' suspension: main armament remains the 90mm gun.

# BMR-600 Infantry Fighting Vehicle

**Armament:** 1 × 7.62mm MG (2,500 rounds carried)
**Crew:** 2 + 16
**Length:** 6.15m
**Width:** 2.49m
**Height:** 2.00m (hull top), 2.36m (inc armament)
**G/clearance:** 0.45m (variable)
**Weight:** 13,000kg (loaded)
**Track:** 2.08m
**Wheelbase:** 1.65m + 1.65m
**Engine:** Pegaso 9157/8 diesel, 306hp at 2,600rpm
**Speed:** 100km/h (road), 10km/h (water)
**Range:** 900km
**Fording:** Amphibious
**Fuel:** 320 litres
**V/obstacle:** 0.8m
**Trench:** 1.2m
**Gradient:** 68%

## Development
The BMR-600 (Blindado Medio de Ruedas) was developed from 1972 to meet the requirements of the Spanish Army with the first prototypes being completed in 1975. After trials between the BMR-600, the French VAB and the Swiss MOWAG Piranha, the Spanish BMR-600 was selected and first production vehicles were delivered to the Spanish Army in 1979.

The hull of the BMR-600 is of all welded aluminium construction with firing ports and vision blocks being provided in the hull sides and rear. The

infantry enter and leave the BMR-600 via a power operated ramp at the rear of the hull. The vehicle is fully amphibious being propelled in the water by two Dowty waterjets mounted on either side at the rear.

An unusual feature of the BMR-600 is that it is fitted with hydropneumatic suspension which allows the driver to adjust the ground clearance to suit the type of ground being crossed, and steering is power assisted on the front and rear axles.

## Variants
The BMR-600 can be fitted with a wide range of armament installations including a cupola-mounted 7.62mm MG, turret-mounted 20mm cannon or a 90mm gun and for trials purposes has already been fitted with a Euromissile HAKO turret with four HOT AGTWs in the ready to launch position. More specialised versions include ambulance, anti-aircraft, cargo, command, maintenance/recovery and mortar towing vehicle. The reconnaissance/scout version, which has a different hull and is fitted with a 25mm turret, is called the VEC.

## Employment
In service with Spanish Army.

*One of the prototypes of the BMR-600 fitted with 7.62mm MG.* Pegaso

# BLR APC                                                      Spain

**Armament:** Depends on role
**Crew:** 3+12
**Length:** 5.65m
**Width:** 2.5m
**Height:** 1.99m (hull top)
**Weight:** 11,000kg (220hp model), 10,625kg (170hp model)
**Track:** 1.96m
**Wheelbase:** 3.15m
**Engine:** Pegaso 9220 6-cylinder water-cooled developing 220hp or Pegaso 9100 6-cylinder water-cooled developing 170hp
**Speed:** 110km/h (road)
**Range:** 800km
**Fording:** 1.1m
**Gradient:** 75%

**Development**
The BLR (Blindado Ligero de Ruedas) has been developed by Pagaso to meet the requirements of both the Spanish Army and police for a vehicle capable of being used in a number of roles including border patrol, airport security and IS operations.

The hull of the BLR is of all welded construction with five bulletproof windows being provided in each

*BLR (4×4) APC without armament installed.*
Pegaso

side of the hull. The personnel can enter and leave the vehicle via four doors, two at the rear and one either side.

The BLR is smoke and gas proof and standard equipment includes a front-mounted winch with a capacity of 4,500kg and a semi-automatic fire extinguishing system for the engine. Each of the four wheels, which have puncture proof Hutchinson O-rings, has a fire extinguishing system. Optional equipment includes smoke or CS gas dischargers, various communications equipment and various turret-mounted MGs.

**Variants**
At present there are no variants of the BLR although it can obviously be converted to other roles such as ambulance and command vehicle.

**Employment**
Production for Spanish police.

# New MBT                                                   Sweden

To design a new MBT to meet the requirements of the Swedish Army a joint development company has been established by Bofors and Hägglund and Söner called UB Utveckling (Hägglund-Bofors Development) with Bofors being responsible for the armament and fire control areas and Hägglund and Söner for the mobility and chassis aspects. The project is still in the very early stages and no prototypes are expected to be completed for some years, although component test rigs may be completed within three years.

The Swedish Army requires a tank weighing around 35tonnes, having a max road speed of 70km/h and a range of at least 500km. Main armament will be a 120mm gun which will be fed by an automatic loader so enabling it to have a three-man crew like the S-tank. For trials purposes a West German Marder MICV chassis has been fitted with an externally mounted 105mm rifled tank gun with the three-man crew all being seated in the hull.

# Stridsvagn 103B MBT

# Sweden

**Armament:** 1 × 105mm automatic gun (50 rounds carried)
3 × 7.62mm MGs — one on commander's cupola, and two on left hull front (2,500 rounds)
2 × 4 barrelled smoke dischargers and 24 smoke grenades
**Crew:** 3
**Length:** 8.9m (inc gun), 7.04m (exc gun)
**Width:** 3.40m
**Height:** 2.50m (inc MG), 2.14m (commanders cupola)
**G/clearance:** 0.50m (max)
**Weight:** 39,000kg (loaded)
**Engines:** One Rolls-Royce K60 multi-fuel developing 240hp at 3,650rpm
One Boeing 553 turbine developing 490shp at 38,000rpm
**Speed:** 50km/h (road)
**Range:** 390km
**Fuel:** 960 litres
**Fording:** 1.50m
**V/obstacle:** 0.90m
**Trench:** 2.30m
**Gradient:** 60%
**G/pressure:** 0.85kg/sq cm

## Development
The Strv 103 (known as the 'S' tank), was first proposed in 1956; feasibility trials were carried out using a Sherman and lkv 103 chassis. In mid-1958 a contract was awarded to the Bofors company to develop the tank while Volvo developed the powerpack and Landsverk the running gear.

The first two prototypes were completed in 1961 but the previous year the Swedish Army placed a pre-production order for 10 vehicles. The prototypes differed from later vehicles as the suspension had no return rollers, no support was provided for the

105mm gun and five MGs were fitted, two either side of the hull firing forwards and one on the commander's cupola.

First production Strv 103s were completed in 1966 and production was completed in 1971 after 300 had been built. The first vehicles built were called the Strv 103A and did not have a flotation screen, other differences included a less powerful turbine. Later models were the Strv 103B. These have the more powerful engine and are fitted with a flotation screen. All Strv 103As have been rebuilt to Strv 103B standards.

The gun is fixed, and aimed in elevation by lowering and raising the road wheels, as the tank has hydro-pneumatic suspension. This gives the gun an elevation of +12° and a depression of −10°. The 105mm gun, which is 11 calibres longer than the British 105mm L7A1 gun, is automatically loaded and can fire APDS, HE or smoke rounds, rate of fire is 10-15 rounds/min.

The tank has a flotation screen permanently mounted under armour. When raised it enables the vehicle to swim at 6km/h with the aid of its tracks. A bulldozer blade is fitted at the front.

## Variants
There are no variants of the Strv 103B although components of the tank are incorporated in the 155mm SP gun and the now defunct VEAK 2 × 40mm AA gun system.

## Employment
In service only with the Swedish Army.

*Strv 103B from the rear with flotation screen lowered.* Bofors

# Ikv 91 Light Tank/Infantry Support Vehicle     Sweden

**Armament:** 1 × 90 Bofors gun, elevation +12°, depression −10° (59 rounds carried)
2 × 7.62mm MGs — coaxial and AA on loader's cupola (4,500 rounds)
2 × 6-barrelled smoke dischargers at rear of turret
**Crew:** 4
**Length:** 8.845m (inc gun), 6.41m (hull only)
**Width:** 3.00m
**Height:** 2.36m (overall)
**G/clearance:** 0.37m
**Weight:** 16,300kg (loaded)
**G/pressure:** 0.46kg/sq cm
**Engine:** Volvo TD 120A, 6-cylinder turbo-charged diesel developing 350hp at 2,200rpm
**Speed:** 69km/h (road), 7km/h (water)
**Range:** 550km (road)
**Fuel:** 405 litres
**Fording:** Amphibious
**V/obstacle:** 0.80m
**Trench:** 2.80m
**Gradient:** 60%

## Development
The contract to develop the Ikv 91 (Infanteri-kanonvagn 91) was awarded to Hägglund and Söner in April 1968. The first of three prototypes was completed and assigned to manufacturer's tests in December 1969, and was delivered to the Army in January 1971. The other two prototypes were completed in 1970. After extensive trials a production order was awarded to Hägglund and Söner in March 1972, with production of the vehicle commencing in 1974. The vehicle has now replaced

*The Ikv 91 light tank/infantry support vehicle; note the smoke dischargers on the rear of the turret and the 7.62mm MG on the loader's cupola.* Hägglund and Söner

the Strv 74, Ikv 102 and Ikv 103 vehicles in the Swedish Infantry Brigades and Norrland Brigades.

The vehicle is fully amphibious being propelled in the water by its tracks. A trim vane is erected at the front of the vehicle before entering the water. The hull is of welded construction and the sides of the hull are of the double-plate type. The vehicle is fitted with an NBC system.

The 90mm Bofors low-pressure gun fires fin stabilised HE and HEAT (m/v 825 m/sec) rounds. The fire control system of the Ikv 91 includes a ballistic computer and a laser rangefinder. The turret has electro-hydraulic traverse and gun elevation but the main armament is not stabilised although provision was made for this to be installed at a later date.

## Variants
Under development, using the chassis of the Ikv 91 tank destroyer is the Anti-tank carrier 551 with Hughes TOW ATGW system and AA carrier 701 with the Bofors RBS-70 SAM system.

## Employment
In service with Swedish Army.

# Pbv 302 APC

## Sweden

**Armament:** 1 × 20mm cannon, elevation +50°, depression −10° (505 rounds carried)
2 ×4 smoke grenade launchers
**Crew:** 2 + 10
**Length:** 5.35m
**Width:** 2.86m
**Height:** 2.50m (inc turret), 2.06m (hull top)
**G/clearance:** 0.40m
**Weight:** 13,500kg (loaded)
**G/pressure:** 0.60kg/sq cm
**Engine:** Volvo THD 100B, 6-cylinder, in-line, turbo-charged diesel developing 280hp at 2,200rpm
**Speed:** 66km/h (road), 8km/h (water)
**Range:** 300km (road)
**Fuel:** 285 litres
**Fording:** Amphibious
**V/obstacle:** 0.61m
**Trench:** 1.80m
**Gradient:** 60%

## Development

In October 1961 a contract was awarded to AB Hägglund with Söner to develop the Pbv 302 (Pansarbandvagn 302). The first two prototypes were completed in December 1962. After extensive trials a production order was awarded to Hägglund and Söner and the first production vehicle was completed in February 1966. Production of the vehicle was completed in December 1971. Components of the Pbv 302 are used in the Ikv 91, Bgbv 82 and Brobv 941 all of which are described later in this section. The hull is of welded construction but the vehicle is not fitted with an NBC system. The Pbv 302 is fully amphibious being propelled in the water by its tracks. Before entering the water the bilge pumps are switched on and the trim vane erected at the front of the vehicle. The

driver, commander and gunner are provided with separate hatches. The crew are provided with two large doors at the rear of the vehicle in addition to roof hatches; the latter are hydraulically operated and allow the crew to fire their weapons.

The 20mm Hispano Suiza cannon has a cyclic rate of fire of 500rpm with three belts each of 135 rounds of HE ammunition and 10 magazines each holding 10 rounds of AP ammunition being carried. Sights are provided for engaging both air and ground targets.

## Variants

The basic vehicle can be used as an ambulance (carrying 4-6 stretchers), load carrier or armoured recovery vehicle (fitted with a winch in the rear compartment). Other variants are:

*Stripbv 3021:* Armoured command vehicle, has four radios, map boards, tables.

*Epbv 3022:* Armoured observation post vehicle. This has a driver, gunner, fire control officer and operators. The commander's hatch has been replaced with a large cupola fitted with a combined binocular and rangefinder.

*Bplpbv 3023:* Armoured fire direction post vehicle. Battery commander's vehicle, has additional radios and fire direction computer.

*Pbv 302 Mark 2 APC:* This was first shown in 1978 but has yet to enter production. Similar to Mark 1 but squad commander has a separate cupola at the rear of the hull that is provided with three periscopes and a single piece hatch cover. Other improvements

*Pbv 302 Mk 2 APC.* Hägglund and Söner

include increased armour protection at the front of the hull, the two trim vanes have added buoyancy aids, improved vision equipment for commander and gunner and Bofors Lyran launcher fitted on top of hull on right side.

*Product Improved Pbv 302:* Hägglund and Söner have stated that the Pbv 302 could be improved with the following modifications. (a) 25mm Oerlikon cannon replacing the 20mm cannon; (b) fitting an automatic Allison HT 740 gearbox (trials have taken place with this modification); (c) Fitting the hydrostatic steering system that has been fitted to the Bgbv 82 and Brobv 941 vehicles; (d) Fitting the later Volvo THD 100C engine developing 310hp; (e) Sloping the sides of the vehicle and fitting firing ports and vision blocks so that the crew can aim and fire their weapons from within the vehicle. About eight men would be carried instead of ten.

**Employment**
Production complete. In service only with the Swedish Army.

# 155mm Bandkanon 1A SP Gun    Sweden

**Armament:** 1 × 155mm fully automatic gun L/50 with one magazine of 14 rounds. Elevation −3° to +40°, traverse 15° left and 15° right
1 × 7.62mm AA MG
**Crew:** 6
**Length:** 11.00m (inc gun) 6.55m (exc gun)
**Width:** 3.37m
**Height:** 3.85m (inc MG), 3.25m (w/o MG)
**G/clearance:** 0.42m (max)
**Weight:** 53,000kg (loaded)
**G/pressure:** 0.85kg/sq cm
**Engines:** One Rolls-Royce K.60 multi-fuel engine developing 240hp at 3,750rpm. One Boeing 502/10MA gas turbine developing 300shp at 38,000rpm
**Speed:** 28km/h (road)
**Range:** 230km (road)
**Fuel:** 1,445 litres
**Fording:** 1.00m
**V/obstacle:** 0.95m
**Trench:** 2.00m
**Gradient:** 60%
**Armour:** 10mm-20mm

**Development/Variants**
The 155mm Bandkanon was developed to meet the

*155mm Bandkanon 1A.* Bofors

requirements of the Swedish Army with the first prototype being completed in 1960. This differed from production vehicles in that they had three track return rollers. Following trials with six pre-production vehicles, production was undertaken by Bofors between 1966 and 1968.

The gun is fully automatic and has a max range of 25,600m and is capable of firing at 14rpm. The magazine holds 14 rounds in two layers of seven. When the ammunition is expended a lorry is brought up with a new magazine. It takes only two minutes to load a new magazine.

The weapon is not fitted with a spade at the rear as its suspension can be locked out when firing, thus providing a very stable firing platform. No variants have been announced, although when the vehicle was first introduced into service it did not have an AA MG.

**Employment**
Used only by the Swedish Army.

# RBS-70 ARMAD SAM System

Sweden

The RBS-70 ARMAD (Armoured Unit Air Defence) has been developed as a private venture by Bofors and uses many components of the RBS-70 man portable air defence system already in use with a number of countries. The prototype of the ARMAD, which was completed in 1981, is based on the chassis of a M113A1 APC but can in fact be fitted to many other types of chassis including the Swedish Ikv 91.

*RBS-70 ARMAD in firing position with radar scanner erected and missile ready for launching.* Bofors

# Bgbv 82 ARV

Sweden

**Armament:** 1 × 20mm cannon, elevation +50°, depression −10°
8 smoke dischargers either side of turret
**Crew:** 4
**Length:** 7.23m
**Width:** 3.25m
**Height:** 2.63m (inc spades), 2.45m (inc turret)
**G/clearance:** 0.45m
**Weight:** 26,500kg (loaded)
**G/pressure:** 0.82kg/sq cm
**Engine:** Volvo THD 100C, 6-cylinder, in-line, diesel, turbo-charged developing 310hp at 2,200rpm

**Speed:** 56km/h (road), 8km/h (water)
**Range:** 400km (cruising)
**Fuel:** 550 litres
**Fording:** Amphibious
**V/obstacle:** 0.60m
**Trench:** 2.50m
**Gradient:** 60%

*Bgbv 82 ARV in travelling order.*
Hägglund and Söner

## Development/Variants

The Bgbv 82 (Bärgningsbandvagn 82) was developed and produced by Hägglund and Söner. The prototype was built in 1968 and a total of 24 was built between April and December 1973. The vehicle has a similar chassis to that of the Brobv 941 Bridgelaying Vehicle. The later Ikv 91 tank destroyer uses components of these two vehicles.

The vehicle can be used as a recovery vehicle, towing vehicle (for example it can tow a disabled S tank), replacement of tank components (the loaded weight of 26,500kg includes a spare S tank powerpack), grading and levelling operations and the transportation of equipment.

The Bgbv 82 has a hull of all-welded construction; its side plates are of double-plate type and the front of the vehicle can withstand attack from 20mm ammunition. Once the flotation screen and trim vane have been erected and the bilge pumps switched on, the Bgbv 82 is fully amphibious being propelled in the water by its tracks.

With the two hydraulically operated anchor spades in the lowered position at the rear of the hull, the hydraulically operated winch has a max capacity, using a three-part pull, of 60,000kg. A hydraulically operated bulldozer blade is fitted at the front of the vehicle and this can be used for both dozing operations and to stabilise the vehicle when the crane or winch is being used.

The vehicle is fitted with infra-red driving lights and there is provision for the fitting of an NBC pack.

## Employment

In service with the Swedish Army.

# Brobv 941 AVLB

Sweden

**Armament:** 2 × 7.62mm MGs
2 × 6-barrelled smoke dischargers
**Crew:** 4
**Length:** 17.00m (with bridge), 6.71m (vehicle only)
**Width:** 4.00m (with bridge), 3.23m (vehicle only)
**Height:** 3.50m (with bridge), 2.75m (vehicle only)
**G/clearance:** 0.41m
**Weight:** 29,400kg (with bridge), 22,400kg (vehicle only)
**G/pressure:** 0.91kg/sq cm (loaded)
**Engine:** Vovlo THD 100C, 6-cylinder, in-line, turbo-charged diesel developing 310hp at 2,200rpm
**Speed:** 56km/h (road), 8km/h (water)
**Range:** 400km
**Fuel:** 550 litres
**Fording:** Amphibious

**V/obstacle:** 0.60m
**Trench:** 2.50m
**Gradient:** 60%

## Development/Variants

The Brobv 941 (Brobandvagn 941) has been designed and manufactured by Hägglund and Söner. It uses the same basic chassis as the Bgbv 82 ARV. The first prototype Brobv 941 was built in 1968 and production vehicles were delivered to the Swedish Army in 1973.

*Brobv 941 bridgelaying vehicle in travelling order.*
Hägglund and Söner

The basic role of the vehicle is that of laying a bridge although it can also transport bridging equipment and can be used for grading operations.

The vehicle is fully amphibious being propelled in the water by its tracks. The only preparation required is to switch on the bilge pumps and lower the trim vane at the front of the vehicle. The bridge is towed behind the vehicle when the vehicle is in the water.

A 15m bridge that weighs 7,000kg is carried; this takes less than five minutes to place in position and can be taken up from the other end. The bridge has a capacity of 50,000kg. The bridgelaying mechanism is journalled in the chassis with two supporting legs and two hydraulic cylinders. The bridge is laid and picked up by a telescopic beam that can be extended to the far pickup point of the bridge.

A dozer blade is mounted at the front of the vehicle, which is used to stabilise the vehicle when the bridge is being put into position. It can also be used to clear river banks so that the bridge can be correctly positioned. The Brobv 941 is fitted with infra-red driving lights and can be fitted with an NBC pack.

**Employment**
In service with the Swedish Army.

# New MBT

Switzerland

After considering proposals from Swiss Industry, the Swiss Government decided in 1979 to select a foreign MBT to meet its future requirements instead of producing a new MBT in Switzerland. Contenders for this contract include Chrysler with the M1, Krauss-Maffei with the Leopard 2, Vickers Defence Systems with the Valiant, Royal Ordnance Factories with the Challenger (or a variant of this tank) and GIAT with the AMX-32. It is expected that whichever tank is selected, production, or at the least, final assembly, will be undertaken in Switzerland but with the initial batch being supplied from abroad for training purposes. The Swiss Army has a requirement for some 450 new MBTs to replace its 150 Pz61 and 320 Centurion MBTs from 1985 to 1987.

# Pz61 and Pz68 MBTs

Switzerland

|  | Pz61 | Pz68 |
|---|---|---|
| Crew: | 4 | 4 |
| Length: (gun forward) | 9.43m | 9.49m |
| (hull) | 6.78m | 6.98m |
| Width: | 3.06m | 3.14m |
| Height: (cupola) | 2.72m | 2.75m |
| G/clearance: | 0.42m | 0.40m |
| Weight: (loaded) | 38,000kg | 39,700kg |
| (empty) | 37,000kg | 38,700kg |
| G/pressure: | 0.85kg/sq cm | 0.86kg/sq cm |
| Speed: (road) | 50km/h | 55km/h |
| Range: (road) | 300km | 350km |
| Fuel: | 760 litres | 710 litres |
| Fording: | 1.10m | 1.10m |
| V/obstacle: | 0.75m | 1m |
| Trench: | 2.60m | 2.60m |
| Gradient: | 70% | 70% |
| Armament calibre: (main) | 105mm | 105mm |
| (sec) | 20mm | 7.5mm |
| (AA) | 7.5mm | 7.5mm |
| Main armament Elev Dep: | +21° −10° | +21° −10° |
| Smoke Dischargers: | 6 | 6 |
| Ammunition: (105mm) | 52 | 56 |
| (20mm) | 240 | — |
| (7.5mm) | 3,000 | 5,200 |
| Engine: | MTU MB 837 V-8 diesel | MTU MB 837 V-8 diesel |
| Bhp/rpm: | 630/2,200 | 660/2,200 |
| Armour: | 60mm (max) | 60mm (max) |

*Pz61 MBT of the Swiss Army.*   Swiss Army

*Pz68 Mk 3 of the Swiss Army.*   Swiss Army

## Development

In 1958 Switzerland built a prototype of a MBT called the Pz58 armed with a Swiss designed 90mm gun. This was followed in 1959 by a second prototype armed with a 20pdr (83.4mm) gun as fitted to the Centurions of the Swiss Army. Ten pre-production tanks were built between 1960 and 1961 armed with the standard 105mm L7 gun and in March 1961 a production order was placed with the Federal Construction Works at Thun for 150 tanks under the designation of the Pz61. These were built between 1965 and 1966.

Between 1971 and 1974 170 Pz68s were delivered to the Swiss Army and these differed from the Pz61 in having the 20mm coaxial cannon replaced by a 7.5mm MG, stabilisation system for the main armament, ammunition resupply hatch in the left side of the turret, more powerful engine, modified transmission and wider tracks with replaceable rubber pads. The Pz68 could also be fitted with deep fording equipment and a stowage basket was mounted at the turret rear. This model was later called the Pz68 Mark 1.

In 1977 50 Pz68 Mk 2s were built which were similar to the Mark 1 but fitted with an alternator, thermal sleeve for main armament and system for extracting carbon monoxide.

Between 1978 and 1979 110 Pz68 Mk 3s were built, these being similar to the Mk 1 and 2 but with a larger turret. In 1978 60 Pz68 Mk 4s were ordered for delivery between 1981 and 1982.

## Variants

*155mm SP Howitzer:* This was developed to the prototype stage but not placed in production.
*Bridgelayer:* This is based on the Pz68 chassis and carries a bridge 18.23m long and 3.79m wide that is launched over the front of the vehicle. Swiss Army designation is the Brückenlegepanzer 68 or Brü Pz68 for short.
*ARV:* This was developed in 1965 and production vehicles are based on the Pz68 chassis. It is called the Entpannungspanzer 65 and is designed to recover disabled vehicles, carry out repairs and do minor engineer work. A dozer blade is mounted at the front of the vehicle. The A frame can lift 15,000kg main winch has a capacity of 25,000kg, also has an auxiliary winch and tow bars, tools, etc. Basic data is armament: 1 × 7.5mm MG and 6 smoke dischargers; Length 7.60m (overall); Height: 3.25m (overall); Width: 3.15m (inc spade); Weight 38,000kg (loaded); Speed: 56km/h; Crew: 5; G, clearance: 0.45m; Gradient: 60%; V/obstacle 0.75m; Fording: 1.10m; Trench: 2.60m.
*AA vehicle:* A prototype of an AA version with twin 35mm guns was developed to the prototype stage, but this was not placed in production.
*Target Tank:* This is a heavily armoured Pz68 and is used for training anti-tank crews. It is called the Pz Zielfz for short.

## Employment

In service only with the Swiss Army.

# MOWAG Improved Tornado MICV     Switzerland

**Armament:** See text
**Crew:** 3 + 7
**Length:** 6.7m
**Width:** 3.15m

*MOWAG Improved Tornado MICV fitted with Oerlikon 25mm turret model GBD-COA which is similar to the GBD-AOA but also has a 7.62mm MG.* MOWAG

**Height:** 1.75m (hull top)
**G/clearance:** 0.45m
**Weight:** 22,000kg (loaded)
**G/pressure:** 0.63kg/sq cm
**Engine:** Detroit Diesel 8V-71T turbocharged diesel developing 390hp at 2,500rpm
**Speed:** 66.1km/h
**Range:** 500km
**Fording:** 1.3m
**V/obstacle:** 0.85m
**Trench:** 2.2m
**Gradient:** 60%

## Development

The Improved Tornado MICV is a further development by MOWAG of the model described in the previous edition of *Armoured Fighting Vehicles of the World* (page 134). The first prototype was completed in 1980 but as this issue went to press production had yet to commence.

A variety of armament stations can be fitted such as an Oerlikon two-man turret model 35mm GDD-AOE (elevation from −15° to +45°) or a Oerlikon one-man turret model 25mm GBD-AOA (elevation −12° to +52°). The troop compartment is at the rear and above this can be mounted two MOWAG designed remote-controlled MG mounts, each of these has a traverse of 230° and is fitted with a 7.62mm MG with an elevation of +60° and a depression of −15°.

Standard equipment on all vehicles includes a power-operated ramp at the rear of the troop compartment and a NBC system, if required passive night vision equipment can be fitted.

## Variants

The Tornado can be adopted to carry out a number of additional roles including ambulance, anti-tank armed with ATGWs, command, fire support, maintenance and recovery, mortar carrier, multiple rocket launcher and reconnaissance.

## Employment

Prototype. Not yet in production.

# MOWAG Piranha Family                    Switzerland

|  | **4 × 4** | **6 × 6** | **8 × 8** |
|---|---|---|---|
| **Crew:** | 9 | 12 | 14 |
| **Length:** | 5.32m | 5.84m | 6.235m |
| **Width:** | 2.5m | 2.5m | 2.5m |
| **Height:** (hull top) | 1.85m | 1.85m | 1.85m |
| **G/clearance:** | 0.5m | 0.5m | 0.5m |
| **Weight:** (loaded) | 7,800kg | 9,600kg | 12,500kg |
| (empty) | 6,700kg | 7,100kg | 8,500kg |
| **Wheelbase:** | 2.42m | 2.04m/1.04m | 1.1m/1.335m/1.04m |
| **Speed:** (road) | 100km/h | 100km/h | 100km/h |
| (water) | 9.5km/h | 10km/h | 10km/h |
| **Range:** | 700km | 600km | 780km |
| **Fuel:** (litres) | 200 | 200 | 300 |
| **Fording:** | Amphibious | Amphibious | Amphibious |
| **V/obstacle:** | 0.5m | 0.5m | 0.5m |
| **Gradient:** | 70% | 70% | 70% |
| **Track:** (front/rear) | 2.18m/2.2m | 2.18m/2.2m | 2.18m/2.2m |
| **Engine:** | 216hp petrol or 190hp diesel | 300hp diesel | 325hp diesel |

## Development

There are three basic models in the Piranha range, these being a 4 × 4, a 6 × 6 and an 8 × 8, all of these share many common components such as axles, wheels and tyres, suspension, hull front and rear, steering and water propulsion system. The first prototype Piranha was completed in 1972 with first production vehicles following in 1976.

The engine and driver are at the front of the hull with the personnel compartment at the rear. The latter is provided with vision blocks and MOWAG firing ports in the hull sides and rear. The Piranha is fully amphibious being propelled in the water by two propellers; all vehicles are provided with an NBC system.

## Variants

*4 × 4:* This is normally armed with a 7.62mm MG which can be aimed and fired from within the vehicle or a turret-mounted 20mm cannon. It normally carries 9 men plus the driver. Variants include a command vehicle, radio and logistics models.

*6 × 6:* When used as an APC it can carry 11 men in addition to the driver. Armament installations available include a 7.62mm MG, 20mm cannon, 90mm gun and a 120mm mortar. This model can also be used as an ambulance, command vehicle or radio vehicle. The 6 × 6 version of the MOWAG Piranha is also built in Canada for the Canadian Armed Forces by the Diesel Division of General Motors Canada. Three versions have been built,

Cougar 76mm Gun Wheeled Fire Support Vehicle (WFSV), Grizzly Wheeled Armoured Personnel Carrier (WAPC), and the Husky Wheeled Maintenance and Recovery Vehicle (WMRV). The Cougar has the same turret as that fitted to the British Alvis Scorpion CVR (T).

*MOWAG Piranha (4×4) APC with remote-controlled MG.* MOWAG

*8 × 8:* This can carry max 14 men plus the driver. Armament installations include a 20 or 30mm cannon, twin 30mm AA guns, 120mm mortar or an 8cm rocket launcher. In addition a remote-controlled 7.62mm MG can be mounted on the roof, towards the rear of vehicle.

**Employment**
In service with a number of countries including Canada (6 × 6) and Greece (4 × 4).

*Piranha (8×8) fitted with one-man Oerlikon turret with 25mm cannon, and remote-controlled 7.62mm MG at rear.* MOWAG

# MOWAG Roland APC
Switzerland

**Data:** APC role
**Armament:** 1 × 7.62mm MG
**Crew:** 3 + 3
**Length:** 4.44m
**Width:** 2.01m
**Height:** 2.03m (turret top), 1.62m (hull top)
**G/clearance:** 0.4m
**Weight:** 4,700kg (loaded), 3,900kg (empty)
**Wheelbase:** 2.5m
**Track:** 1.71m (front), 1.655m (rear)
**Engine:** Chrysler 8-cylinder petrol engine developing 202hp at 3,900rpm
**Speed:** 110km/h
**Range:** 550km
**Fuel:** 154 litres
**Fording:** 1m
**V/obstacle:** 0.4m
**Gradient:** 60%

*MOWAG Roland APC.*   MOWAG

### Development/Variants
The Roland APC has been one of the more successful of the numerous armoured vehicles designed by the MOWAG Company. The vehicle can be adopted to fulfil a wide variety of roles including use as an APC, internal security vehicle, command and radio vehicle, ambulance or supply carrier. The basic vehicle is armed with a 7.62mm MG which can be aimed and fired from within the turret, other armament installations are available however.

Optional equipment for the Roland includes a ventilation system, obstacle clearing blade, smoke dischargers, bullet proof tyres, special firing ports in the hull sides and rear, night vision equipment and an obstacle clearing blade mounted on the front of the hull.

### Employment
In service with a number of countries including Argentina, Greece and Peru.

# MOWAG Grenadier Multi-Purpose Vehicle
Switzerland

**Armament:** See below
**Crew:** 1 + 8
**Length:** 4.84m
**Width:** 2.3m
**Height:** 2.12m (turret), 1.7m (hull top)
**G/clearance:** 0.4m
**Weight:** 6,100kg (loaded), 4,400kg (empty)
**Wheelbase:** 2.5m
**Track:** 1.99m (front), 2m (rear)
**Engine:** 8-cylinder petrol developing 202hp at 3,900rpm
**Speed:** 100km/h (road), 9/10km/h (water)
**Range:** 550km
**Fuel:** 180 litres
**Fording:** Amphibious
**V/obstacle:** 0.4m
**Gradient:** 60%
**Armour:** 8mm

### Development/Variants
The Grenadier multi-purpose vehicle was designed as a private venture by MOWAG of Kreuzlingen with first prototype being completed in 1966 and first production vehicle being completed in 1967. The

vehicle is no longer in production. The vehicle has a hull of all welded steel construction and it is fully amphibious being propelled in the water by a single three bladed propeller at the rear of the hull, steering in the water is accomplished by two rudders, these being operated by the steering wheel. Two bilge pumps are provided.

When being used as an APC it can carry a total of nine men including the driver. Other roles include reconnaissance vehicle, ambulance, command and radio vehicle, supply carrier and internal security vehicle. Various armament installations are available including a turret-mounted 20mm cannon, remote-

*MOWAG Grenadier with 8cm rocket launchers.* MOWAG

controlled 7.62mm MG, 8cm multiple rocket launcher.

Optional equipment includes bulletproof tyres, MOWAG firing ports in the sides and rear of the hull, smoke dischargers, night vision equipment and an air conditioning system.

**Employment**
In service with undisclosed countries.

# MOWAG MR 8-01 Series APC          Switzerland

**Armament:** See text
**Crew:** 2 + 5
**Length:** 5.31m
**Width:** 2.2m
**Height:** 2.22m (turret), 1.88m (hull top)
**G/clearance:** 0.5m (hull), 0.3m (axles)
**Engine:** Chrysler R361 6-cylinder petrol developing 161hp
**Weight:** 8,200kg

**Wheelbase:** 2.60m
**Track:** 1.95m
**Speed:** 80km/h (road)
**Range:** 400km
**Fording:** 1.1m
**Gradient:** 60%

*SW1s of the West German Border Police.* MOWAG

**Development/Variants**

In 1959 the Swiss MOWAG Company sold 20 of these vehicles to the German Border Police. Subsequently production of these was undertaken in Germany by Büssing and Henschel and about 600 were built. The Border Police use two basic models. The first is designated the SW1 (Geschützer Sonderwagen 1) Kfz-91; this has a crew of seven and is not normally armed. The second model is the SW11 (Geschützer Sonderwagen 11) Kfz-91; this has a crew of four and is armed with a turret-mounted 20mm cannon with four smoke dischargers either side of the turret. Some of these vehicles have been transferred to the German Police for use in the internal security role, many of these have been fitted with an obstacle clearing blade at the front of the hull. Other models developed by MOWAG to the prototype stage included the MR 8-90 with a turret-mounted 20mm cannon, MR 8-23 with a 90mm Mecar gun, MR 8-30 with twin 80mm Oerlikon Rocket Launchers; and finally the MR 9-32 which had a slightly different rear hull and carried a 120mm mortar.

**Employment**

In service only in the FRG.

# MOWAG Taifun Tank Destroyer     Switzerland

*Mockup of MOWAG Taifun 105mm tank destroyer.*
MOWAG

**Armament:** 1 × 105mm gun, elevation +18°, depression −12°, traverse 15° left and right (50 rounds carried)
1 × 7.5mm or 7.62mm AA MG (4,000 rounds carried)
1 × flare launcher
1 × 6 smoke dischargers
**Crew:** 4/5
**Length:** 9.33m (gun forward), 6.7m (hull)
**Width:** 3.15m
**Height:** 2.1m (roof)
**G/clearance:** 0.45m
**Weight:** 26,500kg (loaded), 24,000kg (empty)
**G/pressure:** 0.7kg/sq cm
**Engine:** Detroit-Diesel 8V-71T turbo-charged diesel developing 575hp at 2,500rpm
**Speed:** 65km/h (road)
**Range:** 400km (road)
**Fuel:** 520 litres
**Fording:** 1.3m
**V/obstacle:** 0.85m
**Trench:** 2.5m
**Gradient:** 60%

**Development**

The Taifun full tracked tank destroyer has been developed by MOWAG as a private venture as a successor to the company's 90mm Gepard tank destroyer which is no longer being marketed. The fighting compartment is at the front of the hull with the engine at the rear. The 105mm L7 series rifled tank gun is mounted in a ball mount at the front of the hull and is laid in both elevation and traverse electro-hydraulically. MOWAG has suggested that the 105mm gun could be replaced by a 120mm weapon and the fire control system could incorporate a laser rangefinder. Standard equipment would include a NBC system, full range of passive night vision equipment, anti-aircraft machine gun, smoke dischargers and a flare launcher.

**Variants**

There are no variants of the Taifun.

**Employment**

Mock up. Not yet in production.

# Challenger MBT

**Armament:** 1 × 120mm L11A5 rifled tank gun (48 rounds carried, separate loading)
2 × 7.62mm MGs — L8A2 coaxial and L37A2 AA (4,000 rounds)
2 × 5 smoke dischargers
**Crew:** 4
**Length:** 11.55m (gun forward), 9.875m (gun rear)
**Width:** 3.518m (overall), 3.42m (tracks)
**Height:** 2.89m (commander's sight)
**Weight:** 62,000kg (loaded), 60,000kg (empty)
**G/pressure:** 0.96kg/sq cm
**Engine:** Rolls-Royce CV12 TCA 12-cylinder 60° direct injection diesel, 1,200hp at 2,300rpm
**Speed:** 60km/h (max)
**Fording:** 1.07m
**V/obstacle:** 0.9m
**Trench:** 3.15m
**Gradient:** 60%

## Development

Following the cancellation of MBT-80 in July 1980 the British Government placed an order with the Royal Ordnance Factory Leeds for 240 Challenger MBTs. It is expected that first production tanks will be completed in 1984 with the first unit being formed the following year.

The Challenger is essentially the FV4030/3 (Shir 2) which was cancelled by Iran in 1979 with modifications to suit British Army requirements.

The Challenger has the British-developed Chobham armour, Marconi Space and Defence Systems Improved Fire Control System (IFCS), Barr and Stroud Tank Laser Sight, passive night vision equipment, NBC pack and a new powerpack. The latter consists of a Rolls-Royce Motors Military Engine Division CV12 TCA diesel developing 1,200hp, David Brown Gear Industries TN37 transmission and a cooling system designed by Airscrew Howden.

The 120mm L11A5 rifled tank gun fires separate loading (projectile and charge) ammunition including APDS-T, DS/T, HESH, SH/PRAC and smoke. In 1976 it was announced that a new range of product improved ammunition was being developed including APFSDS, product improved APDS, HEAT, product improved HESH and product improved smoke.

## Employment

On order for the British Army.

*One of the prototypes of the FV4030/3 MBT undergoing trials.* Royal Ordnance Factories

# Khalid MBT

**Weight:** 58,000kg
**Length:** 8.39m (hull)
**Width:** 3.518m
**Height:** 3.012m

## Development

In 1974 the Iranian Government ordered 125 Shir 1 (FV4030/2) and 1,225 Shir 2 (FV4030/3) MBTs from the UK. This order was cancelled in 1979 by the new Iranian Government before deliveries could commence from the Royal Ordnance Factory Leeds.

The FV4030/2 is basically the late production Chieftain fitted with a new powerpack and the Marconi Space and Defence Systems Improved Fire

Control system. The powerpack consists of a Rolls-Royce Motors Military Engine Division CV12 TCA diesel developing 1,200hp, David-Brown Gear Industries TN37 transmission and a cooling system designed by Airscrew Howden. The commander is provided with a day/night sight manufactured by

*One of the prototypes of the FV4030/2, or Khalid, MBT.* Rolls-Royce

Pilkington PE and the gunner has a Barr and Stroud Tank Laser Sight.

# Chieftain MBT                                          UK

**Armament:** 1 × 120mm gun L11A5, elevation +20°, depression −10° (53 rounds carried)
2 × 7.62mm MGs — L8A1 coaxial and L37A1 AA (6,000 rounds carried)
2 × 6 barrelled smoke dischargers
**Crew:** 4
**Length:** 10.79m (gun forward), 7.52m (hull only)
**Width:** 3.66m (inc searchlight), 3.50m (over skirts)
**Height:** 2.89m (inc commander's MG)
**G/clearance:** 0.51m
**Weight:** 54,100kg (loaded), 51,460kg (empty)
**G/pressure:** 0.843kg/sq cm
**Engine:** Leyland L60 No 4 Mk 6A, 6-cylinder, multi-fuel engine developing 730hp at 2,100rpm
**Speed:** 48km/h (road)
**Range:** 500km (road), 300km (cross-country)
**Fuel:** 950 litres
**Fording:** 1.07m
**V/obstacle:** 0.914m
**Trench:** 3.15m
**Gradient:** 60%
**Armour:** 150mm (est)

## Development
The Chieftain (FV4201) was developed to replace the Centurion MBT. The first prototype Chieftain was completed in 1959, and was first shown to the public in 1961. In May 1963, the Chieftain was accepted for service and two production lines were set up, one at the Royal Ordnance Factory, Leeds and the other at Vickers Elswick Works.

Just under 2,000 Chieftains of all types were built, with final deliveries being made to Kuwait by Vickers in 1979.

The Chieftain is fitted with a full range of night vision equipment and an NBC system, it can be fitted with a hydraulically operated dozer blade at the front of the hull if required.

When originally introduced into British Army service, the 120mm rifled L11 series gun, which uses separate loading ammunition, was aimed using a 12.7mm RMG. These have now been removed following the installation of a Barr and Stroud laser rangefinder. All front line British Army Chieftains are now being retrofitted with Marconi Space and Defence Systems Integrated Fire Control System.

## Variants
*Mk 1:* This was introduced in 1965 for training purposes, 585bhp engine.
*Mk 1/2:* This is a Mk 1 modified to Mk 2 standards for training purposes.
*Mk 1/3:* This is a Mk 1 with a new powerpack, for training purposes.
*Mk 1/4:* This is a Mk 1/2 with a new powerpack, modified RMG used for training.
*Mk 2:* This was the first model to enter service in 1966, 650bhp engine.
*Mk 3:* This entered service in 1969 and has an improved auxiliary generator, improved engine and a No 15 Mk 2 cupola with L37 MG.
*Mk 3/G:* Prototype with turret air breathing.

*Chieftain ARV for Iran with hydraulic crane.*
Vickers Defence Systems Ltd

*Chieftain MBT of the British Army in Canada.*
MoD (Army)

*Mk 3/2:* This is a modified Mk 3/G.

*Mk 3/S:* Modified Mk 3/G (production), turret air breathing.

*Mk 3/3:* This is a Mk 3 with extended range RMG (2,500m), laser rangefinder, improved engine and a new air cleaner system.

*Mk 3/3(P):* This is a Mk 3/3 with a number of modifications for Iran.

*Mk 4:* Prototype only, had additional fuel and less RMG ammunition.

*Mk 5:* This is a Mk 3/3 with many improvements including an improved engine and gearbox, increased ammunition stowage (64 rounds carried).

*Mk 5/5 (K):* is Mk 5 for Kuwait.

*Mk 5/5(P):* This is a Mk 5 for Iran with modifications.

*Mk 6:* This is the Mk 2 with new powerpack and modified RMG.

*Mk 7:* This is Mk 3, Mk 3/G, Mk 3/2 and Mk 3/S with modified RMG and improved powerpack.

*Mk 8:* Mk 3/3 with above modifications.

*Mk 9:* Mk 6 with IFCS.

*Mk 10:* Mk 7 with IFCS.

*Mk 11:* Mk 8 with IFCS.

*Mk 12:* Mk 5 with IFCS.

*FV4030:* Based on Chieftain chassis, this has a new powerpack. See separate entry.

*Chieftain ARV:* Armed with a 7.62mm MG (cupola mounted) and 20 smoke dischargers, the ARV has a crew of four. It has two winches, each of the double capstan type to give sustained pulls to the front of the vehicle of 90 tonnes and 3 tonnes respectively. A hydraulic operated dozer blade is fitted at the front of the vehicle. Basic data is as follows: Length: 8.57m; Width: 3.53m (over blade); Height: 2.79m; Fuel: 9.55 litres; Weight: 56,000kg; Speed: 42.4km/h (road); Range: 400-500km (road).

*Chieftain Bridgelayer (FV4205):* This can carry either a No 8 tank bridge which can be used to span a gap of up to 22.86m and is carried in the folded position, or a No 9 tank bridge which can be used to span a gap of up to 12.192m and is carried in the ready-to-launch position. Both bridges are launched hydraulically over the front of the vehicle and take about 3min to lay in position. Each is manned by three Royal Engineers Basic data is as follows: Length: 13.74m; Width: 4.16m; Height: 3.93m; Weight: 53,300kg.

*Chieftain Assault Vehicle Royal Engineers (FV4203):* Project only.

**Employment**

Production of the Chieftain has now been completed. In service with Iran (and ARV), Kuwait, Oman and UK (and ARV and AVLB)

# Vickers Valiant MBT                                    UK

**Armament:** 1×105mm gun, elevation +20°, depression −10° (60 rounds carried)
2×7.62mm MGs — coaxial and AA (3,000 rounds carried)
2×6-barrelled smoke dischargers
**Crew:** 4

**Length:** 9.53m (gun forwards), 7.51m (hull)
**Width:** 3.3m

*Prototype of the Vickers Valiant armed with 105mm L7A3 rifled tank gun.* Vickers

**Height:** 2.64m (turret top), 3.24m (commander's sight)
**G/clearance:** 0.457
**Weight:** 43,600kg (loaded), 41,000kg (empty)
**G/pressure:** 0.81kg/cm sq
**Engine:** General-Motors 12V-71T 12-cylinder diesel developing 915bhp at 2,500rpm
**Speed:** 59km/h (road)
**Range:** 603km (road)
**Fuel:** 1,000 litres
**Fording:** 1.1m
**V/obstacle:** 0.914m
**Trench:** 3m
**Gradient:** 60%

## Development

The Valiant MBT has been developed as a private venture by Vickers Defence Systems Limited specifically for the export market and was shown for the first time at the 1980 British Army Equipment Exhibition.

The Valiant has a Condor commander's day/night sight, laser rangefinder, Marconi Radar SFC 600 fire control system, passive periscope for the driver, NBC system and a fire extinguishing system.

The hull of the Valiant is of all welded aluminium construction to which a layer of Chobham armour can be added, the turret is of all welded steel construction which can also have a layer of Chobham armour. The tracks and suspension are protected by removable Chobham armour side skirts.

Optional equipment includes a Rolls-Royce Condor diesel in place of the Detroit Diesel, 12.7mm AA MG and a fire detection system.

## Variants

Under development is the Universal Turret which can be armed with a standard 105mm L7A3 or 120mm L11A5 rifled tank gun, or a Rheinmetall 120mm smooth bore tank gun, with various other types of fire control system fitted. An ARV and a bridgelayer based on the chassis of the Valiant are under development.

## Employment

Development complete. Ready for production.

# Vickers Mk 1 MBT

## UK

**Data:** Mk 1 (*Mk 3*)
**Armament:** 1 × 105mm L7A1 gun, elevation +20°, depression −7° (*−10°*). 44 (*50*) rounds carried
1 × 12.7mm RMG (600 rounds)
2 × 7.62mm MGs — coaxial and AA (3,000 rounds)
**Crew:** 4
**Length:** 9.728m (*9.788m*) (gun forward), 7.920m (*7.561m*) (hull only)
**Width:** 3.168m
**Height:** 2.640m (*3.099m*) (W/o AA MG), 2.438m (*2.476m*) (turret roof)
**G/clearance:** 0.406m (*0.432m*)
**Weight:** 38,600kg (*38,700kg*) (loaded), 36,000kg (*36,900kg*) (empty)
**G/pressure:** 0.86kg/sq cm (*0.79kg/sq cm*)
**Engine:** Leyland L60 Mk 4B, 6-cylinder, water-cooled multi-fuel engine developing 650bhp at 2,670rpm (*General Motors 12V-71T turbocharged diesel developing 720bhp at 2,500rpm*)
**Speed:** 48km/h (*50km/h*)
**Range:** 480km (*600km*)
**Fuel:** 1,000 litres
**Fording:** 1.143m
**V/obstacle:** 0.914m
**Trench:** 2.438m
**Gradient:** 60%
**Armour:** 25mm-80mm

## Development

In August 1961 an agreement was signed between Vickers Limited and the Indian Government. Under this agreement Vickers undertook to design an MBT and also set up a production line in India; some tanks were also to be built in Britain. The first prototype was completed early in 1963. The tank uses the engine and transmission of the Chieftain, gun of the late Centurion (also used in the Leopard, Pz61 and so on), and a suspension based on the cancelled FV300 series. Production commenced at Vickers Elswick works in 1964 and the first British-built tank was delivered to India in 1965. In the meantime a factory was built at Avadi, near Madras, and the first Indian-built tank was completed in 1966.

Initial production Vickers Mk 1 MBTs, called the Vijayanta by India, used many components supplied from the United Kingdom. But since then India has undertaken production of most of the components of the tank and by 1979 over 1,000 had been built with production continuing.

Vickers offered many options for the Mk 1 including passive night vision equipment for commander, gunner and driver, NBC system, various fire control systems and a collapsible flotation screen. When the latter was erected the tank was propelled in the water by its tracks at 6km/h.

## Variants

*Mk 2:* This was a project only and was basically a Mk 1 with two BAC Swingfire ATGW missiles mounted either side of the turret rear.

*Mk 3:* This entered production for Kenya in 1978 with first production vehicles being completed in 1979. Main improvements over the Mk 1 can be summarised as a new turret with a cast front welded to armour plate for increased armour protection, new Vickers V800 powerpack consisting of General Motors 12V-71T turbocharged diesel and TN12 transmission, new commander's cupola incorporating Condor day/night sight and a fire control system incorporating a Barr and Stroud laser rangefinder. The 105mm L7 series gun has an

*Vickers Mk 3 MBT for Kenya.*
Vickers Defence Systems

elevation of +20° and a depression of −10°.
*VARV:* The Vickers ARV entered production for
Kenya in 1979 with first production vehicles
following in 1980. It is based on hull of Vickers Mk 3
MBT but with a new superstructure, the main winch

has a capacity of 25 tonnes which can be increased
to 65 tonnes. An earth anchor is mounted at the front
of the hull and some vehicles are fitted with a
hydraulic crane for changing the V800 powerpack in
the field.

**Employment**
India (Mk 1), Kenya (Mk 3 and VARV), Nigeria
(ordered Mk 3, ARVs and bridgelayers in 1981), and
Kuwait (Mk 1)

# Centurion MBT                                                UK

**Data:** Mk 13
**Armament:** 1 × 105mm L7A2 gun, elevation
+20°, depression −10° (64 rounds carried)
1 × 12.7mm RMG (600 rounds)
2 × 7.62mm MGs — coaxial and AA (4,750 rounds)
2 × 6-barrelled smoke dischargers
**Crew:** 4
**Length:** 9.854m (inc gun), 7.823m (excl gun)
**Width:** 3.39m
**Height:** 3.009m (w/o AA MG)
**G/clearance:** 0.51m
**Weight:** 51,820kg (loaded)
**G/pressure:** 0.95kg/sq cm
**Engine:** Rolls-Royce Meteor Mk 1VB, 12-cylinder,
liquid cooled petrol engine developing 650bhp at
2,550rpm
**Speed:** 34.6km/h (road)
**Range:** 190km (road)
**Fuel:** 1,037 litres
**Fording:** 1.45m, 2.74m (with kit)
**V/obstacle:** 0.914m
**Trench:** 3.352m
**Gradient:** 60%
**Armour:** 17mm-152mm

**Development**
The Centurion was developed from 1944 under the
designation of the A41 heavy cruiser with the first
prototypes being completed in 1945. First
production Centurions were completed by ROF
Woolwich in 1946. Production was also undertaken
by ROF Leeds, Vickers at Elswick and Leyland Motors
at Leyland and over 4,000 were built before
production was finally completed in 1961. The
Centurion was replaced in the British Army by the
Chieftain.

The Centurion chassis has been used as a basis
for many prototype vehicles including the FV4004
Conway, FV4005 Tank Destroyer FV4019
Flamethrower, FV3802 25pdr and FV3805 5.5in SP
guns. The British Aircraft Corporation (GW Division)
did have a project to fit Swingfire ATGW to the
vehicle, but this only reached mock-up stage.
Centurions can be fitted with a dozer blade on the
front of the vehicle. A summary of Centurion tanks
still in service is listed below.

**Variants**
*Mk 3:* 20 pdr (83.4mm) gun with 65 rounds,
7.92mm Besa coaxial MG, Meteor Mk 1VB engine.
Most were re-built to Mk 5 standards.
*Mk 5:* Based on Mk 3 hull but with 7.62mm coaxial
MG. Vickers were design parents. Could tow a trailer
with additional fuel.
*Mk 5/1:* Mk 5 uparmoured, designated FV4011.
*Mk 5/2:* Mk 5 upgunned with 105mm gun.
*Mk 6:* Mk 5 upgunned and up armoured, also has
additional fuel in hull rear.
*Mk 6/1:* Mk 6 with infra-red driving and fighting
equipment, stowage basket on rear of turret.
*Mk 6/2:* Mk 6 with 12.7mm RMG for 105mm gun.
*Mk 7:* Designated FV4007, design parents were
Leyland Motors. Armament is a 20pdr gun with 61
rounds, 7.62mm coaxial MG, fume extractor on
barrel, additional fuel.
*Mk 7/1:* Mk 7 uparmoured, designated FV4012.
*Mk 7/2:* Mk 7 upgunned with 105mm.
*Mk 8:* Based on Mk 7 hull, 20pdr gun with 63 ready
rounds, fume extractor on barrel. Meteor 1VC
engine, contrarotating cupola with raisable roof for
commander, resilient gun mantlet. New elevating
gear.

*Mk 8/1:* Mk 8 uparmoured.

*Mk 8/2:* Mk 8 upgunned with 105mm.

*Mk 9:* Mk 7 upgunned and up armoured, designated FV 4015.

*Mk 9/1:* Mk 9 with infra-red driving and fighting equipment, stowage basket on rear of the turret.

*Mk 9/2:* Mk 9 with RMG for 105mm.

*Mk 10:* Mk 8 upgunned and uparmoured, designated FV4017. Armed with 105mm L7A1 gun with 70 rounds, new control equipment for gun, impact resisting trunions, automatic stabilisation when vehicle exceeds 6.43km/h.

*Mk 10/1:* Mk 10 with infra-red driving and fighting equipment and stowage basket on rear of turret.

*Mk 10/2:* Mk 10 with RMG for 105mm.

*Mk 11:* Mk 6 with RMG, infra-red driving and fighting equipment and a stowage basket on the rear of the turret.

*Mk 12:* Mk 9 with infra-red driving and fighting equipment, RMG and stowage basket on the rear of the turret.

*Mk 13:* Mk 10 with RMG and infra-red driving and fighting equipment.

*Vickers Modified Centurions (1973):* In May 1973 Vickers demonstrated a Centurion MBT which had been fitted with a new powerpack based on a GM 12V-71T diesel engine with a power output of 720bhp and a new gun control and stabilisation system.

Optional equipment includes new TN12 semi-automatic transmission, new final drives, new commander's cupola, revised ventilation system, laser rangefinder and passive night vision equipment. Switzerland and Sweden have both upgraded two of their Centurions to this standard but neither country has yet decided to retrofit their entire fleet of Centurions to this standard.

*ARV Centurion Mk 2 (FV4006):* This is a Mk 3 Centurion with an armoured superstructure, its equipment includes a winch (max capacity 90,000kg pro rata), spades at the rear, tools and so on. Armament is a 7.62mm MG and 10 smoke dischargers. Data: Length: 8.96m; Width: 3.39m; Height: 2.89m; Weight: 50,295kg (loaded), 47,250kg (empty); Crew: 4.

*Tank, Beach, ARV, Centurion (BARV) (FV4018):* This is basically a Centurion with no turret and fitted with a superstructure. It is capable of operating in 2.895m of water. Data: Length: 8.08m; Width: 3.402m; Height: 3.45m; Weight: 40,643kg (loaded), 37,848kg (empty); Crew: 4.

*Tank Assault Vehicle, Royal Engineers (AVRE) Mk 5 (FV4003):* This is armed with a 165mm demolition

*Centurion Mk 8 with 20pdr (83.4mm) gun.*
MoD (Army)

charge projector as well as a coaxial MG. At the front of the vehicle is a hydraulically operated dozer blade and it can also carry a fascine. It can tow a trailer fitted with the Giant Viper mine clearance equipment. Data: Length: 8.686m (inc blade): Width: 3.39m (w/o blade); 3.962m (with blade); Height 3.00m; Weight: 51,800kg (loaded), 49,600kg (empty).

*Tank, Bridgelayer, Centurion Mk 5 (FV4002):* This is fitted with a single span bridge that can be laid across gaps up to 13.72m wide, this takes only two minutes to lay. Data of the vehicle with bridge is: Length: 16.3m; Width: 4.267m; Height: 3.88m; Weight: 50,485kg (loaded), 48,760kg (empty); Crew 2-3.

*Centurion target tank:* Used in UK and BAOR for training crews with anti-tank weapons.

## Employment

*Austria:* Uses Centurion turrets in static defence role.

*Denmark:* These have a 12.7mm M2 AA MG and most have been fitted with a 105mm gun to bring them up to Mk 5/2 standard.

*India:* India used Mk 5 and Mk 7 Centurions but these are now up for sale.

*Centurion AVRE Mk 5.*   MoD (Army)

*Israel:* Details of Israeli Centurions will be found under Israel.

*Jordan:* Has used Mk 3, Mk 5 and Mk 7, many of which have been upgunned to 105mm. Some are now being fitted with new diesel powerpack and a new fire control system.

*Netherlands:* Will be replaced by Leopard 2 MBTs by 1986. Most have been fitted with L7 gun and RMG to bring them up to Mk 5/2 standard. Also in use are Mk 5, Mk 5 bridgelayer with American scissors type bridge, Mk 2 ARV and tankdozer.

*Kuwait:* Uses Mk 8/1

*South Africa:* Uses Mk 3 and Mk 5 obtained from India, Iraq, Jordan and UK at various times, many have been updated with new powerpack.

*Sweden:* Mk 3 was known as Strv 81 but when fitted with a 105mm L7 series gun became the Strv 102, Mk 10 (Strv 101) and Mk 2 (ARV) Bgbv 81).

*Switzerland:* Mk 3 (Pz55), Mk 60 (Pz60), Mk 7 (Pz57), most of which have 105mm guns, and Mk 2 ARV (Entpannungspanzer 56).

# Comet Cruiser Tank UK

**Armament:** 1 × 77mm gun, elevation +20°, depression −12° (61 rounds carried)
2 × 7.92mm MGs — coaxial and bow (5,175 rounds)
2 × 6-barrelled smoke dischargers
**Crew:** 5
**Length:** 7.66m (inc gun), 6.55m (exc gun)
**Width:** 3.073m
**Height:** 2.67m
**G/clearance:** 0.4m
**Weight:** 33,250kg
**G/pressure:** 0.97kg/sq cm
**Engine:** Rolls-Royce Meteor Mk 3, 12-cylinder (V-12), water-cooled petrol engine developing 600hp at 2,500rpm
**Speed:** 51.5km/h (road)
**Range:** 240km (road)

*Comet.* MoD (Army)

**Fuel:** 527 litres
**Fording:** 1.04m
**V/obstacle:** 0.914m
**Trench:** 2.438m
**Gradient:** 60%
**Armour:** 14mm-102mm

### Development/Employment
The Comet was designed by Leyland Motors under the designation of the A34 with first production tanks being completed in 1944. A total of 1,200 were completed by May 1945. It is no longer used by the British Army although a few remain in service with Burma and South Africa.

# FV601 Alvis Saladin Mk 2 Armoured Car UK

**Armament:** 1 × 76mm gun, elevation +20°, depression −10°, (42 rounds carried)
2 × 7.62mm — coaxial and AA (2,750 rounds)
2 × 6-barrelled smoke dischargers
**Crew:** 3
**Length:** 5.284m (inc gun), 4.93m (exc gun)
**Width:** 2.54m
**Height:** 2.19m (w/o MG)
**G/clearance:** 0.426m
**Weight:** 11,590kg (loaded), 10,500kg (empty)
**Track:** 2.038m
**Wheelbase:** 1.524m + 1.524m
**G/pressure:** 1.12kg/sq cm
**Engine:** Rolls-Royce B.80 Mk 6A, 8-cylinder petrol engine developing 170hp at 3,750rpm
**Speed:** 72km/h (road)
**Range:** 400km (road)
**Fuel:** 241 litres

**Fording:** 1.07m, 2.13m (with kit)
**V/obstacle:** 0.46m
**Trench:** 1.52m
**Gradient:** 46%
**Armour:** 8mm-32mm

### Development
Design of the Saladin dates to 1947 but it was not until 1954 that the prototype vehicle was completed with the first production models following in 1958, production of the Saladin was completed in 1972. Production being undertaken by Alvis Limited of Coventry.

The Saladin uses many components of the FV603 Saracen APC, one of the differences being that the Saracen has its engine in the front, and the Saladin has its engine in the rear.

## Variants

The production vehicle was the Mk 2, its full designation being FV601(C) Armoured Car 76mm (Alvis Saladin Mk 2 6 × 6). BAC and Alvis modified a Saladin to carry a single Swingfire anti-tank missile either side of the turret and two reserve missiles at the rear of the vehicle. This, however, was a project only. Also tested in 1966 was a Saladin fitted with a flotation screen, this enabled the vehicle to cross rivers, being propelled in the water by its wheels. It did not progress further than trials. The German Border Police use the FV601(D). This has no coaxial MG and has German type lights and six German smoke grenade launchers either side of the turret. Its German designation is SW-111 Kfz-93, Geschützer Sonderwagen 111.

## Employment

Bahrain, Federal German Border Police, Ghana, Indonesia, Jordan, Kenya, Kuwait, Lebanon, Libya, Oman, Nigeria, Portugal, Sierra Leone, Sudan, Tunisia, United Arab Emirates, UK (few), Yemen Arab Republic (North) and Peoples Democratic Republic of Yemen (south)

*Alvis Saladin FV601.*  MoD (Army)

# Scorpion Family CVR(T)s                                     UK

|  | FV101 | FV102 | FV103 | FV104 | FV105 | FV106 | FV107 |
|---|---|---|---|---|---|---|---|
| **Crew:** | 3 | 3 | 3 + 4 | 3 + 4 | 5/6 | 3 | 3 |
| **Length:** | 4.794m | 4.826m | 4.93m | 5.067m | 4.8m | 4.788m | 4.572m |
| **Width:** | 2.235m | 2.242m | 2.242m | 2.242m | 2.242m | 2.43m | 2.432m |
| **Height:** | 2.102m | 2.21m | 2.26m | 2.416m | 2.559m | 2.254m | 2.096m |
| **Weight:** (loaded) | 8,000kg | 8,346kg | 8,172kg | 8,664kg | 8,664kg | 8,738kg | 7,756kg |
| **G/pressure:** (kg/sq cm) | 0.36 | 0.345 | 0.338 | 0.358 | 0.358 | 0.358 | 0.338 |
| **Speed:** (road) | 80.5km/h | 80.5km/h | 80.5km/h | 72.5km/h | 72.5km/h | 72.5km/h | 80.5km/h |
| **Range:** (road) | 644km | 483km | 483km | 483km | 483km | 483km | 644km |
| **Fuel:** (litres) | 423 | 350 | 386 | 395 | 395 | 404 | 423 |
| **Fording:** | 1.067m | 1.067m | 1.067m | 1.067m | 1.067m | 1.067m | 1.067m |

**G/clearance:** All 0.356m; **V/obstacle:** All 0.50m; **Trench:** All 2.057m; **Gradient:** All 60%; **Engine:** All Jaguar 6-cylinder water-cooled petrol engine developing 190bhp at 4,750rpm

*FV101 Scorpion CVR(T).*  Alvis

## Development

The Scorpion was preceded by a vehicle known as the TV 15000 and a Mobile Test Rig (MTR). In September 1967, Alvis of Coventry was awarded a contract to build 17 prototype Scorpions. The first prototype was completed in January 1969, and in September 1969, prototypes were shown to the public and Press. The first production order was awarded to Alvis in May 1970, and the vehicle entered production in 1971, the first production Scorpion being completed early in 1972. In 1970 a co-production order was signed between the UK and Belgium, under which Belgium received a total of 701 members of the Scorpion family which were assembled in Belgium.

The basic role of the Scorpion is that of reconnaissance and for this reason the vehicle is equipped with a complete range of day and night observation, driving and fighting systems. An NBC system is fitted. The vehicle can be made amphibious in several minutes by erecting a flotation screen around the top of the hull, the vehicle is propelled in the water by its tracks at 6.5km/h. A propeller can be fitted which increases the vehicle's water speed to 9.6km/h. Most British Army Scorpions have now had their flotation screens removed. The Scorpion is of all welded aluminium armour construction and uses the same engine as the Fox CVR(W). Scorpion can also be fitted with the ZB 298 Radar System, Radiac system and navigational aids. The vehicle is air-portable by such aircraft as the C-130 (2 vehicles) or CH-53A helicopter.

## Variants

*FV101 Scorpion:* This is armed with a 76mm gun with an elevation of +35° and a depression of −10°, a 7.62mm MG is fitted and this can be used as a ranging gun, two four-barrelled smoke dischargers are fitted. 40 rounds of 76mm and 3,000 rounds of 7.62mm ammunition are carried. For trials purposes an Alvis Scorpion has been fitted with a Belgian Cockerill 90mm gun. Undergoing trials is a Scorpion with a Perkins turbocharged diesel developing 200bhp at 2,600rpm.

*FV102 Striker:* This is an ATGW vehicle. Mounted on the top of the hull, towards the rear is a launching bin containing five British Aerospace Swingfire ATGW with a range of 4,000m, a further five missiles are carried inside the vehicle. A 7.62mm MG is cupola mounted and smoke dischargers are mounted on the front of the vehicle.

*FV103 Spartan:* This is a small APC and would be used to carry assault troops or engineers. It could also be used to support other members of the family for example carrying spare missiles or ammunition. It is armed with a cupola-mounted 7.62mm MG and smoke dischargers. The Spartan can be fitted with other armament installations including turret mounted twin 20mm cannon for use in the AA role, TOW ATGW launcher, MILAN turret with two MILAN ATGWs in the ready-to-launch position and a HOT turret with two HOT ATGWs in the ready-to-launch position. There is a separate entry for the Alvis Stormer APC.

*FV104 Samaritan:* This is an ambulance and has a raised roof, no armament is fitted. It can carry four stretcher patients, six sitting patients or three sitting and two stretchers, in addition to its crew.

*FV105 Sultan:* This is a command vehicle and has a similar hull to that of the FV104. Additional radios are fitted as are mapboards. A penthouse can be erected at the rear of the vehicle to give additional working space. It is armed with a pintle-mounted 7.62mm MG.

*FV106 Samson:* This is a recovery vehicle and has an internally mounted winch with a maximum capacity of 12,000kg and 229m of wire rope. This is driven from the main engine and has a variable speed. Anchors are provided at the rear of the vehicle.

*FV107 Scimitar:* This has the same hull and turret as the Scorpion but it is armed with a 30mm Rarden cannon and a 7.62mm MG. The gun has an elevation of +35° and a depression of −10°. 165 rounds of 30mm and 3,000 rounds of 7.62mm ammunition

*FV102 Striker launching a Swingfire ATGW.*
MoD (Army)

*FV107 Scimitar armed with 30mm Rarden cannon as fitted on the Fox armoured car.* MoD (Army)

are carried. Two four-barrelled smoke dischargers are fitted either side of the turret front.

**Employment**

In service with Belgium (all versions), Brunei, Honduras, Iran, Ireland, New Zealand, Nigeria, Tanzania, Thailand, Philippines, United Arab Emirates and the UK (Army and RAF Regiment).

# Fox CVR(W) UK

**Armament:** 1 × 30mm Rarden cannon, elevation +40°, depression −14° (96 rounds carried in clips of three)
1 × 7.62mm coaxial MG (2,600 rounds)
2 × 4-barrelled smoke dischargers
**Crew:** 3
**Length:** 5.359m (gun forward), 4.242m (hull)
**Width:** 2.134m
**Height:** 2.20m (overall), 1.98m (turret top)
**G/clearance:** 0.30m
**Weight:** 6,386kg (loaded), 5,733kg (empty)
**Track:** 1.753m
**Wheelbase:** 2.464m
**G/pressure:** 0.46kg/sq cm
**Engine:** Jaguar 4.2 litre, 6-cylinder petrol engine developing, 190hp at 5,000rpm
**Speed:** 104km/h (road), 5km/h (water)
**Range:** 434km (road)
**Fuel:** 145 litres
**Fording:** 1m
**V/obstacle:** 0.50m
**Trench:** 1.22m (with channels)
**Gradient:** 58%

**Development**

The Fox is the development of the Ferret scout car. Design work on the Fox (FV721) started in 1965/1966. Prototypes were built by the Daimler Company at Radford, Coventry, the first prototype

being completed in November 1967. The vehicle was first shown to the public in October 1969. The production contract was awarded to the Royal Ordnance Factory at Leeds and the first production vehicle was completed in May 1973.

*CVR(W) Fox.* Simon Dunstan

As built, all Fox supplied to the British Army were fitted with a collapsible flotation screen. This could be quickly erected by the crew to enable the vehicle to propel itself across rivers by its wheels at a speed of 5km/h. These have now been removed from British Army Fox vehicles.

The hull and turret of the Fox are constructed of welded aluminium armour. Equipment includes an NBC system, navigation system and a full range of day and night vision and fire control devices. The engine of the Fox is also used in the CVR(T) Scorpion and the 30mm Rarden cannon is also used in the Scimitar vehicle. This 30mm cannon can fire a APDS round or standard Oerlikon HE, AP or Practice rounds. Cyclic rate of fire is 90rpm, max range is about 4,000m. Single shots or three round bursts can be fired and the spent ammunition cases are ejected outside the vehicle. The ZB298 Radar System can be fitted to the vehicle if required.

**Variants**

The FV722 Vixen, Combat Vehicle Reconnaissance (Wheeled) Liaison was cancelled in the December 1974 defence cuts.

The Panga is a private venture by the Royal Ordnance Factories and is essentially a Fox with the 30mm Rarden two-man turret removed and replaced by a Peak Engineering one man turret armed with a 7.62mm or a 12.7mm MG.

**Employment**

Iran, Kenya, Nigeria, Saudia Arabia and the UK.

# Ferret Family Light Scout Cars                                      UK

*Ferret Mk 1* (left) *and Ferret Mk 2/3.*   MoD (Army)

**Crew:** 2-3 (Mk 1/1, Mk 4), 3 (Mk 1/2); 2 (Mk 2/3, Mk 2/6)
**Length:** 3.84m, 4.095m (Mk 4)
**Width:** 1.91m, 2.13m (Mk 4)
**Height:** 1.45m (Mk 1/1), 1.65m (Mk 1/2), 1.88m Mk 2/3, Mk 2/6), 2.336m (Mk 4)
**G/clearance:** 0.33m, 0.43m (Mk 4)
**Weight:** Loaded — 4,210kg (Mk 1/1), 4,370kg (Mk 1/2), 4,395kg (Mk 2/3), 4,560kg (Mk 2/6), 5,400kg (Mk 4)
Empty — 3,510kg (Mk 1/1), 3,660kg (Mk 1/2), 3,684kg (Mk 2/3), 3,680kg (Mk 2/6), 4,725kg (Mk 4)

**Track:** 1.55m, 1.75m (Mk 4)
**Wheelbase:** 2.286m
**Engine:** Rolls-Royce B60 Mk 6A 6-cylinder water-cooled petrol engine developing 129bhp at 3,750rpm
**Speed:** 93km/h, 80km/h (Mk 4) (road)
**Range:** 300km (road)
**Fuel:** 96 litres
**Fording:** 0.914m (w/o kit)
**V/obstacle:** 0.406m
**Trench:** 1.22m (with channels)
**Gradient:** 46%
**Wheelbase:** 2.286m

**Development**

The Ferret was designed by Daimler from 1948 as the replacement for the famous Dingo scout car with the first prototype being completed in 1949. The first production vehicles were Mk 2s which were completed in mid-1952 with the first production Mk 1s following later the same year.

Production continued until 1971 by which time 4,409 vehicles had been built. Further development of the Ferret by Daimler resulted in the Fox for which there is a separate entry.

**Variants**

*Mk 1/1 FV 701 (J) Scout Car Liaison:* This is the basic open topped version and is armed with a Bren LMG or a 7.62mm MG. A trials version existed with a flotation screen.

*Mk 1/2 (FV 704) Scout Car Liaison:* This is a Mk 1/1 with a small turret with a flat roof and it is armed with a Bren LMG.

*Mk 2/2:* This is a Mk 2 with an extension collar between the top of the vehicle and the MG turret. The Mk 2 has a 2-door MG turret and the Mk 2/1 is a Mk 1 with a 2-door MG turret.

*Mk 2/3 FV 701 (H) Scout Car Reconnaissance:* This is similar to the Mk 1/1 except that it has a 7.62mm MG in a turret with an elevation of +45° and a depression of −15°, traverse being 360°; 2,500 rounds of 7.62mm ammunition are carried. This vehicle can also be fitted with the ZB 298 Radar System. The Ferret Mk 2/4 and Mk 2/5 have additional armour.

*Mk 2/6 FV 703 Scout Car Reconnaissance (Guided Weapon):* This is the Mk 2/3 built with a Vigilant wire

guided anti-tank missile mounted either side of the turret with a common elevating mechanism. Two spare missiles are carried in place of the spare wheel. The missiles can be controlled from within the vehicle or away from the vehicle with the aid of a combined sight/controller and separation cable. The missiles have a range of 200m to 1,375m.

*Mk 2/7:* This is a Mk 2/6 but with its missile equipment removed and used as a reconnaissance vehicle.

*Mk 3 Scout Car Liaison:* This is a Mk 1/1 but with modified suspension, larger wheels and a flotation screen.

*Mk 4 FV 711 Scout Car Reconnaissance:* This is a rebuilt Mk 2 and has stronger suspension units, disc brakes, larger wheels and tyres. A flotation screen can be quickly erected and the vehicle is propelled in the water by its wheels at a max speed of 3.8km/h.

*Mk 5 FV 712 Scout Car Reconnaissance/Guided Weapon:* This model, armed with British Aerospace Swingfire ATGWs is no longer in service.

**Employment**

In service with: Bahrain, Burma, Burundi, Cameroon, Central African Empire, Gabon, Gambia, Ghana, Indonesia, Jordan, Kuwait, Libya, Madagascar, Malaysia, New Zealand, Nigeria, Portugal, Qatar, Rhodesia, Saudi Arabia, Somalia, South Africa, Sri Lanka, Sudan, United Kingdom, Upper Volta, Yemen Arab Republic (North), People's Democratic Republic of Yemen (South) and Zambia.

# Shorland Armoured Patrol Car  UK

**Armament:** 1 × 7.62mm MG (1,500 rounds carried)
2 × 4 smoke dischargers (optional)
**Crew:** 3
**Length:** 4.597m
**Width:** 1.778m
**Height:** 2.286m
**G/clearance:** 0.21m (min)
**Weight:** 3,360kg (loaded), 2,931kg (empty)

**Track:** 1.358m
**Wheelbase:** 2.768m
**G/pressure:** 2.4kg/sq cm
**Engine:** Rover 6-cylinder petrol engine developing 91bhp at 4,500rpm

*Shorland Mk 4 armoured patrol car armed with smoke dischargers.*   Shorts

**Speed:** 88.5km/h (road)
**Range:** 257km (standard tank) 514km (long range tank)
**Fuel:** 64 litres (standard), 128 litres (long range)
**V/obstacle:** 0.23m
**Trench:** not applicable
**Armour:** 8.25mm-11mm

## Development

The Shorland was conceived, prototype built, and placed in production in 1965. The vehicle is essentially a 2.77m wheelbase modified Land Rover chassis with an armoured body, in addition the engine and radiator have been armoured. The Shorland was first used by the Royal Ulster Constabulary, since then however the British Army have taken over the vehicles. Shorland is recognised by the British Army as an Internal Security Vehicle.

## Variants

The first model to enter production was the Mk 1. This had hull armour of 7.25mm and was powered by a 4-cylinder Rover petrol engine developing 67bhp at 4,000rpm. This was followed by the Mk 2

which had a 4-cylinder petrol engine developing 77bhp at 4,000rpm.

The Mk 3 has a thicker hull armour of 8.25mm which is resistant to the standard 7.62mm NATO round, also, it is powered by a 6-cylinder petrol engine developing 91bhp at 4,500rpm.

The latest version to enter production is the Mk 4, shown for the first time in 1980. This has improved armour protection and is powered by a V-8 3.5 litre petrol engine coupled to permanent four-wheel drive.

The SB 303 is the Mk 3 with a modified turret for anti-hijack patrols at airports and other high risk areas while the SB 404 is similar but based on Mk 3. There is a separate entry for the SB 301 and SB 401 APCs.

## Employment

The Shorland is in service with some 35 countries including Argentina, Botswana, Brunei, Burundi, Guyana, Libya, Malaysia, Seychelles, Thailand, United Arab Emirates and the UK (Northern Ireland only).

# MCV-80 MICV                                          UK

**Armament:** 1 × 30mm Rarden cannon
1 × 7.62mm coaxial MG
2 × 4 smoke dischargers
**Crew:** 10
**Length:** 5.42m
**Width:** 2.8m
**Height:** 2.82m (inc turret)
**G/clearance:** 0.5m
**Weight:** 20,000kg
**Engine:** Rolls-Royce CV8 TCE V-8 diesel developing 800bhp at 2,300rpm
**Speed:** 75km/h (max)
**Range:** 500km
**V/obstacle:** 0.75m
**Trench:** 2.5m
**Gradient:** 60%
*Note:* Above specifications are provisional

## Development

The MCV-80 (Mechanised Combat Vehicle 80) is being developed by GKN Sankey as the replacement for the FV432 and is expected to enter service between 1985 and 1986. The British Army has a requirement for between 1,800 and 2,000 vehicles. The hull is of all welded construction with the driver being seated at the front left and the engine compartment to his right. The two man turret, designed by Vickers is in the centre of the vehicle with the troop compartment at the rear. There is no provision for the infantry to use their small arms from within the vehicle.

*MCV-80 with two-man turret armed with a 30mm Rarden cannon and a 7.62mm coaxial MG.*
GKN Sankey

The MCV-80 is fitted with an NBC system and a full range of passive night vision equipment, but is not amphibious.

**Variants**
Projected variants include: Platoon vehicle with GPMG turret, Command vehicle with GPMG turret, Command vehicle with Rarden turret, Mortar vehicle with GPMG, Artillery command post with GPMG turret, Engineer combat vehicle with GPMG turret and EMI Ranger anti-personnel mine laying system, Recovery vehicle with front mounted spade and GPMG, Repair vehicle with crane and GPMG.

**Employment**
Under development

# FV432 Series APC                                                UK

**Armament:** 1 × 7.62mm GPMG and 2 × 3-barrelled smoke dischargers
**Crew:** 2 + 10
**Length:** 5.251m (overall), 4.87m (hull)
**Width:** 2.80m (overall)
**Height:** 2.286m (inc MG), 1.879m (hull roof)
**G/clearance:** 0.406m
**Weight:** 15,280kg (loaded), 13,740kg (empty)
**G/pressure:** 0.78kg/sq cm
**Engine:** Rolls-Royce K60 No 4 Mk 4F, multi-fuel, 240bhp at 3,750rpm
**Speed:** 52km/h (road), 6.6km/h (water)
**Range:** 480km (road)
**Fuel:** 454 litres
**Fording:** Amphibious
**V/obstacle:** 0.609m
**Trench:** 2.05m
**Gradient:** 60%
**Armour:** 6mm-12mm

**Development**
The FV432 was developed from the earlier FV420 series. The first prototype FV432 was completed in 1961 and production commenced in 1963. Production was undertaken by GKN Sankey and has now been completed. Prototype FV432s were powered by a B81 petrol engine and were called Trojans. First production FV432s were the Mk1 and Mk1/1, followed by Mk2 and Mk2/1. The FV432 is made amphibious by erecting a screen and is propelled in the water by its tracks. It is fitted with an

*FV432 used as an artillery command vehicle.*
Christopher F. Foss

NBC system and has infra-red driving lights. The FV433 Abbot uses components of the FV432.

**Variants**
The FV432 can be adopted for the following roles:
*Mortar:* 81mm mortar with a traverse of 360°, 160 rounds of ammunition, crew of six, laden weight 16,400kg.
*Command:* Has mapboards, additional radios. Crew of seven, laden weight 15,500kg. A large tent can be erected at the rear of the vehicle to give additional working space.
*Recovery:* Fitted with a winch, winch sub-frame, earth anchor, 107m of cable, max line pull 2 part tackle 18,299kg. Winch is driven from the PTO on the engine transfer case.
*Wombat:* Can be fired mounted or dismounted, 14 rounds of ammunition are carried, crew of four, weight 15,870kg.
*Load Carrier:* Can carry 3,670kg of cargo.
*Minelayer:* Can tow the Bar minelaying equipment and can be fitted with the Ranger anti-personnel minelayer system.
*Ambulance:* Can carry four stretchers (two each side), or two stretchers on one side and five seated patients on the other side. Crew of two.
*Carl Gustaf:* Bar across fighting compartment on which is mounted a Carl Gustaf anti-tank weapon.

*Artillery Control:* Fitted with the FACE (Field Artillery Computer Equipment).
*Radar:* Can be fitted with the ZB298 ground surveillance radar.
*Navigation:* Can be fitted with navigation equipment.
*Cymbeline:* Fitted with the EMI Cymbeline mortar locating radar, this version has replaced the FV436 Green Archer mortar locating radar.
*GPMG:* Many FV432s have been fitted with a Peak Engineering turret armed with a 7.62mm GPMG.
*Rarden:* A few FV432 APC fitted with a turret-mounted Rarden cannon are in service with the Berlin brigade.
*Sonic Detection:* The Royal Artillery use the FV432 fitted with the Plessey Sound Ranging Link to locate enemy artillery positions.

**The following variants use a modified FV432 hull:**

*FV434 Carrier, Maintenance, Full Tracked:* This version is fitted with an HIAB crane and carries special tools and equipment. Crew is four, data as for FV432 except: Length: 5.72m; Weight: 17,750kg (loaded), 15,040kg (empty); Height 2.83m (travelling); Width: 2.84m. Its crane can lift 1,250kg at 3.96m radius to 3,050kg at 2.26m radius.

*FV 438 Swingfire Launcher Vehicle:* This version has two launcher boxes for the Swingfire ATGW. A total of 14 missiles is carried. It also carries a 7.62mm GPMG. It has a crew of three. Data is similar to the basic FV 432 except: Height: 2.705m; Weight 16,200kg (loaded), 14,520kg (empty).

*FV439 Signals Vehicles:* The Royal Signals use various models of the FV432 designated the FV439 fitted with communications equipment, many of these have a large aerial mounted on the roof.

**Employment**
Used only by the British Army.

# Alvis Stormer APC

UK

**Armament:** Depends on role
**Crew:** 3+8 (max 1+11)
**Length:** 5.3m
**Width:** 2.375m, 2.654m (with appliqué armour)
**Height:** 2.364m
**G/clearance:** 0.362m
**Weight:** 10,689kg (loaded), 8,740kg (empty)
**G/pressure:** 0.37kg/sq cm
**Engine:** Perkins T6/3544 6-cylinder turbocharged diesel developing 200bhp at 2,600rpm
**Speed:** 72km/h (road), 6.5km/h (water)
**Range:** 800km (road)
**Fuel:** 405 litres
**V/obstacle:** 0.46m
**Trench:** 1.8m
**Gradient:** 60%

**Development**
In the late 1970s the Royal Ordnance Factory Leeds built the prototype of a full tracked APC called the FV4333. This was essentially a Spartan APC with a wider and longer hull, additional roadwheel each side and its original petrol engine replaced by a more powerful diesel engine. In 1980 Alvis purchased the marketing and manufacturing rights from the ROF and in 1981 named the vehicle the Stormer, so becoming the 8th member of the Alvis Scorpion family of CVR(T).

Like the Spartan, the Stormer is of all welded aluminium armour construction and is fully amphibious being propelled in the water by its tracks at a speed of 6.5km/h or by a propeller kit at a speed of 9.6km/h. A full range of night vision equipment is installed as is an NBC system.

**Variants**
The first prototype was fitted with a Number 16 cupola armed with a single 7.62mm GPMG but a wide range of other armament installations can be fitted including a turret armed with 20mm or 30mm cannon, 76mm or 90mm gun, twin 20mm AA guns or various types of ATGW including MILAN and HOT. The vehicle can also be adopted for a wide range of other roles such as ambulance, cargo carrier and command vehicle.

**Employment**
Development complete. Ready for production.

*Infantry dismount from the prototype of the Alvis Stormer APC.* Alvis

# FV603 Alvis Saracen APC UK

**Armament:** 2 × 7.62mm MGs — one in turret, elevation +45°, depression −15°, one on ring mount at rear (3,000 rounds carried)
2×3-barrelled smoke dischargers
**Crew:** 2+10
**Length:** 5.233m (overall)
**Width:** 2.539m
**Height:** 2.463m
**G/clearance:** 0.432m
**Weight:** 10,170kg (loaded), 8,640kg (empty)
**Track:** 2.038m
**Wheelbase:** 1.524m + 1.524m
**G/pressure:** 0.98kg/sq cm
**Engine:** Rolls-Royce B80 Mk 6A, 8-cylinder petrol engine developing 160hp at 3,750rpm
**Speed:** 72km/h (road)
**Range:** 400km
**Fuel:** 200 litres
**Fording:** 1.07m, 1.98m (with kit)
**V/obstacle:** 0.46m
**Trench:** 1.52m
**Gradient:** 42%
**Armour:** 8mm-16mm

## Development

The FV603 Saracen APC was designed shortly after the end of World War 2 with Alvis of Coventry completing the first prototype and first production vehicles in 1952. Production of the Saracen, which uses many automotive components of the FV601 Saladin armoured car and FV622 Stalwart high mobility load carrier, continued until 1972.
    The Saracen has been replaced in the British Army by the tracked FV432 APC although a number are still used in the IS role in Northern Ireland.

## Variants

The full designation of the Saracen is Carrier Personnel Wheeled APC Mk 2 (Alvis Saracen 6×6). The Mk 1 had a slightly different turret and other minor differences. The basic vehicle can be quickly adopted for use as an ambulance, load carrier or engineer vehicle. The FV603(C) incorporates reverse flow cooling enabling the vehicle to operate in the Middle East. This is distinguishable from the basic vehicle by its different arrangement of engine covers and the large cover over the radiator.

*FV 604 Command Post:* This is a Saracen without its turret, modified to carry additional radios, extra batteries, auxiliary charging equipment, map boards, the seating arrangements have also been modified. Some times an LMG is fitted on a ring mount slightly forward to where the turret was. Some FV603s have been converted to FV604 standards but retaining their turrets.

*FV610 Command Post.* This is similar to the FV604 but its height has been increased to 2.36m as this is intended to be used in the static role for longer periods. Additional working space is obtained by erecting tentage at the rear of the vehicle (FV604 is similar). This vehicle can be fitted with the Field Artillery Computer Equipment. Laden weight is 10,620kg.

*Other Projects/Variants:* There was a project to fit Swingfire ATGW to a Saracen but this progressed only as far as the mock up stage. An FV610 vehicle was used as a test vehicle for the GS No 9 Mk 1 Radar called Robert, this did not however, enter service. Some Saracens were built without roofs for operation in the Middle East.

## Employment

In service with Hong Kong (police), Indonesia, Jordan, Kuwait, Libya, Lebanon, Nigeria, Qatar, South Africa, Sudan, Thailand, United Arab Emirates and the UK.

*FV603 Saracen APC.* MoD (Army)

# Short SB301 APC UK

*Short SB301 APC with Shorland armoured patrol car in background.* Simon Dunstan

**Armament:** None
**Crew:** 2+6
**Length:** 4.292m
**Width:** 1.778m
**Height:** 2.159m
**G/clearance:** 0.21m
**Weight:** 3,545kg (loaded)
**Track:** 1.358m
**Wheelbase:** 2.768m
**Engine:** 6-cylinder Rover water-cooled petrol engine developing 91bhp at 4,500rpm
**Speed:** 96km/h
**Range:** 368km
**Fuel:** 50 litres (standard), 100 litres (long range)
**Armour:** 6.35mm

## Development

The Short SB 301 armoured personnel carrier has been designed by Short Brothers of Belfast, Northern Ireland, to meet a requirement for a simple and reliable APC for use in IS operations, and to operate with the Shorland armoured patrol car. The first prototype was completed in 1973 with production vehicles following in 1974.

The SB 301 is essentially a modified long wheel base Land-Rover chassis with a new armoured body. The six passengers are carried in the rear of the hull and a total of eight firing ports are provided. The hull is of all welded construction whilst the floor is of glass reinforced plastic. The basic vehicle is unarmed although four smoke/tear gas dischargers can be mounted each side of the roof if required. Optional equipment includes various radio installations and run-flat tyres.

## Variants

The latest model is the SB 401 which is based on the new V-8 (3.5 litre) powered LWB Land-Rover chassis. The engine is coupled to a permanent four-wheel drive that provides firm tyre grip in all weathers as well as giving increased engine braking, ensures equal tyre wear and extends component life.

# Sankey IS Vehicles

UK

|  | AT 104 | AT 105 |
|---|---|---|
| Crew: | 2+9 | 2+8 |
| Length: | 5.486m | 5.169m |
| Height: (cupola) | 2.489m | 2.628m |
| G/clearance: (hull) | 0.457m | 0.36m |
| Weight: (loaded) | 8,900kg | 10,670kg |
| (empty) | 8,000kg | 8,640kg |
| Speed: (road) | 80km/h | 96km/h |
| Range: | 640km | 510km |
| Fuel: | 160 litres | 160 litres |
| Fording: | 0.7m | 1.12m |
| Engine: | 6-cylinder Bedford petrol (134bhp) or 6-cylinder diesel (186bhp) | 6-cylinder Bedford diesel (164bhp) |

## Development
In 1971, GKN Sankey of Wellington, Shropshire, designed a 4×2 IS vehicle called the AT 100, this was not placed in production and was followed by the AT 104 (4×4) in 1972 and then by the AT 105 (4×4) in 1974. Both of these vehicles use standard Bedford automotive components with a new hull of all welded steel construction, this varies in thickness from 6mm to 12.5mm, firing ports are provided in the hull sides and rear. A wide range of equipment can be fitted including an air-conditioning system, heater, search-light, grenade launchers, winch barricade removers and so on. A variety of armament installations is available including Peak Engineering P1 turret with a single 7.62mm GPMG or a Peak Engineering P2 turret with twin 7.62mm GPMGs.

## Variants
Basic model of the AT 105 is designated the AT 105-P and has a fixed cupola for the commander. The AT 105-E has the machine gun turret, AT 105-MR is the mortar carrier with 81mm mortar, AT 105-C is the command vehicle while AT 105-A is the unarmed ambulance version.

## Employment
AT 104s are used by the Dutch State Police and the Royal Brunei Malaya Regiment, but production has now been completed. The AT 105 is the current production model and is in service with Bahrain, Malaysia, Oman and the UK (three for evaluation), and other undisclosed countries.

*Sankey AT 105 IS vehicle.* GKN Sankey

*Sankey AT 104 IS vehicle.* GKN Sankey

133

# FV1611 Humber 1Ton Armoured Truck UK

**Crew:** 2+6/8
**Length:** 4.93m
**Width:** 2.05m
**Height:** 2.12m
**Weight:** 5,790kg (loaded), 4,770kg (empty)
**Track:** 1.713m
**Wheelbase:** 2.743m
**Engine:** Rolls-Royce B60 6-cylinder petrol engine developing 120hp at 3,750rpm
**Speed:** 64km/h (road)
**Range:** 400km
**Fuel:** 145 litres

## Development/Variants

The FV1611 was developed from the earlier FV1609A armoured truck which in turn was based on the chassis of the Humber FV1601A one-ton cargo truck. The chassis was made by Humber and the body by Sankey Limited or the Royal Ordnance Factory at Woolwich. The basic vehicles are:

*FV1611:* Used to transport personnel and stores, was also used to tow the Green Archer Mortar Locating Radar system.

*FV1612:* This is a radio vehicle and has a crew of three, driver, commander and radio operator.

*FV1613:* Ambulance version. Crew of two, driver and medical orderly. Can carry three stretcher or eight sitting, or one stretcher and four sitting patients.

*FV1620:* Hornet/Malkara vehicle is no longer in service having been replaced by the Ferret Mk 5, this in turn has now been phased out of service.

*Humber 1 ton armoured 4×4 truck.* MoD (Army)

## Employment

Used only by the British Army for IS operations in Northern Ireland. Between 1972/73 most were uparmoured to provide increased protection against attack from 7.62mm armour piercing rounds. These and other modifications have pushed the weight of the vehicle up to around 7,000kg. Specialised versions of the Pig are also used in Northern Ireland and some have been fitted with searchlights and tear gas launchers.

# Abbot SP Gun UK

| | Abbot | V/E Abbot |
|---|---|---|
| **Crew:** | 4 | 4 |
| **Length:** (overall) | 5.84m | 5.714m |
| (hull) | 5.709m | 5.333m |
| **Width:** | 2.641m | 2.641m |
| **Height:** | 2.489m | 2.489m |
| **G/clearance:** | 0.406m | 0.406m |
| **Weight:** (loaded) | 16,556kg | 15,900kg |
| (empty) | 14,878kg | 14,200kg |
| **G/pressure:** | 0.89kg/sq cm | 0.81kg/sq cm |
| **Speed:** (road) | 48km/h | 48km/h |
| **Range:** (road) | 390km | 390km |
| **Fuel:** | 386 litres | 386 litres |
| **Fording:** | 1.219m | 1.117m |
| **V/obstacle:** | 0.609m | 0.609m |
| **Trench:** | 2.057m | 2.057m |
| **Gradient:** | 60% | 60% |
| **Armament:** (main) | 105mm | 105mm |
| (AA) | 7.62mm | — |
| **Ammunition:** (main) | 40 | 36 |
| (AA) | 1,200 | — |
| **Armour:** | 6mm-12mm | 6mm-12mm |

## Development

Development of the Abbot commenced in 1958, the design parents being Vickers Limited. The first of 12 prototypes was completed in 1961. After trials a production order was awarded to Vickers Limited. The Abbot was in production at Vickers Elswick Works from 1964 until 1967. The Abbot uses many components of the FV432 series of APCs.

## Variants

*Abbot (FV433):* The Abbot is armed with a 105mm gun in a turret with a traverse of 360°, the gun has an elevation of +70° and a depression of −5°. Sustained rate of fire is 12rpm. The gun has a max range of 17,000m and seven different types of projectile are available. A 7.62mm AA MG is mounted for the use of the commander and there are three smoke dischargers mounted either side of the turret. The Abbot is fitted with an NBC system and infra-red driving lights. A flotation screen is carried around the top of the hull, and when erected enables the vehicle to cross rivers. It is propelled in the water by its tracks at about 5km/h. The Abbot is powered by a Rolls-Royce K60 Mk 4G, 6-cylinder, in-line, multi-fuel engine developing 240bhp at 3,750rpm.

*Value Engineered Abbot:* The first prototype was completed in 1971 and it has been built at Vickers Elswick Works for the Indian Army. The Value Engineered Abbot is basically a standard Abbot with non-essential equipment removed, more economical components have been used. It lacks such items as the NBC system and the flotation screen as a number of armies have no requirement for these. Any of these components could be added at a later date. It must be emphasised that there has been no degradation of standards or materials. The Value Engineered Abbot is powered by a Rolls-Royce K60 Mk 60G/1, 6-cylinder, in-line diesel engine developing 213bhp at 3,750rpm.

*Falcon:* The Falcon twin 30mm SP AA was a private venture between Vickers and the British Manufacture and Research Company and was armed with twin 30mm cannon. It is no longer being offered.

*Abbot 105mm SP gun with turret traversed left.* MoD (Army)

### Employment

Abbot is used by the British Royal Artillery. Value Engineered Abbot is used by the Indian Army although a few are also used by the British Army.

# FV180 Combat Engineer Tractor                           UK

**Crew:** 2
**Length:** 7.544m (overall), 5.334m (hull)
**Width:** 2.896m (bucket)
**Height:** 2.667m (overall)
**G/clearance:** 0.457m
**Weight:** 18,000kg
**G/pressure:** 0.435kg/sq cm
**Engine:** Rolls-Royce C6TFR 6-cylinder in-line diesel developing 320hp at 2,100rpm
**Speed:** 56km/h (road), 8km/h (water)
**Fuel:** 430 litres
**Fording:** 1.829m
**V/obstacle:** 0.61m
**Trench:** 2.06m
**Gradient:** 60%

### Development/Variants

The FV180 Combat Engineer Tractor (CET) has been developed by the Military Vehicles and Engineering Establishment to meet the requirements of the Royal Engineers. The first test rigs were completed in 1968 with seven prototypes following in 1973/74. It entered production at the Royal Ordnance Factory at Leeds and entered service with the British Army in 1978. It has taken over some of the roles now being carried out by the Centurion AVRE. Its crew of two consists of the driver and operator and is normally driven with the bucket to the rear. The latter is hydraulically operated and can be used for a variety of roles. These include the preparing of river crossings, preparation of gun and tank pits as well as clearing battlefield obstacles. A crane can be installed in the bucket if required. A hydraulic winch with 107m of rope is provided and this can be led out either the front or rear of the hull. If the CET becomes stuck in a river or similar obstacle, then it can launch its earth anchor. This is rocket propelled

and is attached to 91m of rope. When emplaced it enables the CET to winch itself out. A NBC system is provided as is passive rather than infra-red driving equipment. No armament is fitted although smoke dischargers are mounted. The CET can also tow a trailer fitted with the Giant Viper mine clearance system. It can ford to a depth of 1.829m without preparation. Flotation equipment designed by FPT Industries of Portsmouth can be quickly installed and it then propels itself in the water by two waterjets, one in each side of the hull. The following equipment can be installed on the Combat Engineer Tractor if required: Pusher bar for launching bridging pontoons; Carrying class 30 and class 50 trackway laying equipment; Jib crane attachment can be installed in the bucket, this has a maximum lifting capacity of 4,000kg.

### Employment

In service with the British Army.

*FV180 Combat Engineer Tractor.* I. V. Hogg

# M1 Abrams MBT

## USA

**Armament:** 1 × 105mm gun, elevation +20°, depression −10° (55 rounds carried)
2 × 7.62mm MGs — coaxial and at loader's station (11,400 rounds)
1 × 12.7mm MG at commander's station (1,000 rounds)
6 smoke dischargers either side of turret
**Crew:** 4
**Length:** 9.766m (gun forward), 7.918m (hull)
**Width:** 3.655m
**Height:** 2.895m (overall), 2.375m (turret roof)
**G/clearance:** 0.482m
**Weight:** 54,432kg (loaded)
**Engine:** Lycoming ACT-1500C gas turbine delivering 1,500hp at 3,000rpm
**Speed:** 72.42km/h (road)
**Range:** 450km
**Fuel:** 1,907 litres
**Fording:** 1.219m (w/o preparation), 2.36m (with preparation)
**V/obstacle:** 1.244m
**Trench:** 2.743m
**Gradient:** 60%

## Development

Following the cancellation of the MBT-70 in 1970, the United States Army went ahead to develop a more austere version called the XM803, but this in turn was cancelled in 1971 owing to rising costs. The army then established a task force at the Armor School at Fort Knox, Kentucky, to formulate a concept for a new MBT, this task was completed in January 1973. In June 1973, contracts were awarded to both Chrysler and General Motors to build prototypes of a new tank called the XM1, or

Abrams as it later became known. These prototypes were completed and handed over to the Army for trials early in 1976. In November 1976, it was announced that the Chrysler entry had been selected for full scale development.

Chrysler then built 11 pre-production vehicles which were completed in 1978. The first production order was for 110 M1 which were procured with fiscal year 1979 funding and the first two production tanks were completed at the Lima Army Tank Centre, Ohio, in February 1980. The fiscal year 1980 request was for 352 vehicles and the Army has a requirement for 7,058 M1s.

First production vehicles have a 105mm M68 gun, as fitted to the M60 vehicle but it is expected that in 1984/85 production vehicles will be fitted with a 120mm Rheinmetall smooth bore gun as fitted to the Leopard 2. The M1 has advanced Chobham type armour and its fire control system includes a computer and a laser rangefinder. Standard equipment includes a NBC system, hull escape hatch and passive night vision equipment.

## Variants
There are no variants of the M1.

## Employment
Entering service with the US Army.

*Chrysler-built XM1 MBT with 105mm gun.*
US Army

# M60 Series MBT

| | M60 | M60A1 | M60A2 |
|---|---|---|---|
| **Crew:** | 4 | 4 | 4 |
| **Length:** (gun forward) | 9.309m | 9.436m | 7.283m |
| (hull) | 6.946m | 6.946m | 6.946m |
| **Width:** | 3.631m | 3.631m | 3.631m |
| **Height:** (overall) | 3.213m | 3.27m | 3.20m |
| **G/clearance:** | 0.463m | 0.463m | 0.463m |
| **Weight:** (loaded) | 46,266kg | 48,987kg | 51,982kg |
| (empty) | 42,184kg | 43,999kg | 41,459kg |
| **G/pressure:** | 0.78kg/sq cm | 0.79kg/sq cm | 0.86kg/sq cm |
| **Speed:** (road) | 48km/h | 48km/h | 48km/h |
| **Range:** (road) | 500km | 500km | 500km |
| **Fuel:** | 1,457 litres | 1,420 litres | 1,457 litres |
| **Fording:** (w/o kit) | 1.219m | 1.219m | 1.219m |
| (with kit) | 2.438m | 2.438m | 2.438m |
| **V/obstacle:** | 0.914m | 0.914m | 0.914m |
| **Trench:** | 2.59m | 2.59m | 2.59m |
| **Gradient:** | 60% | 60% | 60% |
| **Calibre:** (main) | 105mm | 105mm | 152mm |
| (coaxial) | 7.62mm | 7.62mm | 7.62mm |
| (AA) | 12.7mm | 12.7mm | 12.7mm |
| **Ammunition:** (main) | 60 | 63 | n/a |
| (coaxial) | 5,950 | 5,950 | 5,560 |
| (AA) | 900 | 900 | 1,080 |
| **Engine:** | see below | see below | see below |
| **Armour:** | 25mm-110mm | 25mm-110mm | 25mm-110mm |

**Development**

Further development of the M48 series resulted in the M60 which was standardised in March 1959. Production was initially undertaken at the Delaware Defense Plant operated by the Chrysler Corporation but from late in 1960 production was transferred to the Detroit Tank Plant also operated by the Chrysler Corporation.

In 1962 the M60 was succeeded in production by the M60A1 and this remained in production until 1978 when its place was taken by the M60A3 which is essentially a M60A3 with improvements to the fire control system and other key areas. By 1980 over

*M60 MBT with turret traversed to rear.* US Army

*M728 CEV based on the M60A1.* MoD (Army)

13,000 M60 series had been completed and final deliveries are expected to be made in 1982 after which the Detroit Tank Plant will tool up as the second source for the M1 MBT.

The main armament of the M60, M60A1 and M60A3 is the 105mm M68 gun which is the British 105mm L7 series manufactured under licence in the United States. Standard equipment includes a full range of night vision equipment and a NBC system. If required it can be fitted with a hydraulically operated dozer blade at the front of the hull, deep fording equipment or mine clearing rollers.

### Variants

*M60:* This is the basic model and has the same turret as the M48A2. It is powered by a Continental AVDS-1790-2A 12-cylinder, air-cooled diesel developing 755hp at 2,400rpm. It has three return rollers and no idler tension wheel or fender dust shields. it is armed with the 105mm M68 in mount M116, this has an elevation of +20° and a depression of −9°, a 7.62mm coaxial MG M73 (now being replaced by a M240 machine gun) and a 12.7mm AA MG M85.

*M60A1:* This has a new turret which has more room as well as giving greater ballistic protection. On the rear of the turret is a stowage basket that extends completely around the rear of the turret, the lower portion of the turret is screened. It has no fender dust shields, nor rear idler tension wheels and three return rollers. It is powered by an AVDS-1790-2A which develops 750hp at 2,400rpm. It has the same armament as the M60 except that its 105mm gun is in mount M140. It also has a more recent fire control system.

*M60A2:* This is an M60A1 hull fitted with a new turret mounting the Shillelagh weapons system.

Development started in April 1964 and the first prototype was completed in September 1965, although trials were unsuccessful production was ordered in September 1966. By the end of 1971 the problems had been solved and on 29 November 1971, a contract was signed for retrofit production of 526 M60A2 tanks along with continued production of the M60A1. The 152mm tube can fire either the Shillelagh missiles or conventional type rounds. It has an elevation of +20° and a depression of −10°, a total of 46 rounds of ammunition are carried of which 13 can be Shillelagh missiles. The type of ammunition carried does, of course, depend on the tactical situation. Also fitted is a coaxial 7.62mm MG, a 12.7mm AA MG and smoke dischargers.

*M60A3:* The M60A3 was developed under the designation of the M60A1E3 and has some of the improvements of late production M60A1s including an add-on-stabilisation system, RISE engine and smoke dischargers either side of the turret. In addition it has a solid state ballistic computer, laser rangefinder, tank thermal sight, top loading air cleaner, AN/VSS-3A searchlight over the main armament, new tracks, tube-over-bar suspension system on the 1st, 2nd and 6th road wheel stations, thermal sleeve for main armament, coaxial MG replaced by M240 (MAG-58), muzzle reference system and an automatic Halon fire-extinguishing system.

*M60 AVLB:* This is similar to the M48 AVLB except that it uses an M60 chassis. The bridge can take a load of 60,000kg and can span a gap of 18.288m. The bridge takes less than 2min to lay; the vehicle has a crew of two. Performance is similar to the M60A1; additional data is: Length: 11.048m (with bridge); Width: 4.012m (with bridge); Height: 4.038m (with bridge); Weight: 55,746kg (with bridge), 41,685kg (vehicle only), 14,470kg (bridge only).

M60A2. US Army

M60A1 MBT showing changed turret design.
US Army

**M728 Combat Engineer Vehicle (CEV):** This vehicle is based on the M60A1 chassis and turret; its development designation was T118E1. The vehicle entered production in 1965 and was issued to the 1st Armored Division in 1968. The vehicle is designed to destroy enemy positions and fortifications, clear roadblocks and obstacles. Armament consists of a 165mm demolition gun, a 7.62mm coaxial MG and a 12.7mm AA MG. Ammunition carried is 30 rounds of 165mm, 2,000 rounds of 7.62mm and 600 rounds of 12.7mm. An A frame is mounted on the front of the vehicle for lifting operations, a winch with a capacity of 11,340kg is provided. A hydraulically operated dozer blade is also provided. Kits for fording and night operations are available. Performance is similar to the M60A1; additional data is as follows: Length: 9.30m (boom erected), 7.88m (with blade); Width: 3.70m (with blade); Height: 3.20m; Weight: 52,163kg (loaded), 48,500kg (empty); G/pressure: 0.87kg/sq cm.

*Teledyne Continental High Performance M60:* This has been developed as a private venture by the General Products Division of Teledyne Continental Motors and is essentially a M60 series MBT fitted with a new powerpack, hydropneumatic suspension and, as an option, applique armour. The powerpack is a AVCR-1790-1B 12-cylinder turbocharged diesel developing 1,200hp at 2,400rpm and is coupled to a West German Renk RK 304 fully automatic transmission. When fitted with this powerpack the vehicle has a max road speed of 74km/h, power-to-weight ratio of 23.1hp/tonne and will accelerate from 0 to 32km/h in 9sec.

**Employment**
Austria (M60A1), Egypt (M60A3), Iran (M60A1), Israel (M60, M60A1, M60A3), Italy (200 built by OTO-Melara and 100 direct from USA), Jordan (M60A1), Morocco (M60A1), Saudi Arabia (M60A1, M60A3), Somalia (unconfirmed), South Korea (few), Singapore, Spain (M60 AVLB only), Sudan (M60A1), USA (M60, M60A1, M60A2 and M60A3) and Yemen Arab Republic (North) (M60A1).

M60A3 MBT. US Army

# M48 Series MBT

USA

| | M48 | M48A1 | M48A2 | M48A3 | M48A5 |
|---|---|---|---|---|---|
| **Crew:** | 4 | 4 | 4 | 4 | 4 |
| **Length:** (gun forward) | 8.444m | 8.729m | 8.686m | 8.686m | 9.436m |
| (hull) | 6.705m | 6.870m | 6.870m | 6.882m | 6.870m |
| **Width:** | 3.631m | 3.631m | 3.631m | 3.631m | 3.631m |
| **Height:** (overall) | 3.241m | 3.130m | 3.089m | 3.124m | 3.086m |
| **G/clearance:** | 0.393m | 0.387m | 0.385m | 0.406m | 0.419m |
| **Weight:** (loaded) | 44,906kg | 47,173kg | 47,173kg | 47,173kg | 48,987kg |
| (empty) | 42,240kg | 43,999kg | 43,999kg | 44,452kg | 46,287kg |
| **G/pressure:** (kg/sq cm) | 0.78 | 0.83 | 0.83 | 0.83 | 0.88 |
| **Speed:** (road) | 42km/h | 42km/h | 48km/h | 48km/h | 48km/h |
| **Range:** (road) | 113km | 113km | 258km | 463km | 499km |
| **Fuel:** (litres) | 757 | 757 | 1,268 | 1,420 | 1,420 |
| **Fording:** (w/o kit) | 1.219m | 1.219m | 1.219m | 1.219m | 1.219m |
| (with kit) | 2.438m | 2.438m | 2.438m | 2.438m | 2.438m |
| **V/obstacle:** | 0.915m | 0.915m | 0.915m | 0.915m | 0.915m |
| **Trench:** | 2.59m | 2.59m | 2.59m | 2.59m | 2.59m |
| **Gradient:** | 60% | 60% | 60% | 60% | 60% |
| **Calibre:** (main) | 90mm | 90mm | 90mm | 90mm | 105mm |
| (coaxial) | 7.62mm | 7.62mm | 7.62mm | 7.62mm | 7.62mm |
| (AA) | 12.7mm | 12.7mm | 12.7mm | 12.7mm | 2×7.62mm |
| **Ammunition:** (main) | 60 | 60 | 64 | 62 | 54 |
| (coaxial) | 5,900 | 5,900 | 5,590 | 6,000 | 10,000 |
| (AA) | 180 | 500 | 1,365 | 630 | inc in above |
| **Engine:** | See below for details | | | | |
| **Armour:** | 25mm-110mm for all models | | | | |

## Development

The M48 was developed from the earlier M47. Design work started in 1950 by the Chrysler Corporation and the first pilot model was completed in December 1951 this being designated T48. Early M48s used the same engine and transmission as the M47. A total of 11,703 M48 series tanks was completed between 1952 and 1959 with production being undertaken by Alco Products at Schenectady, Chrysler at the Delaware Defense Plant, Fisher Body

*M48A2GA2 of West German Army with 105mm gun and other modifications.*   West German Army

Division of General Motors Corporation and Ford Motor Company at Livonia. Further development of the M48 resulted in the M60 MBT which entered production at the Chrysler operated Delaware Defense Plant in 1959, production was however transferred to the Detroit Tank Plant, also operated by Chrysler, the following year. Automotive components of the M48 tank were also used in the M88 ARV and the M53 and M55 SP guns.

## Variants

*M48 and M48C:* This was the first production model and has a small driver's hatch; the commander has a MG in an open mount, five return rollers and no idler. The M48C is similar except that it has a hull of mild steel and is not suitable for combat. The gun has an elevation of +19° and a depression of −9°, this being the same for all the M48 series. The vehicle is powered by a Continental AV1790-5B, −7, −7B or −7C, 12-cylinder, air-cooled petrol engine developing 810hp at 2,800rpm. It has no fender dust shields and either a T or cylindrical blast deflector on the barrel.

*M48A1:* This has a large driver's hatch, a commander's cupola complete with MG, fender dust shields, rear track idler wheel and five support rollers, and a T type blast deflector. It is powered by a Continental AV-1790-7C petrol engine developing 810hp at 2,800rpm.

*M48A2 and M48A2C:* Development of the M48A2 started in 1954 and it was designated T48E2, the prototype was completed in 1955. The improvements over the earlier vehicle included an engine with a fuel-injection system, improved engine deck, constant pressure turret control system, improved fire control system. It could also be fitted with additional fuel tanks which give it a range of 400km. The first production order went to Alco Products of Schenectady, New York, in 1956. A later contract was awarded to Chrysler Delaware Defense Plant (Lenape Ordnance Modification Centre) Newark, Delaware. The main difference between the M48A2 and the M48A2C is in vision and fire control equipment, the only visual difference between them is the absence of the track tension idler wheels on the M48A2C. Both are powered by a Continental AV-1790-8, 12-cylinder, air-cooled petrol engine developing 825bhp at 2,800rpm. Other distinguishing features are three return rollers, raised rear engine covers, stowage basket on the turret rear and a 'T' blast deflector.

*M48A3:* Development designation M48A1E2, this has only three support rollers (although some may be seen with five), no track idler wheel, T blast deflector, fender dust shields. It is powered by a Continental AVDS-1790-2A, 12-cylinder, air-cooled diesel engine developing 750bhp at 2,400rpm. Other improvements include an improved fire control system and some vehicles have been fitted with a circular ring with vision blocks between the roof of the turret and the base of the commanders cupola.

*M48A4:* The M48A4 programme has been cancelled.

*M48A5:* The US Army has brought 1,864 M48A1 and M48A3 tanks up to a new standard known as the M48A5. These have a 105mm M68 gun, new commander's low profile cupola, two single 7.62mm MGs mounted on the roof and, in the case of M48A1 conversions, the petrol engine has been replaced by a AVDS-1790-2D engine. Many other countries have also brought their M48s up to the M48A5 standard.

*M67:* The M67 was standardised in 1955, development designation was T67 and a total of 74 was built for the USMC. It is a modified M48A1. The 90mm gun has been replaced by an M7-6 flamethrower gun. This has a slightly shorter tube and is slightly larger in diameter than the standard 90mm tube. The headlamps are slightly lower as the flamethrower has an elevation of +45° and a depression of −12°.

*M67A1:* This is an M48A2 modified for use by the United States Army. It is similar to the above except that it has an M7A16 flame gun.

*M67A2:* This is an M48A3 for use by the USMC. It has the M7A16 flame gun with a range of 100-250m depending on the weather conditions. *Note:* At the time of writing none of the flamethrower tanks was in service, they are however held in reserve.

*M48 AVLB:* The M48 AVLB (Armoured Vehicle Launched Bridge) is based on the hull of the M48A2. Early M48 AVLBs were fitted with two MG turrets each fitted with a 12.7mm MG but these have been removed. The scissors bridge is laid hydraulically and can cross ditches up to 18.29m in width. Additional data is: Crew: 2; Length: 11.048m; Width: 4.002m; Height: 4.038m; Weight: 55,746kg.

*Bulldozer:* An hydraulic bulldozer blade can be fitted to the M48 series. The width of the blade is 3.71m and two types of blade are available: M8 for the M48, M48C and M48A1; this has a weight of 3.98 tonnes. M8A1 for the M48A2 and other members of the family, weight 3.81 tonnes.

*DIVADS:* The M48 chassis also used as the basis for the M48 Division Air Defense Gun System described elsewhere in this book.

*(Note:* The M48 tanks have been updated a number of times in their lives and it is very difficult to distinguish between models)

**Employment**

It is in service with FRG (inc 105mm armed versions), Greece, Iran (inc M48A5), Israel (inc 105mm versions), Jordan, South Korea (inc M48A5), Morocco, Norway, Pakistan (inc M48A5), Portugal (M48A5), Somalia, Spain, Thailand (M48A5), Taiwan, Tunisia, Turkey, USA and Vietnam.

*M48A5 with 105mm gun and two pintle-mounted 7.62mm MGs.   US Army*

# M47 Medium Tank

*M47 of the Spanish Army.* Mazarrasa

**Armament:** 1 × 90mm M36 gun, elevation +19°,
depression −5° (71 rounds carried)
2 × 7.62mm M1919A4E1 MGs — coaxial and bow
(4,125 rounds)
1 × 12.7mm AA MG (440 rounds)
**Crew:** 5
**Length:** 8.508m (inc gun), 6.307m (hull only)
**Width:** 3.51m
**Height:** 3.35m (inc AA MG), 2.95m (w/o AA MG)
**G/clearance:** 0.469m
**Weight:** 46,170kg (loaded), 42,130kg (empty)
**G/pressure:** 0.935kg/sq cm
**Engine:** Continental AV-1790-5B, 7 or 7B,
12-cylinder, air-cooled petrol engine developing
810bhp at 2,800rpm
**Speed:** 58km/h (road)
**Range:** 130km
**Fuel:** 875 litres
**Fording:** 1.219m
**V/obstacle:** 0.914m
**Trench:** 2.59m
**Gradient:** 60%
**Armour:** 12.7mm-115mm

## Development
The M47 was developed during the Korean War. It is
basically a modified M46 chassis with a T42 turret
mounting a T119 gun. The M46 chassis was given a
better cooling system, improved hull armour and
different electrical equipment. M47s were built by
the Detroit Tank Arsenal and the American
Locomotive Company. M47s may be seen with two
types of blast deflector, one has a T type and the
other a cylindrical type.

## Variants
*M102 Combat Engineer Vehicle:* With 165mm gun,
none remain in service.
*T66 Flamethrower Tank:* Trials only.
*French M47 with 105mm gun:* The French DTAT has
fitted an M47 with the complete gun of the AMX-30
MBT.
*Italian M47 with 105mm gun:* OTO-Melara has
rebuilt an M47 with the 105mm gun of the M60 as
well as fitting the vehicle with the engine,
transmission and electrical system of the M60.
Project only, no production undertaken.
*M47 with Swingfire ATGW:* This was shown at the
Farnborough Air Display in 1966 and was a proposal
only.
*M47 with bridge:* The Italian Company of Astra SpA
of Piacenza has built a bridgelayer on an M47
chassis. At each end of the bridge is a ramp that can
be used as a pile, thus allowing two bridges to be
used.
*Korean ARV:* The Korean Army have adopted a
number of M47s so that they can be used as ARVs.
The gun has been removed and an A frame fitted on
the glacis plate with the winch inside the turret, the
rope being taken out through the manlet where the
main gun was fitted.
*Spanish M47 with new engine:* Chrysler (Spain) is
carrying out a major modification programme which
includes the installation of a Continental AVDS-
1790-2A diesel engine. When this conversion has
been completed the vehicle is known as the M47E.

## Employment
Austria, Belgium (reserve), Greece, Iran, Italy, Jordan,
Pakistan, Portugal, South Africa (reported), South
Korea, Somalia, Spain, Taiwan, Turkey and
Yugoslavia.

# Sherman Medium Tank

USA

| | M4A1 (WET) | M4A2 (WET) | M4A3 (WET) | M4A3E8 |
|---|---|---|---|---|
| **Crew:** | 5 | 5 | 5 | 5 |
| **Length:** | 7.39m | 7.39m | 6.273m | 7.518m |
| **Width:** | 2.717m | 2.653m | 2.667m | 2.667m |
| **Height:** | 3.425m | 3.425m | 3.374m | 3.425m |
| **G/clearance:** | 0.43m | 0.43m | 0.43m | 0.43m |
| **Weight:** (loaded) | 32,044kg | 33,320kg | 31,574kg | 32,284kg |
| **G/pressure:** (kg/sq cm) | 1.02 | 1.05 | 1.00 | 0.72 (wide tracks) |
| **Speed:** (road) | 39km/h | 45km/h | 42km/h | 48km/h |
| **Range:** (cruising) | 160km | 160km | 160km | 160km |
| **Fuel:** (litres) | 651 | 560 | 636 | 636 |
| **Fording:** | 1.066m | 1.016m | 0.914m | 0.914m |
| **V/obstacle:** | 0.609m | 0.609m | 0.609m | 0.609m |
| **Trench:** | 2.286m | 2.286m | 2.286m | 2.286m |
| **Gradient:** | 60% | 60% | 60% | 60% |
| **Calibre:** (main) | 76mm | 76mm | 75mm | 76mm |
| (coaxial) | 7.62mm | 7.62mm | 7.62mm | 7.62mm |
| (bow) | 7.62mm | 7.62mm | 7.62mm | 7.62mm |
| (AA) | 12.7mm | 12.7mm | 12.7mm | 12.7mm |
| **Ammunition:** (main) | 71 | 71 | 104 | 71 |
| (7.62mm) | 6,250 | 6,250 | 6,250 | 6,250 |
| (AA) | 600 | 600 | 600 | 600 |
| **Elevation:** | All have an elevation of +25° and depression −10° | | | |
| **Engine:** | R-975-C4 | GMC 6046D | Ford GAA | Ford GAA |
| **Bhp/rpm:** | 400/2400 | 375/2100 | 450/2600 | 460/2600 |
| **Armour:** | 12mm-75mm | 12mm-75mm | 12mm-75mm | 12mm-75mm |

## Development

The Sherman was developed under the designation of the T6 and entered production early in 1942. Production was undertaken by the American Locomotive Company, Baldwin Locomotive Company, Detroit Tank Arsenal (Chrysler Corporation), Federal Machine and Welding Company, Fisher Tank Division of General Motors, Ford Motor Company, Lima Locomotive Works, Montreal Locomotive Works (Canada), Pacific Car and Foundry Company, Pressed Steel Car Company and the Pullman Standard Car Manufacturing Company. A total of 48,064 Shermans was built by June 1945.

The Sherman chassis was also used as the basis for the M7 Priest 105mm SP howitzer and the M10 and M36 tank destroyers, there are separate entries for these vehicles. Details of the many versions of the Sherman developed by Israel are given under Israel.

## Variants

*Recovery vehicle, fully tracked, M32 and M32A1:* The M32B1 used M4A1 chassis, M32B2 used M4A2, M32B3 used M4A3 and the M32B4 used the M4A4 chassis. All vehicles have an A frame, winch with a maximum capacity of 27.22 tonnes and a full range of tools and other recovery equipment. Basic data is: Crew: 4; Length: 5.82m (overall); Height: 2.467m; Width: 2.616m; Engine: Continental R-975-C1, 350bhp at 2,400rpm; Armament: 1×81mm mortar, 1×7.62mm bow MG, 1×12.7mm AA MG; weight 28,123kg (loaded); speed: 41.8km/h; Range: 165km.

*Argentina still uses the famous Sherman Firefly.*

*M32 ARV of the JGSDF.* K. Nogi

*Recovery Vehicle, full tracked, Medium M74:* This is a postwar development and is a rebuild based on M4A3 chassis. Equipment fitted includes a blade at the front, A frame, winch, tools, blocks and so on. Basic data is: Crew: 4; Length: 7.95m (overall); Height: 3.095m (exc MG); Width: 3.09m; Weight: 42,525kg (loaded); Engine: Ford GAA, 8-cylinder petrol engine, 450hp at 2,600rpm; Armament: 1×3.5in rocket launcher, 1×7.62mm bow MG, 1×12.7mm AA MG; Fuel: 636 litres; Gradient: 60%;

Fording: 0.91m; V/obstacle: 0.61m; Speed: 34km/h. *Sherman Firefly:* This was a British development and was a Sherman with its original 76mm gun replaced by the 17pdr gun, modified turret fitted with a bustle and bow MG deleted for additional ammunition stowage capacity.

**Employment**
Argentina (including Firefly), Austria (M32 ARV only), Brazil (and M32 and M74 ARVs), Chile, Colombia, Ecuador, Greece (M32 and M74 ARVs only), Israel (and M32 ARV), Japan (M32 ARV only), Pakistan, Spain (M74 ARV only), Paraguay, Turkey (M74 only), Yugoslavia (Firefly, M32 and M74 ARVs).

# M551 General Sheridan Light Tank/ Reconnaissance Vehicle

USA

**Armament:** 1×152mm M81 launcher, elevation +19.5°, depression −8° (20 conventional rounds, 10 Shillelagh missiles carried)
1×7.62mm M73 coaxial MG (3,080 rounds)
1×12.7mm M2 MG at commander's cupola (1,000 rounds)
8 grenade launchers (four either side of turret)
**Crew:** 4
**Length:** 6.299m
**Width:** 2.819m
**Height:** 2.946m (inc MG)
**G/clearance:** 0.48m
**Weight:** 15,830kg (loaded), 13,589kg (empty)
**G/pressure:** 0.49kg/sq cm
**Engine:** Detroit Diesel 6V53T, 300hp at 2,800rpm
**Speed:** 70km/h (road), 5.8km/h (water)
**Range:** 600km (road)
**Fuel:** 598 litres

**Fording:** Amphibious
**V/obstacle:** 0.838m
**Trench:** 2.54m
**Gradient:** 60%

**Development**
The development of the Sheridan dates back to 1959 and the first prototype, the XM551, was completed in 1962. Production was undertaken by the Allison Division of the General Motors Corporation at the Cleveland Automotive Plant. The first production vehicle was completed in June 1966 and production continued until 1970 by which time 1,700 had been built. The M551, officially known as the Armored Reconnaissance/Airborne Assault Vehicle, was developed to replace the M41 light tank and the M56 90mm SP anti-tank gun.

In 1978 a decision was taken to phase the

*M551 Sheridan; note ammo boxes on sides of turret.* Allison Division of GMC

majority of M551s out of service and by late 1980 it only remained in service with one battalion, this being attached to the 82nd Airborne Division.

The Sheridan has a number of interesting features including a hull of welded aluminium armour, turret of steel; it is fully amphibious, although a small flexible barrier system is erected around the vehicle before entering the water.

The most interesting part of the Sheridan is its weapons system; this consists of a launcher that can fire Shillelagh missiles, which have a range of some 3,000m or a variety of conventional rounds including HEAT-T-MP with a m/v of 683m/sec, white

phosphorus, TP-T and canister with a m/v of 683m/sec and an effective range of 400m.

Night vision equipment is provided for the commander, gunner and driver and an infra-red searchlight is mounted to the left of the main armament. All vehicles have an NBC system.

In 1971 the Hughes Aircraft Corporation was awarded a contract for production of the AN/VVG-1 laser rangefinder for the M551, vehicles with this are designated the M551A1.

**Variants**
There are no variants of the M551 in service although there have been many projects some of which reached the prototype stage.

**Employment**
In service only with the US Army.

# M41 Light Tank                    USA

**Armament:** 1 × 76mm M32 gun, elevation +19°, depression −10° (57 rounds carried)
1 × 7.62mm M1919A4E1 coaxial MG (5,000 rounds)
1 × 12.7mm M2 AA MG (2,175 rounds)
**Crew:** 4
**Length:** 8.212m (inc gun), 5.819m (exc gun)
**Width:** 3.198m
**Height:** 3.075m (with MG), 2.726m (w/o MG)
**G/clearance:** 0.45m
**Weight:** 23,495kg (loaded)
**G/pressure:** 0.72kg/sq cm
**Engine:** M41 and M41A1, Continental or Lycoming

AOS-895-3; M41A2 and M41A3, Continental or Lycoming AOS1-895-5, 6-cylinder, air-cooled petrol engine, super-charged, developing 500hp at 2,800rpm
**Speed:** 72km/h (road)
**Range:** 161km
**Fuel:** 530 litres
**Fording:** 1.016m (w/o kit), 2.44m (with kit)
**V/obstacle:** 0.711m
**Trench:** 1.828m
**Gradient:** 60%
**Armour:** 12mm-38mm

## Development/Variants

Further development of the T37 Phase II light tank resulted in the T41 and the T41E1. The latter was standardised as the M41 light tank in mid-1950. Production of the M41 was undertaken by the Cadillac Motor Car Division of General Motors Corporation at the Cleveland Tank Arsenal with the first production vehicles being completed in mid-1951. A total of 5,500 M41s was built. In the US Army the M41 was replaced by the M551 Sheridan.

The M41 and M41A1 are the same except that the M41A1 has later traversing and elevating mechanism. This gives the tank commander control of both the turret and the guns; in the M41 the commander has only power control of the turret. The M41A2 and M41A3 have the later traversing and elevating mechanism and also double the fuel injection engine. Many components of the M41 are used in the M42, M44 and M52. There were also a number of experimental vehicles on the M41 chassis, including one with a Sheridan development turret.

The M41A1s used by Denmark are fitted with an

*M41 fitted with NAPCO Industries powerpack consisting of GM 8V71T engine and CD500 transmission.* Christoper F. Foss

AEG infra-red searchlight type B30A and infra-red sighting device B8V (ELTRO). The QM41 is a remote controlled model for use in air-surface missile trials.

For trials purposes Cockerill of Belgium have replaced the 76mm gun of an M41 with a 90mm gun. Brazil has also fitted an M41 with a Cockerill 90mm MkII gun which is made under licence in Brazil by ENGESA. For trials purposes the Spanish Army has fitted an M41 chassis with a HAKO turret with HOT ATGWs.

## Employment

Brazil, Chile, Denmark, Japan, New Zealand, Philippines, Portugal, Spain, Taiwan, Thailand, Tunisia, Turkey and Vietnam.

# M24 Chaffee Light Tank

## USA

**Armament:** 1 × 75mm M6 gun, elevation +15°, depression — 10° (48 rounds carried)
1 × 12.7mm M2 AA MG (440 rounds)
2 × 7.62mm MGs — coaxial and bow (3,750 rounds)
**Crew:** 4/5
**Length:** 5.486m (inc gun), 5.028 (exc gun)
**Width:** 2.95m

**Height:** 2.77m (inc MG), 2.46m (commander's cupola)
**G/clearance:** 0.457m
**Weight:** 18,370kg (loaded), 16,440kg (empty)
**G/pressure:** 0.78kg/sq cm
**Engines:** 2 × Cadillac Model 44T24 petrol, V-8, water-cooled, developing 110hp at 3,400rpm (each)
**Speed:** 55km/h (road)

**Range:** 281km (road), 173km (cross country)
**Fuel:** 416 litres
**Fording:** 1.02m
**V/obstacle:** 0.91m
**Trench:** 2.44m
**Gradient:** 60%
**Armour:** 10mm-38mm

## Development

In April 1943 the Cadillac Motor Car Division of General Motors Corporation commenced design work on a new light tank under the designation of the T24 as the replacement for the M5 light tank. The first two prototypes were completed in October 1943 with first production tanks following in April 1944. The T24 was not standardised as the M24 until some months after production had already commenced.

The Cadillac Motor Car Division of General Motors Corporation at Detroit and Massey Harris at Milwaukee built a total of 4,070 M24s by 1945. The M24, commonly known as the Chaffee, was replaced in the US Army in the 1950s by the M41 light tank.

## Variants

The M24 chassis was also used as the basis for the M19 twin 40mm SP AA gun system, M37 105mm SP howitzer and the M41 155mm SP howitzer. As far as it is known, none of these remain in service today.

*M24 with 90mm gun:* To extend the life of the M24 Chaffee tanks in the 1990s, Thune-Eureka of Norway and the DTAT of France have carried out a major overhaul of the vehicle to bring it up to the latest standards.

The 75mm gun has been replaced by a 90mm gun (for which 41 rounds of ammunition are carried), the bow MG has been removed for increased ammunition stowage, the 7.62mm coaxial MG has been replaced by a 12.7mm MG, the original engines and transmission have been replaced by a General Motors 6V-53T diesel and an Allison MT 650 transmission with torque converter, four smoke dischargers have been fitted either side of the turret, new tracks and shock absorbers have been fitted, as has a laser rangefinder and night vision equipment. Road speed is increased to 57km/h and max range on roads has been increased to 400km. A total of 54 was rebuilt between 1973-6 in Norway for the Norwegian Army under the designation NM-116. This conversion is now being offered by NAPCO Industries.

## Employment

Greece, Laos, Norway, Portugal, Pakistan, Taiwan, Thailand and Uruguay.

*Modified M24 of the Norwegian Army.*
Norwegian Army

# M3 and M5 Light Tanks; M8 SP Howitzer USA

| | M3A1 | M5A1 | M8 |
|---|---|---|---|
| Crew: | 4 | 4 | 4 |
| Length: | 4.54m | 4.84m | 4.438m |
| Width: | 2.24m | 2.29m | 2.24m |
| Height: | 2.30m | 2.30m | 2.30m |
| G/clearance: | 0.42m | 0.35m | 0.42m |
| Weight: (loaded) | 12,927kg | 15,397kg | 15,694kg |
| G/pressure: (kg/sq cm) | 0.74 | 0.88 | 0.88 |
| Speed: (road) | 56km/h | 58km/h | 58km/h |
| Range: (cruising) | 120/145km | 160km | 160km |
| Fuel: | 212 litres | 310 litres | 310 litres |
| Fording: | 0.91m | 0.91m | 0.91m |
| V/obstacle: | 0.61m | 0.46m | 0.46m |
| Trench: | 1.83m | 1.62m | 1.62m |
| Gradient: | 60% | 60% | 60% |
| Armament: (main) | 37mm | 37mm | 75mm |
| (coaxial) | 7.62mm | 7.62mm | — |
| (bow) | 7.62mm | 7.62mm | — |
| (AA) | 7.62mm | 7.62mm | 12.7mm |
| Ammunition: (main) | 108 | 147 | 46 |
| (7.62mm) | 6,890 | 6,500 | — |
| (12.7mm) | — | — | 400 |
| Engine: | see below | see below | see below |
| Armour: | 10mm-44mm | 10mm-63mm | 10mm-44mm |

## Development/Variants

*M3:* The M3 was developed from the earlier M2 and saw service with the British Army from 1941. The above data relates to the M3A1 which was powered either by a Continental W670-9A, 7-cylinder petrol engine developing 250hp at 2,400rpm. This gives the tank a range of 120km. Or a Guiberson Model T-1020-4, 9-cylinder diesel engine, developing 220hp at 2,200rpm. This gives it a range of 145km. In addition to the fuel carried internally an additional 151 litres of fuel could be carried in external jettisonable tanks. The 37mm gun has an elevation of +20° and a depression of −10°. The later M3A3 had an all-welded hull, increased fuel capacity (386 litres), additional stowage box at the rear, sand shields, additional ammunition stowage. This was made possible as the glacis plate was extended forward and the sponsons lengthened to the rear of the vehicle.

*M5:* Developed from the M3, the M5 was originally designated M3, but this was changed to avoid confusion. It was powered by two V-8 Cadillac Series 42 petrol engines developing 110hp at 3,200rpm. The later M5A1 had an improved turret with a radio bulge at the rear and the AA gun repositioned on the right side of the turret.

*M8:* This is an M5 chassis and hull fitted with a new turret mounting a 75mm howitzer with an elevation of +40° and a depression of −20°. The range of the gun was about 8,786m. The same turret was fitted to the LVT(A)4.

## Employment

*M3:* Brazil (most modified, see entry under Brazil), Colombia, Ecuador, Guatemala, Mexico (and M8), Paraguay, Uruguay.

*M3A3 light tanks (World War 2 photograph).*
US Army

# Lynx C & R Carrier

**Armament:** 1 × 12.7mm MG (1,155 rounds carried)
1 × 7.62mm MG (2,000 rounds)
2 × 3 smoke grenade launchers
**Crew:** 3
**Length:** 4.597m
**Width:** 2.413m
**Height:** 2.171m (inc cupola), 1.651m (hull top)
**G/clearance:** 0.406m
**Weight:** 8,775kg (loaded), 7,725kg (air-drop)
**G/pressure:** 0.48kg/sq cm
**Engine:** GMC Detroit Diesel 6V53 6-cylinder diesel, 215hp at 2,800rpm
**Speed:** 70.8km/h (road), 5.6km/h (water)
**Range:** 523km
**Fuel:** 303 litres
**Fording:** Amphibious
**V/obstacle:** 0.61m
**Trench:** 1.473m
**Gradient:** 60%
**Armour:** 38mm (max)

## Development
The Command and Reconnaissance Vehicle (sometimes called the M113½) was developed by FMC as a private venture with the first prototype being completed in 1963. It was not adopted by the US Army who instead selected the M114 which has now been phased out of service. Main automotive components of the Command and Reconnaissance vehicle are identical to the M113A1 APC but the C&R has a different layout with the engine at the rear, lower profile hull and four instead of five road wheels either side.

*Lynx C&R carrier of the Canadian Armed Forces without armament fitted.* Michael Ledford

The C&R has the commander and driver located side by side. This model was ordered by the Netherlands and the first production vehicle was completed in September 1966. The 250 vehicles used by the Netherlands Army have now been refitted with an Oerlikon KBD turret fitted with a 25mm KBA-B cannon.

When Canada purchased the vehicle, they requested certain changes, such as the commander and driver placed in tandem. They named their vehicle Armoured, Full-Tracked, Command and Reconnaissance Carrier, Lynx, the first production vehicle for Canada was completed in May 1968.

The vehicle is fully amphibious being propelled in the water by its tracks. It has infra-red night driving lights but no NBC system.

## Variants
In addition to the armament installations employed by Canada and the Netherlands, the vehicle can be fitted with many other types of armament including turret with twin 7.62mm MGs, single 12.7mm MG or a 20mm cannon, pedestal-mounted 7.62mm or 12.7mm MG or 20mm/25mm cannon, 106mm M40 type recoilless rifle or ATGWs such as TOW.

## Employment
Canada and Netherlands.

149

# M8 Armoured Car; M20 Utility Vehicle          USA

**Armament:** M8 — 1 × 37mm gun, 1 × 7.62mm coaxial MG, 1 × 12.7mm AA MG
M20 — 1 × 12.7mm AA MG
**Ammunition:** M8 — 80 rounds of 37mm, 1,500 rounds of 7.62mm and 400 rounds of 12.7mm
M20 — 1,000 rounds of 12.7mm
**Crew:** 4 (2-6)
**Length:** 5.003m
**Width:** 2.54m
**Height:** 2.25m (M20 2.31m)
**G/clearance:** 0.29m
**Weight loaded:** 7,892kg (M20 7,937kg)
**Track:** 1.93m
**Wheelbase:** 2.032m + 1.219m
**Engine:** Hercules JXD 6-cylinder petrol developing 110hp at 3,000rpm
**Speed:** 90km/h
**Range:** 560km
**Fuel:** 212 litres
**Fording:** 0.61m
**V/obstacle:** 0.3m
**Gradient:** 60%
**Armour:** 3-20mm

## Development/Variants

The M8, also called the Greyhound, was designed and built by the Ford Motor Company with a total of 8,523 M8 armoured cars and 3,791 M20 armoured utility cars being built between 1943 and 1945.

The M20 has the same hull as the M8 but the turret has been replaced by an open topped superstructure on top of which is a ring-mounted 12.7mm (0.50in) M2HB MG.

NAPCO Industries Incorporated of Minneapolis are now offering a retrofit package for the M8/M20 which replaces the original engine and transmission with a Detroit Diesel 4-53N engine and the Allison AT-545 automatic transmission.

## Employment

Benin (and M20), Brazil, Cameroon, Colombia, Guatemala, Laos, Madagascar, Mexico, Morocco, Niger (and M20), Paraguay, Peru, Senegal (and M20), South Korea, Taiwan, Togo (and M20), Upper Volta (and M20), Venezuela and Yugoslavia.

*M8 Greyhound 6×6 armoured car.* US Army

# Cadillac Gage Commando Scout          USA

**Data:** Model with 1m turret and twin 7.62mm MGs
**Armament:** dependent on role
**Crew:** 1 + 1 (or 1 + 2)
**Length:** 4.699m
**Width:** 2.057m
**Height:** 2.235m
**Weight:** 6,577kg
**Track:** 1.651m
**Wheelbase:** 2.667m

**Engine:** Cummins V-6 diesel developing 149hp at 3,300rpm
**Speed:** 88.5km/h
**Range:** 800km
**Fuel:** 208 litres
**Fording:** 1.168m
**V/obstacle:** 0.609m
**Gradient:** 60%

Cadillac Gage Commando Scout with 12.7mm M2 HB MG. Cadillac Gage

## Development

The Commando Scout has been developed as a private venture by the Cadillac Gage company who also manufacture the V-150 Commando range of multi-mission vehicles and was first shown in 1977. At the time of writing the vehicle had not been placed in production.

The vehicle can be fitted with a wide range of armament installations including a 1m turret with twin 7.62mm MG (with 1,600 rounds of ammunition), 1m turret with one 7.62mm and one 12.7mm MG, one 1m turret with twin 12.7mm MGs or a 1m turret with one 20mm (or 30mm) cannon

with a coaxial 7.62mm MG (400 rounds of 20mm and 3,200 rounds of 7.62mm ammunition).

The vehicle does not have any amphibious capability and is not provided with a NBC system or any night vision equipment.

## Variants

*Anti-tank* Fitted with a Hughes TOW ATGW system and six missiles

*Anti-tank* Fitted with an American M40 106mm recoilless rifle and 15 rounds of ammunition

*Command* Fitted with rear-mounted pod, additional communications equipment and a pintle-mounted 7.62mm MG

## Employment

Development complete. Ready for production.

# Dragoon 300 Multi-Mission Vehicle  USA

**Armament:** Dependent on role
**Crew:** 9 (typical)
**Length:** 5.588m
**Width:** 2.438m
**Height:** 2.642m (turret), 2.133m (hull)
**G/clearance:** 0.692m (hull)
**Weight:** 11,830kg (loaded), 9,072kg (empty)
**Track:** 1.981m
**Wheelbase:** 2.794m
**Engine:** Detroit Diesel 6V53T, 6-cylinder turbocharged diesel developing 300bhp at 2,100rpm
**Speed:** 116km/h (road), 5.5km/h (water)
**Range:** 1,045km
**Fuel:** 341 litres
**Gradient:** 60%

## Development/Variants

The Dragoon 300 family of multi-mission vehicles was designed by the Verne Corporation with the first prototype being completed in 1978. These were followed by a pre-production batch of 17 vehicles which were completed by the Dominion Manufacturing Company. Marketing of the Dragoon is carried out by the Arrowpointe Corporation.

The Dragoon 300 family have the same engine and many other automotive components as the M113A2 APC and the axles, suspension, brakes, steering, electrical and hydraulic system of the M809 (6×6) 5-ton truck.

When being used as an APC it can carry a maximum of 11 fully equipped men plus a two-man crew. A wide range of armament systems can be

151

*Dragoon 30 multi-mission vehicle with 90mm
Cockerill gun.*

installed including turret/pintle-mounted 7.62mm or
12.7mm MGs, turret-mounted 20mm or 25mm
cannon, turret-mounted 90mm gun (Cockerill or
Mecar), and ATGWs such as TOW or Dragon. More

specialised versions would include ambulance,
command and a 81mm mortar carrier.

The vehicle is fully amphibious being propelled in
the water by its wheels and standard equipment
includes a front mounted winch, heater and run flat
tyres.

**Employment**
Development complete. Ready for production.

# Cadillac Gage Commando V-300 Multi-Mission Vehicle    USA

**Armament:** See below
**Crew:** 3 + 9 (typical)
**Length:** 6.4m
**Width:** 2.54m
**Height:** 1.981m (hull top), 2.692m (with 90mm
turret)
**G/clearance:** 0.533m (max)
**Weight:** 12,700kg (max)
**Track:** 2.198m (front), 2.167m (rear)
**Wheelbase:** 2.209m + 1.524m
**Engine:** V-8-555 diesel developing 250bhp at
3,000rpm
**Speed:** 88.51km/h (road), 4.8km/h (water)
**Range:** 644km
**Fuel:** 284 litres
**V/obstacle:** 0.609m
**Gradient:** 60%

**Development**
The Commando V-300 (6×6) multi-mission vehicle
has been developed as a private venture by the
Cadillac Gage Company who currently manufacture
the Commando V-150 (4×4) range of multi-mission
vehicles used by many countries.

The hull is of all welded steel construction and
provides protection from 7.62mm small arms fire
with firing ports and vision blocks being provided in
the sides and rear.

The V-300 is fully amphibious being propelled in
the water by its wheels. Standard equipment
includes 'Commando Special' run-flat combat
tubeless tyres, automatic transmission, two speed
transfer case with spline engagement clutch for axle
drive, silent locking differentials and a winch with a
capacity of 9,072kg with 45.72m of cable.

The V-300 can be fitted with a variety of armament installations including: One-man turret with twin 7.62mm MGs; One-man turret with one 7.62mm and one 12.7mm MGs; One-man turret with 20mm cannon and coaxial 7.62mm MG; Two-man turret with 76mm gun and coaxial 7.62mm MG;

Two-man turret with 90mm gun and coaxial 7.62mm MG; Emerson turret as fitted to M901 Improved TOW Vehicle with two Hughes TOW ATGW in ready to launch position.

**Variants**
In addition to the various armament installations the vehicle can also be used for other roles such as command and recovery.

**Employment**
Development complete. Ready for production.

*Cadillac Gage Commando V-300 multi-mission vehicle fitted with two-man turret with 76mm gun, coaxial 7.62mm MG and AA 7.62mm MG.*
Cadillac Gage

# Cadillac Gage Commando Multi-Mission Vehicle    USA

| | V-100 | V-150 | V-200 |
|---|---|---|---|
| **Crew:** (according to role) | 12 | 12 | 12 |
| **Length:** | 5.689m | 5.689m | 6.12m |
| **Width:** | 2.26m | 2.26m | 2.438m |
| **Height:** (over hull) | 1.93m | 1.981m | 1.981m |
| **G/clearance:** (axles) | 0.406m | 0.381m | 0.431m |
| **Weight:** (loaded) | 7,370kg | 9,888kg | 12,730kg |
| **Speed:** (road) | 100km/h | 88km/h | 96km/h |
| (water) | 4.8km/h | 4.8km/h | 4.8km/h |
| **Range:** (road) | 665km | 643km | 600km |
| **Fuel:** | 303 litres | 303 litres | 379 litres |
| **Fording:** | Amphibious | Amphibious | Amphibious |
| **V/obstacle:** | 0.609m | 0.609m | 0.609m |
| **Gradient:** | 50% | 60% | 60% |
| **Engine:** | Petrol (200hp) | Diesel (202hp) | Petrol (275hp) |
| **Track:** | 1.866m | 1.914m/1.943m | 2.038m/2.076m |
| **Wheelbase:** | 2.667m | 2.667m | 3.263m |

*Note:* The crew, weight loaded and weight empty depend on the role and type of armament fitted.

## Development

The V-100 Commando was developed as a private venture by the Cadillac Gage Company of Detroit, Michigan with the first prototype being completed in March 1963 and first production vehicles being completed in January 1964.

The V-100 was used on a large scale in Vietnam and was originally designated the XM706 by the US Army before it was standardised as the M706.

All members of the Commando family are fully amphibious being propelled in the water by their wheels, are fitted with a front mounted winch and are provided with vision blocks and firing ports to enable the crew to fire their weapons from within the vehicle in safety. By early 1981 over 4,000 Commando vehicles had been built and further development has resulted in the V-300 (6×6) Commando for which there is a separate entry.

## Variants

*V-100:* The following models were available:
(a) Fitted with a turret mounting twin 7.62mm MGs with 1,000 ready rounds and 9,000 rounds in reserve, and 12 smoke dischargers.
(b) Fitted with turret-mounted 7.62mm and 12.7mm MG, and 12 smoke dischargers.
(c) Fitted with a pod for use in the command/APC role.
(d) Open-topped model on which could be fitted turret, pod, or single 7.62mm MG.
(e) Police, rescue, riot control or fire fighting vehicle.
(f) Fitted with TOW missile launcher.
(g) Fitted with turret-mounted 7.62mm minigun.
(h) Fitted with Dragon anti-tank weapons.
(i) 81mm mortar carrier.
(j) Recovery vehicle.

*V-150:* The V-150 Commando was announced in 1971 and has now replaced both the V-100 and V-200 in production. The following models are currently available:
(a) APC with pintle-mounted 7.62mm MG and carrying 12 men including commander, gunner and driver.
(b) Fitted with one-man turret armed with twin 7.62mm or one 7.62mm and one 12.7mm MG.
(c) Fitted with 1m turret armed with twin 7.62mm or one 7.62mm and one 12.7mm MGs.
(d) Fitted with 1m turret armed with 20mm cannon, coaxial 7.62mm MG.
(e) Fitted with two-man turret armed with 20mm Oerlikon cannon, 7.62mm coaxial MG and 7.62mm AA MG.
(f) Fitted with General Electric turret with one six-barrelled 20mm Vulcan AA gun.
(g) Fitted with two-man turret armed with 76mm gun (as fitted in Scorpion), coaxial 7.62mm and 7.62mm AA MGs.
(h) Fitted with two-man turret armed with 90mm gun, coaxial 7.62mm and 7.62mm AA MGs.
(i) Fitted with 81mm M29 mortar firing through the roof, plus 7.62mm MGs.
(j) Fitted with Hughes TOW ATGW system with seven missiles being carried.
(k) Command vehicle with 7.62mm MG.
(l) Base security vehicle with 7.62mm MGs.
(m) Police Emergency Rescue Vehicle (ERV).
(n) Recovery vehicle with A-frame, heavy duty winch and wide range of tools.

*V-200:* This was first shown in 1969 and has been produced in the following roles:
(a) Personnel carrier seating 12 men, armed with 7.62mm MGs.
(b) Armed with 90mm gun, 7.62mm coaxial MG, 7.62mm AA MG and 12 smoke dischargers.
(c) Armed with a turret-mounted 20mm gun, 7.62mm coaxial MG, 7.62mm AA MG, 12 smoke dischargers. Crew of 11.
(d) Mortar vehicle with 81mm mortar, 7.62mm MGs and a crew of five.
(e) 120mm mortar carrier, crew of seven and 7.62mm MGs.
(f) Recovery vehicle, crew of eight, armed with 7.62mm MGs. Also fitted with an A frame.

## Employment

Bolivia (V-100), Cameroon (V-150), Ethiopia (V-150), Gabon (V-150), Guatemala (V-150), Haiti (V-150), Indonesia (V-150), Jamaica (V-150), Malaysia (V-150), Oman (V-150), Saudi Arabia (V-150), Singapore (V-150 and V-200), Somalia (V-150), Sudan (V-150), Thailand (V-150), Tunisia (V-150), Turkey (V-150), USA (V-100) and Vietnam (V-100).

*Cadillac Gage V-150 Commando fitted with two-man turret armed with 20mm Oerlikon cannon, 7.62mm coaxial and 7.62mm AA MG and smoke dischargers.* Cadillac Gage

*Cadillac Gage V-200 fitted with two-man turret
armed with a Mecar 90mm gun.* Cadillac Gage

# M2 IFV; M3 Cavalry Fighting Vehicle    USA

**Data:** M2
**Armament:** 1 × 25mm cannon, elevation +60°, depression −10° (900 rounds carried)
1 × 7.62mm coaxial MG (4,400 rounds)
Twin launcher for Hughes TOW ATGW (7 TOWs)
2 × 4 smoke dischargers
**Crew:** 3 + 6
**Length:** 6.453m
**Width:** 3.2m
**Height:** 2.972m (overall), 2.565m (turret roof)
**G/clearance:** 0.457m
**Weight:** 22,045kg (loaded), 18,869kg (empty)
**Engine:** Cummins VTA-903 8-cylinder turbocharged

diesel developing 500hp at 2,400rpm
**Speed:** 66km/h (road), 7.2km/h (water)
**Range:** 483km
**Fuel:** 662 litres
**Fording:** Amphibious
**V/obstacle:** 0.914m
**Trench:** 2.54m
**Gradient:** 60%

*M2 IFV with twin TOW launcher raised on left side of turret.* US Army

## Development

After many false starts in the 1960s, in November 1972 the FMC Corporation were awarded a contract to design and develop a new IFV called the XM723. Prototypes were built between 1973 and 1975 but in 1976 a decision was taken to redesign the vehicle to incorporate a two-man turret with a twin TOW ATGW launcher as well as designing a variant for the reconnaissance role. The latter was required as the Armored Reconnaissance Scout Vehicle (ARSV) project was cancelled after prototypes had been completed by FMC (tracked) and Lockheed Missiles and Space (6×6).

The complete project was then renamed the Fighting Vehicle System (FVS) with the Infantry Fighting Vehicle being called the XM2 and the Cavalry Fighting Vehicle being called the XM3. Following successful trials with prototype vehicles these were standardised as the M2 and M3 and first production vehicles were completed by FMC in 1981.

The vehicles have an all-welded aluminium hull with spaced laminate armour added to the hull front, sides and rear for increased protection and each is fully amphibious being propelled in the water by its tracks and is fitted with a NBC system and passive night vision equipment.

## Variants

*M3 Cavalry Fighting Vehicle:* This is almost identical to the M3 but has only a five-man crew and no firing ports, it carries additional ammunition.
*Fighting Vehicle Systems Carrier:* This uses automotive components of the M2/M3 and has a fully armoured three man cab at the front and a cargo area at the rear. Its first application is for the Vought Multiple Launch Rocket System.

## Employment

In service with the US Army.

# Armoured Infantry Fighting Vehicle          USA

**Armament:** 1×25mm cannon, elevation +50°, depression −10° (324 rounds carried)
1×7.62mm coaxial MG (1,840 rounds)
6 smoke dischargers
**Crew:** 3+7
**Length:** 5.258m
**Width:** 2.819m
**Height:** 2.794m (inc turret), 1.854m (front, hull top)
**G/clearance:** 0.432m
**Weight:** 13,687kg (loaded), 11,405kg (empty)
**G/pressure:** 0.67kg/sq cm
**Engine:** Detroit Diesel 6V53T, V6 turbocharged diesel developing 264hp at 2,800rpm

**Speed:** 61km/h (road), 6.3km/h (water)
**Range:** 490km
**Fuel:** 416 litres
**Fording:** Amphibious
**V/obstacle:** 0.635m
**Trench:** 1.625m
**Gradient:** 60%
**Armour:** Aluminium and steel

*AIFV of the Netherlands Army with which it serves under the designation YPR-765 PRI.*   Dutch Army

## Development

In 1967, FMC Corporation built two XM765s for the United States Army. These vehicles used a number of M113 components and were tested in the USA and Korea. FMC developed this vehicle further as a private venture with the end result being the AIFV, the prototype of which was completed in 1970. The vehicle has been changed and improved in many ways, including additional steel armour attached to the hull (with a gap between it and the aluminium armour), a power-operated turret with a 25mm automatic cannon and a coaxial 7.62mm MG, five firing ports for individual weapons (two each side and one at the rear), an engine turbo-charger that increases the hp from 215 to 264, and new high-capacity shock absorbers. The vehicle uses the improved T130E1 track adapted for use on the M113A1. A unique torsion bar and tube suspension system results in superior cross-country performance.

The AIFV is fully amphibious being propelled in the water by its tracks. Standard equipment includes a full range of night vision equipment and optional equipment includes a NBC system and a heater for the troop compartment.

## Variants

The AIFV can be adopted for a wide range of roles and variants used by the Netherlands army include command, radar (British ZB 298), radar/command, ambulance, 120mm mortar tractor, cargo vehicle, anti-tank vehicle with same launcher with TOW ATGWs as fitted to the American M901 Improved TOW Vehicle, and recovery.

## Employment

In service with Netherlands and Philippines and on order for Belgium.

# M113 Series APC                                             USA

|  | M106 | M106A1 | M113 | M113A1 | M125A1 | M132A1 | M577A1 |
|---|---|---|---|---|---|---|---|
| **Crew:** | 6 | 6 | 2+11 | 2+11 | 5 | 2 | 5 |
| **Length:** | 4.93m | 4.93m | 4.87m | 4.87m | 4.87m | 4.87m | 4.87m |
| **Width:** | 2.86m | 2.86m | 2.69m | 2.69m | 2.69m | 2.69m | 2.69m |
| (reduced) | 2.54m | 2.54m | 2.54m | 2.54m | 2.54m | 2.54m | 2.54m |
| **Height:** (overall) | 2.50m | 2.50m | 2.50m | 2.50m | 2.50m | 2.43m | 2.68m |
| (reduced) | 2.02m | 2.02m | 2.02m | 2.02m | 2.02m | 2.29m | 2.54m |
| **G/clearance:** | 0.41m | 0.41m | 0.41m | 0.41m | 0.41m | 0.41m | 0.41m |
| **Weight:** (loaded) | 10,750kg | 11,996kg | 10,258kg | 11,156kg | 11,261kg | 10,840kg | 11,513kg |
| (empty) | 8,790kg | 9,005kg | 8,960kg | 9,702kg | 10,539kg | 9,475kg | 10,865kg |
| **G/pressure:** (kg/sq cm) | 0.57 | 0.59 | 0.50 | 0.55 | 0.55 | 0.54 | 0.57 |
| **Speed:** (road) | 64.4km/h | 67.6km/h | 64.4km/h | 67.6km/h | 67.6km/h | 68.4km/h | 67.6km/h |
| (water) | 5.8km/h | 5.6km/h | 5.6km/h | 5.8km/h | 5.8km/h | 5.8km/h | 5.8km/h |
| **Range:** | 298km | 483km | 321km | 483km | 483km | 490km | 595km |
| **Fuel:** (litres) | 322 | 360 | 320 | 360 | 360 | 360 | 454 |
| **Fording:** | AMP | AMP | AMP | AMP | AMP | AMP | AMP |
| **V/obstacle:** | 0.61m | 0.61m | 0.61m | 0.61m | 0.61m | 0.61m | 0.61m |
| **Trench:** | 1.68m | 1.68m | 1.68m | 1.68m | 1.68m | 1.68m | 1.68m |
| **Gradient:** | 60% | 60% | 60% | 60% | 60% | 60% | 60% |
| **Armament:** | 12.7mm | 12.7mm | 12.7mm | 12.7mm | 12.7mm | 7.62mm | None |
| **Ammunition:** | 1,000 | 1,000 | 2,000 | 2,000 | 1,000 | 2,000 | None |
| **Engine:** | Chry | GMC | Chry | GMC | GMC | GMC | GMC |

*Note:* The Chrysler engine is a Model 75M petrol engine developing 209hp at 4,000rpm and the GMC engine is a Detroit Diesel Model 6V53 diesel developing 215hp at 2,800rpm. Max armour is 38mm.

## Development

In 1956 the development of a light airportable APC commenced and prototypes were built both in aluminium (the T113) and steel (the T117). Following trials the T117 was dropped and further development of the T113 resulted in the T113E1 which was subsequently standardised in 1960 as the M113. First production vehicles were completed by FMC Corporation at their San Jose, California, facility in 1960.

Following trials with a diesel-engined model, the T113E2, this was standardised as the M113A1 in

1963 and replaced the M113 in production from late 1964. This model has a greater operational range than the earlier M113 as well as a reduced risk of fire.

The latest model to enter production is the M113A2 with improvements to its cooling system and suspension, as well as fuel tanks mounted externally at the rear of the hull instead of inside.

By 1981 over 70,000 members of the M113 family had been built in the USA and further development of the M113 as a private venture by FMC has resulted in the AIFV for which there is a separate entry. The M113 and M113A1 have also been manufactured under licence in Italy by OTO-Melara and they have also developed an improved version for the Italian Army called the Infantry Armoured Fighting Vehicle.

The M113 is of all welded aluminium construction and is fully amphibious being propelled in the water by its tracks, before entering the water trim vane is erected at the front of the hull and the bilge pumps switched on. All vehicles have infra-red night vision equipment although many now have passive night vision equipment. Listed below are the more important variants of the M113. In addition there are many local variants.

### Variants

*Mortar Carrier M106 and M106A1:* The M106 has a petrol engine and the M106A1 a diesel engine. It is armed with a 107mm (4.2in) mortar which has a traverse of 89° and fires through a three part circular hatch in the roof. A mortar base and stand are carried externally on the left side of the vehicle enabling the mortar to be fired away from the vehicle. The M106 carried 93 rounds and the M106A1 carries 88 rounds of 107mm mortar ammunition. The Swiss have some with 120mm mortars of Swiss design.

*APC M113 and M113A1:* This is the basic vehicle. In its normal role it carries 12 infantrymen. A wide range of kits are available to adapt it for various roles, these include ambulance, cargo, dozer vehicle, fitters' vehicle, recovery vehicles. It can be fitted with HOT, TOW, MILAN anti-tank missile systems. Another model in service is the ACAV (Armoured Cavalry Assault Vehicle) which is armed with a 12.7mm and two 7.62mm MGs. Each of these MGs is protected by an armoured shield. The German and Danish Armies have M113s modified to carry British Green Archer mortar locating radar system.

Many countries have modified the M113 to meet their own specific requirements, for example Australia uses the following models: M113A1 APC/Light Reconnaissance Vehicle, M113A1 APC (Ambulance), M113A1 Fire Support Vehicle (Scorpion turret), M113A1 Fire Support Vehicle (Saladin turret), M577A1 Armoured Command Vehicle, M125A1 APC (Mortar), M806A1 (ARV Light), M113A1 (APC (F) (Carrier, Repair Fitters) and M548 (Tracked Load Carrier). The German Army has a number of M113s with 120mm mortars.

*Mortar Carrier M125, M125A1 and M125A2:* This is armed with an 81mm mortar mounted on a baseplate giving the mortar a traverse of 360°. It fires through the three part circular hatch in the roof, baseplate and stand are carried externally enabling the mortar to be fired away from the vehicle. 114 rounds of 81mm mortar ammuntion are carried. First production vehicles were delivered in 1966.

*Self-Propelled Flamethrower M132A1:* This is armed with a turret mounting a 7.62mm M73 MG and a M10-8 flame gun, the turret has a traverse of 360° elevation being +55° and depression −5°. The flamethrower has a max firing range of 180m and a sustained duration of 32sec. The vehicle is supported in action by the M45 (a modified M548) vehicle which carries additional fuel for the flame gun. This model is not currently deployed by the US Army.

*M163 Vulcan Air Defense System:* This is a Vulcan 20mm cannon mounted on a M113A1 chassis, the chassis in this case is designated M741. The Vulcan gun has six barrels and has two rates of fire, 1,000 or 3,000rpm, thus allowing it to be used against both ground and air targets. The turret has a traverse of

*M113A1 APC.* US Army

360°, elevation being +85° and depression −5°. In addition to being used by the US Army it is also in service with Ecuador, Israel, Morocco, Thailand, Tunisia and North Yemen.

*Command Post M577, M577A1 and M577A2:* Both petrol- and diesel-engined models. This is basically an M113 or an M113A1 with a higher hull. The vehicle is fitted with additional radios, mapboards, tables and so on; it also fitted with an NBC system. A tent can be erected at the rear of the vehicle to give additional working space. The first production M577 was completed in 1962.

*XM734 MICV:* This was basically an M113 with firing ports in the sides of the vehicle. Trials only.

*XM765 MICV:* Two of these were built for the US Army in 1967 by FMC. It had firing ports, additional armour and a turret-mounted gun. It was further developed by FMC into the AIFV.

*M548 Cargo Carrier:* Development commenced in May 1963 and the vehicle entered production in 1967. It uses the engine and suspension of the M113A1 APC. Its role is to carry cargo and ammunition in the battle zone. It is fully amphibious and is armed with a 7.62mm or 12.7mm MG. A recovery vehicle was designated XM696 but this did not enter service.

In addition to being used for applications such as the Tracked Rapier, M727 HAWK, M730 Chaparral and Lance SSM system, the M548 tracked vehicle is also used for a wide range of other applications such as carrying and dispensing mines and as the basis for the Oerlikon twin 35mm GDF-CO2 SP AA gun system.

*M727 HAWK:* This is a M548 chassis with three Raytheon HAWK surface-to-air missiles at the rear of the hull. It is only used by the United States and Israel.

*M730 Chaparral:* This is a M548 chassis with four Chaparral surface-to-air missiles in the ready-to-launch position and entered service with the US Army in 1968. It is also used by Ecuador, Greece, Israel, Morocco, Spain, Taiwan and Tunisia.

*M806 ARV:* This is the ARV version of the M113A1 with internal winch with a maximum capacity of 9,070kg, two spades at the rear of the hull and a roof-mounted auxiliary crane.

*M901 ITV:* The M901 Improved TOW vehicle entered service with the US Army in 1979 and is a M113A1 with an elevating launcher for two TOW ATGWs with a further 10 missiles being carried internally for rapid reloading.

*Lance SSM:* A modified M548 chassis is used for the Vought Lance surface-to-surface missile system. The launch vehicle is the M752 (chassis M667) while the launcher/transporter which carries the two reserve missiles is designated the M688.

*Tracked Rapier:* This was originally developed by British Aerospace Dynamics for the Iranian Army but this order was subsequently cancelled. It consists of an M548 with an armoured cab with eight Rapier surface-to-air missiles in the ready to launch position at the rear. It has recently been ordered by the British Army.

*Lynx C&R Vehicle:* This was developed using components of the M113. For this vehicle there is a separate entry.

*M132A1 flamethrower.* US Army

## Employment

Argentina, Australia, Belgium, Bolivia, Brazil, Canada, Chile, Costa Rica, Denmark, Ecuador, Egypt, El Salvador, Ethiopia, FRG, Guatemala, Greece, Haiti, Israel, Italy, Jordan, Kampuchea, Kenya, South Korea, Kuwait, Laos, Lebanon, Libya, Morocco, Netherlands, New Zealand, Norway, Pakistan, Peru Philippines, Portugal, Saudi Arabia, Singapore, Somalia, Spain, Sudan, Switzerland, Taiwan, Thailand, Tunisia, Turkey, USA, Uruguay, Vietnam, Yemen Arab Republic (North) and Zaire.

*M577A1 command vehicle of the Canadian Armed Forces.* Canadian Armed Forces

159

M106A1 107mm (4.2in) mortar carrier.  US Army

M901 Improved TOW Vehicle launching Hughes
TOW ATGW.  Emerson Electronics

# M59 APC

USA

**Armament:** 1 × 12.7mm M2 MG (2,205 rounds
carried)
**Crew:** 2 + 10
**Length:** 5.613m
**Width:** 3.263m, 3.149m (min)
**Height:** 2.768m (inc cupola), 2.387m (hull top)
**G/clearance:** 0.457m
**Weight:** 19,323kg (loaded), 17,916kg (empty)
**G/pressure:** 0.51kg /sq cm
**Engine:** 2 × GMC Model 302, 6-cylinder, water-
cooled, in-line, petrol engines developing 127hp at
3,350rpm (each)
**Speed:** 51.50km/h (road), 6.9km/h (water)
**Range:** 164km (road)
**Fuel:** 518 litres
**Fording:** Amphibious
**V/obstacle:** 0.46m
**Trench:** 1.676m
**Gradient:** 60%
**Armour:** 16mm

## Development
In 1951 the FMC Corporation designed a full tracked
APC powered by two Cadillac engines under the
designation of the T59. This was soon followed by
the T59E1 which was powered by two General
Motors Corporation Model 302 petrol engines. This
was standardised as the M59 in 1953 and between
1954 and 1959 the FMC Corporation built just over
4,000 M59s.

The M59 is fully amphibious being propelled in
the water by its tracks, infra-red driving lights are
fitted. There are hatches in the roof and a single
ramp at the rear of the vehicle.

## Variants
The basic vehicle was armed with a pintle-mounted
12.7mm MG; some models were fitted with a
cupola-mounted 12.7mm MG and these vehicles
were known as M59A1s.

Experimental models of the M59 included a

missile carrier, recoilless rifle carrier and the LVTP6 amphibious vehicle for the United States Marines. The basic M59 could also be used as a load carrier, command vehicle or ambulance.

The M84 was armed with a 4.2in mortar and had a cupola-mounted 12.7mm MG and a crew of six men. The contract for the M84 ran from May 1956 until May 1958 and a total of 21.7million dollars was spent on the programme.

*M59 APC fitted with 106mm recoilless rifle.*
*US Army*

### Employment
The M59 has been replaced in the United States Army by the M113. The vehicle is still in service with Brazil, Greece and Turkey.

# M75 APC                                                           USA

**Armament:** 1 × 12.7mm M2 MG (1,800 rounds carried)
**Crew:** 2 + 10
**Length:** 5.193m
**Width:** 2.84m
**Height:** 3.041m (with MG), 2.775m (inc cupola)
**G/clearance:** 0.457m
**Weight:** 18,828kg (loaded), 16,632kg (empty)
**G/pressure:** 0.57kg/sq cm
**Engine:** Continental AO-895-4, 6-cylinder, air-cooled petrol, developing 295hp at 2,600rpm
**Speed:** 71km/h (road)
**Range:** 185km
**Fuel:** 568 litres
**Fording:** 1.219m, 2.032m (with kit)
**V/obstacle:** 0.457m
**Trench:** 1.676m
**Gradient:** 60%
**Armour:** 25mm (max)

### Development
After the end of World War 2 the T12 series of full tracked APCs was developed and one of these, the T18E1, was standardised as the Vehicle, Armored Infantry, Full Tracked, M75. A total of 1,729 M75s was built by International Harvester and FMC between 1951 and 1954. Some of the automotive components of the M75 were also used in the M41 light tank, including the engine and tracks.

The M75 suffered from a number of disadvantages including its size and lack of amphibious capability. It was soon replaced in US Army service by the M59 APC.

The vehicle was fitted with infra-red driving lights. The crew was provided with roof hatches and there were two doors at the rear of the vehicle.

### Variants
There were few minor differences between production batches. Experimental vehicles included the T64 mortar carrier (with a 4.2in mortar) and a T73 Infantry Vehicle.

### Employment
Belgian Army.

*M75 APC.  US Army*

# Armoured Half-Track Vehicles USA

| | M2 | M3 | M3A1 | M4A1 | M9A1 | M16 |
|---|---|---|---|---|---|---|
| **Crew:** (total) | 10 | 13 | 13 | 6 | 10 | 5 |
| **Length:** (overall) | 6.146m | 6.34m | 6.337m | 6.194m | 6.32m | 6.501m |
| **Width:** | 2.196m | 2.22m | 2.22m | 2.22m | 2.19m | 2.159m |
| **Height:** | 2.26m | 2.501m | 2.692m | 2.26m | 2.31m | 2.616m |
| **G/clearance:** | 0.28m | 0.28m | 0.28m | 0.28m | 0.28m | 0.28m |
| **Weight:** (loaded) | 8,980kg | 9,072kg | 9,298kg | 9,135kg | 9,348kg | 9,810kg |
| (empty) | 6,940kg | 7,030kg | 6,940kg | 7,144kg | 7,756kg | 8,450kg |
| **Speed:** (road) | 73km/h | 73km/h | 73km/h | 73km/h | 73km/h | 64km/h |
| **Range:** (road) | 242km | 321km | 321km | 321km | 321km | 250km |
| **Fuel:** | 227 litres | 227 litres | 227 litres | 227 litres | 227 litres | 227 litres |
| **Fording:** | 0.812m | 0.812m | 0.812m | 0.812m | 0.812m | 0.812m |
| **Gradient:** | 60% | 60% | 60% | 60% | 60% | 60% |
| **Armament:** | 12.7mm | — | 12.7mm | — | 12.7mm | 12.7mm(4) |
| | 7.62mm | 7.62mm | 7.62mm | 7.62mm | 7.62mm | — |
| **Mortar:** | — | — | — | 81mm | — | — |
| **Engine:** | White | White | White | White | I.H.C. | White |
| **Bhp/rpm:** | 147/3,000 | 147/3,000 | 147/3,000 | 142/3,000 | 124/3,000 | 142/3,000 |
| **Armour:** | 7-13mm | 7-13mm | 7-13mm | 7-13mm | 7-13mm | 7-13mm |

Full designations and manufacturers are as follows:
Car, Half-Track, M2 (Autocar Company, White Motor Company);
Carrier, Personnel, Half-Track, M3 and M3A1 (Autocar Company, Diamond T Motor Company, White Motor Company);
Carrier, 81mm Mortar, Half-Track, M4A1 (White Motor Company);
Carrier, Half-Track, M9A1 (International Harvester Company);
Carriage, Motor, Multiple Gun, M16 (White Motor Company).

*Half-track armed with 12.7mm M2HB MG.*
Armor Magazine

## Development/Variants

The United States developed half-track vehicles in the 1930s and they were produced in large numbers by various manufacturers during World War 2. The above listing is only a selection of those that may be found in service. The dimensions vary on whether the vehicle has a winch or roller mounted at the front, whether a 12.7mm MG is fitted and whether racks are fitted on the sides of the vehicle. Many local modifications are in service; refer also to the section on Israel.

## Employment

Argentina, Colombia, Guatemala, Israel, Japan, Madagascar, Mexico, Morocco, Paraguay, Senegal, Taiwan and Yugoslavia.

# Cadillac Gage Commando Ranger APC    USA

**Armament:** depends on role
**Crew:** 2 + 6
**Length:** 4.699m
**Width:** 2.019m
**Height:** 1.981m
**G/clearance:** 0.203m
**Weight:** 4,848kg (max loaded)
**Track:** 1.689m
**Wheelbase:** 2.946m
**Engine:** Dodge 360 CID V-8 liquid cooled petrol developing 180hp at 3,600rpm
**Speed:** 112.65km/h (road)
**Range:** 482km
**Fuel:** 121 litres
**V/obstacle:** 0.254m
**Gradient:** 60%

## Development
The Commando Ranger APC has been developed as a private venture by the Cadillac Gage Company who also manufacture the Commando V-150 range of multi-role 4 × 4 vehicles. In 1979 the USAF ordered the Ranger to meet its requirements for a Security Police Armored Response/Convoy Truck for patrolling airfields and missile bases. The first production vehicle was handed over on 24 April 1980. The USAF, who call the vehicle the Peacekeeper, has a total requirement for 810 vehicles of this type.
When being used as an APC it can carry six fully equipped men in addition to its two-man crew. It can also be fitted with a pintle-mounted 7.62mm MG with 200 rounds of ready use ammunition or a Cadillac Gage turret with twin 7.62mm or one 7.62mm and one 12.7mm MGs, with an elevation of +55°, depression −14°, and total turret traverse of 360°.
Standard equipment includes firing ports, vision blocks, combat tyres, air conditioning system while

*Cadillac Gage Commando Ranger APC: note 7.62mm MG provided with a shield.*   Cadillac Gage

optional equipment includes a front-mounted winch, radio, spotlights, flashing lights, public address system, grenade launchers and a 24V electrical system.

## Variants
*Ambulance:* Crew of two can carry two stretcher patients plus two sitting patients.
*Command:* Crew of two plus command staff, additional communications equipment and map boards.

## Employment
In service with USAF.

# Lancer Armoured Patrol Vehicle    USA

**Armament:** Depends on role
**Crew:** 4
**Length:** 4.42m
**Width:** 1.792m
**Height:** 1.727m
**G/clearance:** 0.22m
**Weight:** 2,812kg
**Track:** 1.481m
**Wheelbase:** 2.54m
**Engine:** Petrol developing 150hp at 3,800rpm
**Speed:** 128km/h
**Range:** 370km
**Fuel:** 70 litres
**Fording:** 0.457m
**Gradient:** 60%
**V/obstacle:** 0.254m

## Development
The Lancer armoured patrol vehicle has been developed as a private venture by the Vehicle Systems Development Corporation of California to meet a known requirement for a reliable and low cost vehicle suitable for a number of roles such as airport security and anti-highjack patrols, anti-terrorist, ambulance, APC, base security and border patrol and reconnaissance and convoy escort duties.
The vehicle is based on an unmodified 4 × 4 commercial truck chassis utilising standard automotive components and suspension.
The crew enter and leave the vehicle via a single door in either side of the hull and a further door in the rear, five spherical firing ports are fitted, two in each side and one in the rear, these enable the crew to use their small arms from within the vehicle in safety.

The body of the Lancer is constructed of ArmaCore™ armour which combines superior ballistic qualities and low weight and the advanced design transparent armour offers excellent exterior visability without the need for special periscopes, visors or shutters to protect the occupants during hostile action. If required the doors can be fitted with special retractable ballistic shields which, when the doors are open, provide full frontal protection for dismounted personnel.

A circular roof hatch is provided to the rear of the commander's and driver's position and on this can be mounted a 7.62mm or a 12.7mm MG.

Standard equipment includes an explosion-proof fuel tank, air conditioning system, runflat tyres, front

*Model of the Vehicle Systems Development Corporation Lancer armoured patrol vehicle.*
Vehicle Systems Development Corp

mounted electrically operated winch and an air conditioning system. Optional equipment includes other types of armament installations and various types of night vision equipment.

**Employment**
Development complete. Ready for production. The Lancer is being marketed by the Arrowpointe Corporation.

# M3A1 4 × 4 Scout Car USA

This was manufactured by the White Motor Company. It is a 4 × 4 vehicle and was used as a radio vehicle, command vehicle, troop carrier and reconnaissance vehicle. Its basic data is as follows:

**Armament:** 1 × 12.7mm and 1 × 7.62mm MGs
**Length:** 5.625m
**Width:** 2.032m
**Height:** 1.993m
**Weight:** 5,920kg (loaded)

**Engine:** Hercules JXD developing 87hp at 2,400rpm
**Speed:** 90km/h (road)
**Range:** 410km
**Fording:** 0.71m
**Gradient:** 60%

**Employment**
Still in service with Guatemala, Liberia, Mexico, Nicaragua, Peru, Uruguay and Yugoslavia.

# LVTP7 Armoured Amphibious Assault Vehicle USA

**Armament:** 1 × 12.7mm M85 MG, elevation +60°, depression −10° (1,000 rounds carried)
**Crew:** 3 + 25
**Length:** 7.94m
**Width:** 3.27m
**Height:** 3.26m (overall), 3.12m (turret)
**G/clearance:** 0.406m
**Weight:** 22,838kg (loaded), 17,441kg (empty)
**G/pressure:** 0.57kg/sq cm
**Engine:** Detroit Diesel model 8V53T, 8-cylinder, developing 400hp at 2,800rpm
**Speed:** 64.37km/h (road), 13.5km/h (water)
**Range:** 482km (land)
**Fuel:** 681 litres
**Fording:** Amphibious
**V/obstacle:** 0.914m
**Trench:** 2.438m
**Gradient:** 70%
**Armour:** 10mm-45mm

## Development
The first prototype was completed in October 1967 and was known as the LVTPX12. A total of 15 prototypes was built by July 1968. These vehicles were armed with a 20mm cannon. Development and production of the vehicle was undertaken by FMC under the supervision of the Naval Ships Systems Command. A production order for the LVTP7 was awarded to FMC in June 1970 and the first vehicle was delivered to the USMC on 26 August 1971 with final deliveries being made in 1974. A total of 942 was built for the USMC, 853 LVTP7, 76 LVTC7 and 54 LVTR7.

The LVTP7 is fully amphibious being propelled in the water by two waterjets. It is constructed of welded aluminium armour. It has torsion bar and tube suspension and is fitted with infra-red driving lights.

## Variants
*LVTP7A1:* All USMC LVTP7s will be brought up to a new standard and designated LVTP7A1. These will have a new powerpack using Cummins VT904/400 engine, improved ventilation, passive night vision equipment, smoke generating capability, automatic fire detection and supression system, PLRS and a secure voice radio installation.

*LVTC7:* Landing Vehicle Tracked, Command Model 7. Prototype built in 1968 as LVTCX2. It is a command vehicle and has a crew of 13, carries additional radios and has an auxiliary power unit. A shelter can be erected if required.

*LVTR7:* Landing Vehicle Tracked, Recovery Model 7. Prototype built in 1968 as the LTRX2. It has a winch, crane, welding equipment, pump, compressor, tools, etc.

*LVTE7:* Landing Vehicle Tracked, Mine Clearing Model 7. Prototype built in 1970 as the LVTX3. Developed to clear paths through minefields. Not placed in production and no further development.

*LVTH7:* Was to be SP 105mm howitzer but not developed to prototype stage.

*Mobile Test Rig:* LVTP7 hull fitted with laser for use in AA role, trials only.

## Employment
Argentina, Italy, South Korea, Spain, Thailand, USA and Venezuela.

*LVTP7 of the USMC.* USMC

# M107 and M110 SP Guns

USA

| | M107 | M110 |
|---|---|---|
| **Crew:** | 5 | 5 |
| **Length:** (in travelling order) | 11.256m | 7.467m |
| (hull w/o spade) | 5.72m | 5.72m |
| **Width:** | 3.149m | 3.149m |
| **Height:** (top of mount) | 2.809m | 2.809m |
| (top of barrel-travelling) | 3.679m | 2.93m |
| **G/clearance:** | 0.466m | 0.44m |
| **Weight:** (loaded) | 28,168kg | 26,534kg |
| (empty) | 25,945kg | 24,312kg |
| **G/pressure:** | 0.81kg/sq cm | 0.76kg/sq cm |
| **Speed:** (road) | 56km/h | 56km/h |
| **Range:** (cruising) | 725km | 725km |
| **Fuel:** | 1,137 litres | 1,137 litres |
| **Fording:** | 1.066m | 1.066m |
| **V/obstacle:** | 1.016m | 1.016m |
| **Trench:** | 2.362m | 2.362m |
| **Gradient:** | 60% | 60% |
| **Armament:** (calibre) | 175mm | 203mm |
| (designation) | M113 | M2A2 |
| (mount) | M158 | M158 |
| **Ammunition:** | 2 | 2 |
| **Engine:** | see below | see below |

*M107 175mm SP gun of the British Royal Artillery.*
Simon Dunstan

## Development

Both the M107 and M110 use a common chassis that was originally designed in the 1950s by the Pacific Car and Foundry Company. This chassis is also used for the M578 ARV and was used for the T245 155mm SP gun, XM701 MICV and T119 and T121 recovery vehicles, none of which reached production.

Production of the M107 and M110 was originally undertaken by Pacific Car and Foundry Company but more recent production has been undertaken by Bowen-McLaughlin York of Pennsylvania. The M107 and M110 each have a total crew of 13 men, five are carried on the gun (driver in the front and two men either side of the gun), and the other eight in an M548 support vehicle which also carries the ammunition. The British Army uses the 6×6 Stalwart for this role. The M107 and M110 use the same engine, transmission and final drive as the M108 and M109. The vehicles do not have AA guns and the driver is the only member of the crew under cover.

## Variants

*M107:* Design dates from 1956 and first prototype completed in February 1958 as the T235; this was fitted with a diesel engine and redesignated the T235E1. The first production M107 was completed in August 1962, the first unit was equipped at Fort Sill, Oklahoma, in January 1963. The gun, which is made by Watervliet Arsenal, New York, has a traverse of 30° left and 30° right, elevation being +65° and depression −2°. It is powered by a General Motors 8V71T 8-cylinder, liquid-cooled diesel developing 405hp at 2,300rpm. The M107 fires an HE projectile to a max range of 32,700m, and no other type of ammunition can be fired. The M107 has now been phased out of service with the US Army in favour of the M110A1 and M110A2 203mm (8in) SP howitzers.

*M110:* Prototype was designated T236 and later T236E1, production dates, manufacturers and engine data are similar to the M107. The 203mm (8in) howitzer has an elevation of +65° and a

depression of −2°, traverse being 30° left and 30° right. Max range is 16,800m and it can fire nuclear or a wide range of conventional shells.
*M110A1/M110A2:* The M110A1 was developed from 1969 and entered service in January 1977. Its major difference over the M110 is that it has a much longer barrel designated the M201 and fires an HE projectile to a max range of 21,300m or an HE RAP projectile to a max range of 29,000m, other types of ammunition can be fired including tactical nuclear. The M110A2 is identical to the M110A1 but is fitted with a double baffle muzzle brake. Loaded weight of

*M110A2 203mm (8in) SP howitzer with double baffle muzzle brake.* US Army

the M110A1 is 28,168kg and overall length is 10.365m.

**Employment**
*M107:* FRG, Greece, Iran, Israel, Italy, South Korea, Netherlands, Spain, Turkey, UK and Vietnam.
*M110:* Belgium, FRG, Greece, Iran, Israel, Jordan, South Korea, Netherlands, Spain, Turkey, UK, USA and Vietnam.

# M55 SP Howitzer

USA

**Armament:** 1×203mm M47 howitzer, elevation +65°, depression −5° (10 rounds carried)
1 × 12.7mm (0.50in) Browning AA MG (900 rounds)
**Crew:** 6
**Length:** 7.908m
**Width:** 3.58m
**Height:** 3.469m (top of cupola), 3.124m (top of turret)
**G/clearance:** 0.469m
**Weight:** 44,452kg (loaded), 30,823kg (empty)
**G/pressure:** 0.78kg/sq cm
**Engine:** Continental Model AV-1790-5B, 5C or 5D, 12-cylinder air-cooled petrol developing 704bhp at 2,800rpm
**Speed:** 48km/h
**Range:** 257km
**Fuel:** 1,438 litres
**Fording:** 1.219m
**V/obstacle:** 1.016m
**Trench:** 2.26m
**Gradient:** 60%
**Armour:** 13-26mm

**Development**
In 1948 the Pacific Car and Foundry Company was awarded a contract to design a 155mm Gun Motor Carriage under the designation of T97 which would also accept a 8in (203mm) howitzer. In 1950 the company was awarded a contract to build prototypes of the T97 and the following year a contract was also awarded for the construction of 203mm SP howitzer under the designation of the T108.

These two prototypes were completed in 1952 with first production vehicles being completed late the same year. The T97 was standardised as the M53 while the T108 was standardised as the M55, or to give the vehicle its correct designation: Howitzer, Heavy, Self-Propelled: Full Tracked, 8-inch, M55. Production continued until 1955 and the following year a decision was taken to convert all M53s into M55s and this was completed by 1958.

*M55 203mm (8in) SP howitzer in action.* US Army

The M55 was replaced in the US Army by the 203mm M110 in the early 1960s.

The engine and transmission is at the front of the vehicle with the turret at the rear. The latter has a traverse of 30° left and 30° right and all of the crew are seated in the turret including the driver. When in action a large spade is lowered down at the rear of the hull. The M55 fires a separate loading HE projectile to a max range of 16,800m. The M55 is not provided with a NBC system and has no amphibious capability.

**Variants**
There are no variants of the M55 in service.

**Employment**
In service with Belgium.

# M108 and M109 SP Howitzers                                  USA

|  | M108 | M109 |
|---|---|---|
| **Crew:** | 5 | 6 |
| **Length:** (gun forward) | 6.114m | 6.612m |
| (vehicle only) | 6.114m | 6.256m |
| **Width:** (overall) | 3.295m | 3.295m |
| (reducable to) | 3.149m | 3.149m |
| **Height:** (inc MG) | 3.115m | 3.289m |
| (w/o MG) | 2.794m | 3.06m |
| **G/clearance:** | 0.451m | 0.467m |
| **Weight:** (loaded) | 22,452kg | 23,786kg |
| (empty) | 18,436kg | 19,730kg |
| **G/pressure:** | 0.71kg/sq cm | 0.766kg/sq cm |
| **Speed:** (road) | 56km/h | 56km/h |
| (water) | 6.43km/h | 6.43km/h |
| **Range:** (cruising) | 390km | 390km |
| **Fuel:** | 511 litres | 511 litres |
| **Fording:** | 1.828m | 1.828m |
| **V/obstacle:** | 0.53m | 0.53m |
| **Trench:** | 1.828m | 1.828m |
| **Gradient:** | 60% | 60% |
| **Armament:** (main) | 105mm | 155mm |
| (AA) | 12.7mm | 12.7mm |
| **Ammunition:** (main) | 87 | 28 |
| (AA) | 500 | 500 |
| **Engine:** | both are powered by a Detroit Diesel Model 8V71T turbo-charged engine developing 405hp at 2,300rpm | |

*M108:* In 1954 development of a 110mm SP howitzer commenced under the designation of the T195 but in 1956 it was decided that the 156mm (later 155mm) T196 SP howitzer would use the same chassis as the T195 and at the same time the 110mm weapon was dropped in favour of a 105mm howitzer. The T196 was followed by the T196E1 which was eventually standardised as the M109.

The prototype T195 was completed in 1958 and the following year a decision was taken to replace the petrol engine by a diesel and the T195 was redesignated the T195E1 and this was standardised as the M108 in December 1961.

Production was undertaken by the Cadillac Motor Car Division of the General Motors Corporation with first production vehicles being completed in October 1962 and final deliveries being made the following year. Only a small number were built as it was decided to concentrate on the 155mm M109 SP howitzer.

The 105mm howitzer fires an HE projectile to a max range of 11,500m and the M103 howitzer can be elevated from −4° to +74°, turret traverse being 360°. Amphibious capabilities are the same as those of the M109.

*M109:* In 1959 the first prototype of the 155mm T196 SP howitzer was completed. This used the same chassis as the 105mm T195 SP howitzer and was powered by a petrol engine. The T196 was then fitted with a diesel engine and redesignated the T196E1. Production of the latter commenced at the Cleveland Tank-Automotive Plant run by the Cadillac Motor Car Division of the General Motors Corporation in 1962 but it was the following year before the T196E1 was standardised as the Howitzer, Medium, Self-Propelled M109.

The turret can be traversed through a full 360° and the howitzer elevated from −3° to +75°. It can fire an HE projectile to a max range of 14,600m and also has a nuclear capability. Flotation equipment consists of nine air bags which are positioned four each side and one at the front of the vehicle, they are inflated in less than two minutes. The tracks propel the vehicle whilst in the water.

*M108 105mm SP howitzer.* US Army

**M109A1:** This is the M109 with longer barrel designated the M185, improved elevation and traverse system and stronger suspension. Classified as Standard A in October 1970 with conversion kits being made available from 1972 and first units becoming operational in 1973. The M109A1 weighs 24,070kg and fires an HE projectile to a max range of 18,100m or a HE RAP to a range of 24,000m.

**M109A2:** This is essentially a M109 built with all of the modifications of the M109A1 but in addition has a redesigned rammer, improved recoil system and a bustle designed to carry an additional 22 projectiles. First production M109A2s were completed by Bowen-McLaughlin-York in 1978.

**M109 (Israel):** These are designated the M109 AL and carry additional ammunition internally and externally. Israel uses the M109A1 as well as the M109.

**M109G:** This is a German model of the M109. Its differences are that it has a horizontal sliding breech-block by Rheinmetall (American M109s have an interrupted screw breech-block), German aiming equipment. Range is 18,500m.

**M109U:** This is the designation of the model used by the Swiss Army which is fitted with a semi-automatic loader of Swiss design enabling it to fire six rounds a minute.

*M109A1 155mm SP howitzer of the British Royal Artillery.* MoD (Army)

**M109 (Italy):** The M109s used by the Italian Army had their ordnance built and installed in Italy by OTO-Melara. For trials purposes OTO-Melara fitted one M109 with a much longer barrel with a fume extractor and a double baffle muzzle brake. This fired an M107 HE projectile to a max range of 22,000m but has not so far been adopted.

**M109 Ammunition Delivery System:** This is currently being tested by the United States Army and is used to supply artillery units with new ammunition.

**Roland:** A modified M109 chassis, designated the XM975 is being used for the US version of the French/German Roland SAM system.

**Employment**

*M108:* Belgium, Brazil, Spain, Taiwan, Tunisia and Turkey.

*M109* and variants: Argentina, Austria, Belgium, Canada, Denmark, Ethiopia, FRG, Greece, Iran, Israel, Italy, Jordan, Kampuchea, South Korea, Kuwait, Libya, Morocco, Netherlands, Norway, Pakistan, Spain, Switzerland, Taiwan, Turkey, UK, USA and Vietnam.

# M44 and M52 SP Howitzers USA

*M44 155mm SP howitzers of the US Army.* US Army

|  | M52 | M44 | M44A1 |
|---|---|---|---|
| **Crew:** | 5 | 5 | 5 |
| **Length:** (overall) | 5.80m | 6.159m | 6.159m |
| **Width:** | 3.149m | 3.238m | 3.238m |
| **Height:** (inc AA MG) | 3.31m | — | — |
| (w/o AA MG) | 3.056m | — | — |
| (with canvas cover) | — | 3.11m | 3.11m |
| **G/clearance:** | 0.49m | 0.48m | 0.48m |
| **Weight:** (loaded) | 24,040kg | 28,349kg | 29,030kg |
| (empty) | 22,588kg | 26,308kg | 26,980kg |
| **G/pressure:** (kg/sq cm) | 0.60 | 0.66 | 0.67 |
| **Speed:** (road) | 56km/h | 56km/h | 56km/h |
| **Range:** (cruising) | 160km | 122km | 122km |
| **Fuel:** | 678 litres | 568 litres | 568 litres |
| **Fording:** | 1.219m | 1.066m | 1.066m |
| **V/obstacle:** | 0.914m | 0.762m | 0.762m |
| **Trench:** | 1.828m | 1.828m | 1.828m |
| **Gradient:** | 60% | 60% | 60% |
| **Armament:** (main) | 105mm | 155mm | 155mm |
| (AA) | 12.7mm | 12.7mm | 12.7mm |
| **Ammunition:** (main) | 102 | 24 | 24 |
| (AA) | 900 | 900 | 900 |
| **Armour:** | 12.7mm (max) | 12.7mm (max) | 12.7mm (max) |
| **Engine:** | see below | see below | see below |

## Development/Variants

*General:* Both the M44 and M52 use components of the M41 light tank including the engine, transmission and auxiliary engine. The layout of the two vehicles is also similar with the engine and transmission at the front and the turret (M52) or gun compartment (M44) at the rear, the latter houses all of the crew including the driver.

*M44:* Development started in 1947 as the T99 and the first prototypes were built in 1950 at Detroit Arsenal. The next model was the T99E1; in 1952 this was redesignated T194. In 1953 it was standardised as the M44. The M44 is armed with a 155mm M45 howitzer in a mount M80, traverse being 30° left and 30° right, elevation being +65° and depression −5°. The vehicle is powered by a Continental AOS-895-3 petrol engine developing 500hp at 2,800rpm. The M44A1 is similar to the M44 but is powered by a Continental AOSI-895-5 petrol engine with a fuel injection system. There is no overhead armour protection for the crew of the M44. A canvas cover can be erected over the fighting compartment if required. When in the firing position a spade is let down at the rear of the vehicle and the back of the fighting compartment folds down to provide a platform for the crew to operate the gun.

*M52:* The first pilot model was designated the T98 and was built at Detroit Arsenal in 1950. This was followed by the T98E1 which was armed with a 105mm howitzer and was subsequently standardised as the M52. The M52 is armed with an M49 105mm howitzer in a mount M85. The turret has a traverse of 60° left and 60° right. Elevation is +65° and depression is −10°. The M52 is powered by a 6-cylinder air-cooled petrol engine; this is a

*M52 105mm SP howitzer of the US Army.*
US Army

Continental AOS-895-3 developing 500hp at 2,800rpm. The M52AI is powered by a Continental AOSI-895-5 with a fuel injection system fitted. This gives the vehicle a max speed of 68km/h.

**Employment**
*M44:* Belgium, Greece, Italy, Japan, Jordan, Spain and Turkey.
*M52:* Greece, Japan and Jordan.

# M7 SP Howitzer

*M7B1 105mm SP howitzer.* Kensuke Ebata

**Data:** M7 *(M7B1)*
**Armament:** 1 × 105mm howitzer, elevation +35°, depression −5°, traverse 30° left and 15° right of centre line (69 rounds carried)
1 × 12.7mm AA MG (300 rounds)
**Crew:** 7
**Length:** 6.02m *(6.18m)* (overall)
**Width:** 2.88m *(2.93m)*
**Height:** 2.946m (inc MG)
**G/clearance:** 0.43m *(0.44m)*
**Weight:** 22,970kg *(22,680kg)* (loaded)
**G/pressure:** 0.73kg/sq cm
**Engine:** See below
**Speed:** 40km/h
**Range:** 137-210km
**Fuel:** 677 litres *(636)* litres
**Fording:** 1.22m *(0.91m)*
**V/obstacle:** 0.61m
**Trench:** 2.286m
**Gradient:** 60%
**Armour:** 12mm-114.3mm

**Development**
In 1941 development commenced of the T32 105mm Howitzer Motor Carriage. This was essentially the chassis of the M3 Sherman with a new superstructure fitted with a standard 105mm M2A1 howitzer. In February 1942 the T32 was standardised as the 105mm Howitzer Motor Carriage M7 and was first used in action by the British Army — who called it the Priest — in North Africa.

Production was undertaken by the American Locomotive Company (M7), Pressed Steel Car Company (M7 and M7B1) and Federal Machinery and Welding Company (M7B2), and a total of 4,267 was built by the end of 1945.

The 105mm howitzer is offset to the right of the M7's centre line and fires the same range of ammunition as the towed 105mm howitzer M2A1 (post World War 2 designation M101) and has a max range of 10,500m.

**Variants**
*M7:* This was based on the M4 chassis and powered by a Continental Model R-975-C1, 9-cylinder, radial petrol engine developing 350hp at 2,400rpm.
*M7B1:* This was based on the M4A3 chassis and powered by a Ford GAA V8 engine developing 450hp at 2,600rpm. It was standardised in September 1942.
*M7B2:* Very few of these were built by Federal Machine and Welder Company.

**Employment**
Used by Argentina, Brazil, Israel (most converted to other roles), Pakistan, Portugal, South Africa, Turkey and Yugoslavia.

# M56 Scorpion SP Anti-Tank Gun

*M56 Scorpion SP anti-tank gun.* US Army

**Armament:** 1 × 90mm gun M54 in mount M88 (29 rounds carried)
**Crew:** 4
**Length:** 5.841m (inc gun), 4.555m (exc gun)
**Width:** 2.577m
**Height:** 2.057m
**G/clearance:** 0.38m
**Weight:** 7,030kg (loaded), 5,783kg (empty)
**G/pressure:** 0.316kg/sq cm
**Engine:** Continental AO1-403-5, 6-cylinder, air-cooled, fuel injection petrol engine developing 200bhp at 3,000rpm
**Speed:** 45km/h (road)
**Range:** 225km (cruising)
**Fuel:** 208 litres
**Fording:** 1.066m (w/o kit), 1.524m (with kit)
**V/obstacle:** 0.762m
**Trench:** 1.524m
**Gradient:** 60%
**Armour:** See below

## Development

Two prototypes of an airportable SP anti-tank gun were built by Cadillac Motor Car Division of the General Motors Corporation under the designation of the T101. With modifications this became the T101E1 which was subsequently standardised as the Gun, Anti-Tank, Self-Propelled: 90mm, M56.

This was manufactured by the Cadillac Motor Car Division of the General Motors Corporation from 1953 to 1959. The main drawback of the M56 was

that when the main armament was fired the forward part of the chassis would tend to lift off the ground and dust would often obscure the gunners' field of view. In the late 1960s the M56, also known as the Scorpion, was replaced by the M551 Sheridan.

The Scorpion is armed with a 90mm gun that fires similar ammunition to the M48 tank. The gun has a vertical sliding breechblock and has an elevation of +15° and a depression of −10°, traverse being 30° left and 30° right. The chassis of the M56 is unarmoured and fabricated from sheeting and rolled sections of aluminium and is riveted and welded together. The only armour on the vehicle is the shield.

## Variants

There are no variants in service although many versions were projected or built as prototypes including: missile carrier, AA vehicle with 4 × 12.7mm MGs, 81mm and 107mm mortar carriers, 106mm recoilless rifle carriers, amphibious armoured personnel carrier. One was also fitted with a gas turbine engine.

## Employment

Morocco.

# M10 and M36 SP Anti-Tank Gun                                             USA

|  | M10 | M10A1 | M36 | M36B1 | M36B2 |
|---|---|---|---|---|---|
| **Crew:** | 5 | 5 | 5 | 5 | 5 |
| **Length:** (hull) | 5.97m | 5.97m | 5.97m | 6.27m | 5.97m |
| **Width:** | 3.05m | 3.05m | 3.05m | 2.55m | 3.05m |
| **Height:** | 2.47m | 2.47m | 3.19m | 2.66m | 3.15m |
| **G/clearance:** | 0.43m | 0.43m | 0.44m | 0.43m | 0.46m |
| **Weight:** (loaded) | 29,940kg | 39,030kg | 27,670kg | 30,840kg | 29,940kg |
| **G/pressure** (kg/sq cm) | 0.86 | 0.85 | 0.95 | 0.96 | 0.86 |
| **Speed:** (road) | 48km/h | 48km/h | 42km/h | 42km/h | 40km/h |
| **Range:** (cruising) | 320km | 260km | 180km | 160km | 180km |
| **Fuel:** | 621 litres | 727 litres | 727 litres | 636 litres | 625 litres |
| **Fording:** | 0.91m | 0.91m | 0.91m | 0.91m | 1.07m |
| **V/obstacle:** | 0.61m | 0.61m | 0.46m | 0.61m | 0.48m |
| **Trench:** | 2.29m | 2.29m | 2.29m | 2.29m | 2.29m |
| **Gradient:** | 60% | 60% | 60% | 60% | 60% |
| **Armament:** (main) | 76.2mm | 76.2mm | 90mm | 90mm | 90mm |
| (bow) | — | — | — | 7.62mm | — |
| (AA) | 12.7mm | 12.7mm | 12.7mm | 12.7mm | 12.7mm |
| **Ammunition:** (main) | 54 | 54 | 47 | 47 | 47 |
| (bow) | — | — | — | 450 | — |
| (AA) | 300 | 300 | 1000 | 1000 | 1000 |
| **Engine:** | GM(2) | Ford GAA | Ford GAA | Ford GAA | GMC(2) |
| **Bhp/rpm:** | 375/2100 | 450/2600 | 450/2600 | 450/2600 | 375/2100 |
| **Armour:** | 12mm-50mm | 12mm-50mm | 12mm-50mm | 12mm-50mm | 12mm-50mm |

## Development/Variants

The above tank destroyers were developed during World War 2 and saw service in Europe from 1943 onwards. The M10, M10A1, M36 and M36B2 all incorporate a Sherman chassis with a new hull and turret. The M36B1 retains the chassis and hull (and the bow MG) of the M4A3, and is fitted with a new turret and gun. The M36 uses an M10A1 chassis and the M36B2 the M10 chassis. A prime mover version of the M10 was called the M35. The British converted many M10s and M10A1s to carry the excellent 17pdr gun. These were called 17 Pounder Self-Propelled Achilles.

## Employment

M10s are still used by South Korea.
M36s are still used by Pakistan (M36B2), South Korea, Turkey, Yugoslavia (M36B2).

*M10 tank destroyer.* US Army

# M18 SP Anti-Tank Gun

USA

**Armament:** 1 × 76mm M1A1 or M1A2 gun, elevation +19.5°, depression −10° (45 rounds carried)
1 × 12.7mm AA MG (840 rounds)
**Crew:** 5
**Length:** 6.654m (inc gun), 5.282m (exc gun)
**Width:** 2.794m
**Height:** 2.57m (inc AA MG)
**G/clearance:** 0.355m
**Weight:** 17,036kg (loaded), 16,114kg (empty)
**G/pressure:** 0.83kg/sq cm
**Engine:** Continental R-975-C4, 9-cylinder, radial petrol engine developing 400hp at 2,400rpm *or* Continental R-975-C1 developing 350hp at 2,400rpm
**Speed:** 88.5km/h (road)

**Range:** 240km (cruising)
**Fuel:** 625 litres
**Fording:** 1.219m
**V/obstacle:** 0.914m
**Trench:** 1.879m
**Gradient:** 60%
**Armour:** 7mm-25mm

**Development/Variants**
In 1942 the Buick Motor Division of the General Motors Corporation started work on a 76mm Gun Motor Carriage. The first six prototypes, designated the T70, were completed in July 1943. Well before this date however, in January 1943, a production order was placed for 1,000 vehicles and the first of these was completed shortly after the prototypes.

The T70 was standardised as the M18 Gun Motor Carriage in 1944 and a total of 2,507 vehicles was built by Buick at their Flint, Michigan facilities by the time production was completed late in 1944. The M18 was commonly known as the Hellcat by the US Army.

Its primary role was of tank hunting and the vehicle relied on its high speed to get itself out of trouble, its armour being very thin.

There were a number of variants on the M18 chassis including the M39 and M44 armoured utility vehicles, none of which are known to remain in service. In addition there were many experimental vehicles.

**Employment**
South Korea, Taiwan, Venezuela and Yugoslavia.

*M18 Hellcat.* US Army

# 40mm DIVADS

USA

To meet the requirements of the United States Army for a Division Air Defense System, Ford Aerospace and the Pomona Division of General Dynamics each built two prototypes for competitive evaluation. These were tested at Fort Bliss and in May 1981 the Army selected the Ford Aerospace entry which is armed with twin 40mm guns mounted on a modified M48A5 tank chassis.

Major sub-contractors to Ford Aerospace are AAI for the turret, Westinghouse for the radar, Bofors for the gun and ammunition, Hughes Aircraft for the laser rangefinder, Kollmorgen for the optical sights, Litton for the attitude reference units and gyros and Garret AiResearch for the primary power unit. The US Army has a total requirement for 618 systems and the first of these should be completed late in 1983.

The 40mm Bofors guns fire three types of ammunition, pre-fragmented high explosive (PFHE), high capacity high explosive (HCHE) and target practice with a total of 560 rounds being carried per vehicle; reload time is only 13 minutes.

The chassis of the DIVADS is almost the same as the M48A5 medium tank but loaded weight is around 60 tonnes and mobility is probably reduced compared to original tank.

**Employment**
Entering production for US Army.

*One of the prototypes of the 40mm DIVADS system mounted on M48A5 chassis.*

# M42 SP AA Gun System

USA

**Armament:** 2 × M2A1 40mm cannon (480 rounds carried)
1 × M1919A4 7.62mm MG (1,750 rounds)
**Crew:** 6
**Length:** 6.356m (inc guns), 5.819m (exc guns)
**Width:** 3.225m
**Height:** 2.847m
**G/clearance:** 0.438m
**Weight:** 22,452kg (loaded)
**G/pressure:** 0.65kg/sq cm
**Engine:** M42 has Continental or Lycoming AOS-895-3, M42A1 has a Continental or Lycoming AOSI-895-5, 6-cylinder air-cooled, supercharged petrol engine developing 500hp at 2,800rpm
**Speed:** 72km/h (road)
**Range:** 161km (road)
**Fuel:** 530 litres
**Fording:** 1.016m
**V/obstacle:** 0.711m
**Trench:** 1.828m
**Gradient:** 60%
**Armour:** 10mm-25mm

## Development/Variants
The M42 was developed from 1951 under the designation of the T141 and uses many components of the M41 light tank developed at the same time. The twin 40mm turret is the same as that fitted to the earlier M19 SP AA gun.

A total of 3,700 M42s was built between 1951 and 1957 by Cadillac Motor Car Division of General Motors Corporation at the Cleveland Tank Plant and ACF Industries of Berwick, Pennsylvania.

The 40mm cannon are mounted in a power-operated turret and have a traverse of 360°, powered elevation is from −3° to +85°, or from −5° to +87° manually. The guns have a cyclic rate of fire of 240rpm and a max effective range of 4,700m

The M42A1 has a fuel injection system fitted to its engine. This increases the power of the engine to 525bhp as well as a small extension in its operating range. In the 1950s an M42 was fitted with a radar system on the right side of the guns; this however did not enter production. The crew of six are seated four in the turret and two in the front of the vehicle.

## Employment
Used by Austria, Japan, Jordan, Lebanon, Saudi Arabia, Taiwan, Thailand, USA and Vietnam.

*M42 of the US Army.* US Army

# M88 Medium ARV

USA

**Armament:** 1 × 12.7mm M2 MG 1,500 rounds carried.
**Crew:** 4
**Length:** 8.267m (inc blade)
**Width:** 3.428m
**Height:** 3.225m (inc MG), 2.921m (ex MG)
**G/clearance:** 0.43m
**Weight:** 50,800kg (loaded)
**G/pressure:** 0.764kg/sq cm
**Engine:** Continental AVSI-1790-6A, 12-cylinder, air-cooled, supercharged petrol engine developing 980bhp at 2,800rpm
**Speed:** 48km/h (road)
**Range:** 360km
**Fuel:** 1,515 litres
**Fording:** 1.42m
**V/obstacle:** 1.066m
**Trench:** 2.616m
**Gradient:** 60%

### Development/Variants
The M88 was designed by Bowen-McLaughlin-York under the designation of the T88 and uses many automotive components of the M48 tank. The three prototypes were followed by 10 pre-production vehicles and a total of 1,075 production M88s was completed between 1961 and 1964.

Following successful trials of the M88E1, this being an M88 fitted with the engine of the M60 tank as well as modified transmission, personnel heater and an APU, a decision was taken to retrofit the entire US Army fleet to this standard, this vehicle then became known as the M88A1, as well as putting the vehicle back in production again. Conversion and new production M88A1s are produced by Bowen-McLaughlin-York at their York facilities.

A hydraulically operated dozer blade is mounted on the front of the vehicle. This can be used for dozing operations or for supporting the vehicle when the boom is being used. The A-type boom at the front of the hull can lift a vehicle weighing up to 5,443kg without using the blade or suspension lockout, 18,143kg using lockout, and 22,680kg when using the blade.

The main winch has 60.96m of cable and a max pull of 40,823kg at 6m/min. The hoist winch has 61m of cable and a max capacity of 22,680kg (bare drum low speed). The winch and hoist are hydraulically operated.

Trials have been carried out with deep fording equipment. This has not however been adopted for service.

### Employment
In service with Austria, Egypt, FRG, Israel, Jordan, Norway, Pakistan, South Korea, Tunisia, USA (Army and Marines) and Yemen Arab Republic (North).

*M88A1 ARV in travelling order.*
Bowen-McLaughlin-York

# M578 Light ARV

USA

**Armament:** 1 × 12.7mm M2 MG (500 rounds carried)
**Crew:** 3
**Length:** 6.444m (inc crane), 5.937m (hull only)
**Width:** 3.149m
**Height:** 2.921m (w/o MG)
**G/clearance:** 0.47m
**Weight:** 24,494kg
**G/pressure:** 0.71kg/sq cm (loaded)
**Engine:** GMC 8V71T Detroit diesel, liquid-cooled, 8-cylinder, turbo-charged, developing 425hp at 1,700rpm
**Speed:** 54.71km/h (road)
**Range:** 725km (cruising)
**Fuel:** 1,137 litres
**Fording:** 1.066m
**V/obstacle:** 1.016m
**Trench:** 2.667m
**Gradient:** 60%

*M578 ARV of the US Army.* Michael Ledford

## Development/Variants

In 1956 the Pacific Car and Foundry Company were awarded a contract to develop a range of full tracked light ARVs, these were the T119 (crane armoured), T120 (crane in unarmoured turret) and the T121 (crane unarmoured), all of which were powered by a petrol engine. The T120 was then fitted with a diesel engine and designated the T120E1, this was standardised as the M578. First production M578s were completed by the FMC Corporation but the vast majority have been manufactured by Bowen-McLaughlin-York, the current manufacturer. The vehicle has a hoisting capacity of 13,620kg, with the crane turret traversed to the rear and the spade in position.

A hydraulically operated spade is mounted at the rear of the M578 and four of the road wheels have an hydraulic bump-stop, during recovery operations the suspension can be locked to provide a more stable platform.

The M578 has two winches, a tow winch with a max capacity of 27,216kg on a bare drum and a hoisting winch with a max capacity of 6,804kg. Standard equipment includes tools, tow bars, hydraulic impact wrench, Acetylene welding and cutting equipment.

## Employment

Bolivia, Brazil, Canada, Denmark, Egypt, Iran, Jordan, Morocco, the Netherlands, Norway, Saudi Arabia, Spain, UK and the USA.

# T-80 MBT

USSR

**Armament:** 1 × 125mm gun (40 rounds carried)
1 × 7.62mm coaxial MG
1 × 12.7mm AA MG
**Crew:** 3
**Length:** 7m (hull)
**Width:** 3.5m
**Height:** 2.3m
**G/clearance:** Variable
**Weight:** 45,000kg
**Engine:** Liquid-cooled diesel developing 750bhp
**Speed:** 70km/h
**Range:** 450km (w/o long range tanks), 650km (with long range tanks)
**Fording:** 1.4m (w/o preparation), 5.5m (with snorkel)
*Note:* Above specification is provisional

## Development

In the late 1970s Western sources stated that the Soviet Union was developing a new MBT for the 1980s and this was subsequently given the Western designation of the T-80. The latter is probably incorrect as this number was allocated by the Soviets to a light tank many years ago.

The T-80 has the same armament as the T-64/T-72 with a three-man crew consisting of a commander, driver and gunner, no loader is required as an automatic loader is fitted. The tank has much improved armour which is said to be comparable to the British developed Chobham armour which gives a high degree of protection against all types of battlefield weapons, including ATGWs. The hydropneumatic suspension gives a much improved cross-country capability. No details of the fire control system of the T-80 are available but is thought to include a stabilisation system, computer, laser rangefinder and a full range of night vision devices of the passive type.

## Variants

There are no known variants of the T-80.

## Employment

Believed to be on troop trials.

# T-64 and T-72 MBTs USSR

**Armament:** 1×125mm gun, elevation of +18°, depression −5° (40 rounds carried)
1×7.62mm coaxial MG (3,000 rounds)
1×12.7mm AA MG (500 rounds)

| | T-64 | T-72 |
|---|---|---|
| **Crew:** | 3 | 3 |
| **Length:** (gun forward) | 9.1m | 9.24m |
| (hull) | 6.4m | 6.9m |
| **Width:** (w/o skirts) | 3.38m | 3.49m |
| (with skirts) | 4.64m | 4.75m |
| **Height:** | 2.3m | 2.37m |
| **G/clearance:** | 0.377m | 0.42m |
| **Weight:** | 38,000kg | 41,000kg |
| **Engine:** | Diesel, 700 or 750hp | Diesel, 750hp |
| **Speed:** (max road) | 70km/h | 80km/h |
| **Range:** (internal fuel tanks) | 500km | 500km |
| (with long range fuel tanks) | 700km | 700km |
| **Fording:** (w/o preparation) | 1.4m | 1.4m |
| (with preparation) | 5.5m | 5.5m |
| **V/obstacle:** | 0.915m | 0.915m |
| **Trench:** | 2.72m | 3.07m |
| **Gradient:** | 60% | 60% |

*T-64 MBT. The main difference between the T-64 and T-72 is that the latter has much larger road wheels. US Army*

*T-72 MBTs on parade in Red Square, Moscow in November 1980. Tass*

## Development

Once the T-62 had entered production the Soviet Union built prototypes of a new MBT called the M-1970 in the West, but this did not enter production. Further development resulted in the T-64 which entered production in the late 1960s and the T-72 which entered production in 1972. The T-64 is only used by the Soviet Union and has now gone out of production. The T-72 is now used on a large scale by the Warsaw Pact and has also been exported, in addition to being built in the Soviet Union it is also built in Czechoslovakia and Poland.

Both the T-64 and the T-72 have a three-man crew as an automatic loader is fitted. Standard equipment includes a complete range of night vision equipment, snorkel for deep fording, provision for laying its own smoke screen and some T-72s have been seen fitted with a dozer blade at the front of the hull. In addition both vehicles can be fitted with various types of mine clearing equipment.

The 125mm smooth bore gun fires APFSDS, HE-Frag and HEAT projectiles and it is possible that the fire control system includes a laser rangefinder. Some reports have indicated that the T-64 and T-72 have advanced armour protection.

## Variants

Command versions of the T-64 and T-72 are designated the T-64K and T-72K, these do not have the AA MG and when used in the static role have a large aerial fitted to the turret held in position by stays.

## Employment

*T-64* USSR only.

*T-72* Algeria, Bulgaria, Czechoslovakia, GDR, Hungary, India, Iraq, Libya, Poland, Romania and the USSR.

# T-62 MBT

USSR

**Armament:** 1×115mm (U-5TS), elevation +17°, depression −4° (40 rounds carried)
1×7.62mm PKT coaxial MG (2,500 rounds)
**Crew:** 4
**Length:** 9.335m (inc gun), 6.63m (exc gun)
**Width:** 3.3m
**Height:** 2.395m
**G/clearance:** 0.425m
**Weight:** 40,000kg (loaded)
**G/pressure:** 0.83kg/sq cm
**Engine:** Model V-12 water-cooled diesel engine developing 580hp at 2,000rpm
**Speed:** 45.5km/h (road)
**Range:** 450km (road)
**Fuel:** 1,360 litres (total)
**Fording:** 1.40m, 5.486m (with snorkel)
**V/obstacle:** 0.80m
**Trench:** 2.85m
**Gradient:** 60%
**Armour:** 20mm-170mm

## Development

The T-62 is a further development of the T-54/T-55 and entered production in 1961. It was seen in public for the first time in May 1965 but unlike the earlier T-54/T-55 it has not been produced under licence in Czechoslovakia or Poland.

Major differences between T-54/T-55 and the T-62 are that the latter has a longer and wider hull, new turret mounted slightly more to the rear, new 115mm smooth bore gun fitted with a fume extractor and a system that ejects the empty cartridge cases out through a hatch in the turret rear.

Standard equipment on all T-62s includes a full range of infra-red night driving and fighting equipment, optional long range fuel tanks, fire extinguishing system and a NBC system. Like all Soviet tanks it can be fitted with a snorkel for deep

fording operations and can lay its own smoke screen by injecting diesel fuel into the exhaust.

The 115mm gun fires the following types of ammunition: APFSDS with a muzzle velocity of 1,680m/sec, HEAT with a muzzle velocity of 1,000m/sec and two types of HE Fragmentation, one with a muzzle velocity of 750m/sec and the other with a muzzle velocity of 780m/sec.

Mine clearing rollers or mine clearing ploughs can be mounted at the front of the hull as can various types of snow ploughs and dozer blades.

## Variants

T-62A has minor modifications including a 12.7mm AA MG on loader's hatch. T-62K is command model with additional communications equipment. T-62M is T-62A with track and drive sprocket of T-72 MBT.

## Employment

In service with Afghanistan, Angola, Algeria, Bulgaria, Cuba, Czechoslovakia, Egypt, Ethiopia, GDR, India, Iraq, Israel, Mozambique, North Korea, Libya, Romania, Somalia, Syria, USSR, Vietnam and Yemen (South).

*T-62 MBT.* Michael Ledford

# T-54 and T-55 MBTs

USSR

**Armament:** 1×100mm D-10T gun, elevation +17°, depression −4° (34 rounds carried)
2×7.62mm SGMT MGs — coaxial and bow operated by driver (3,000 rounds)
1×12.7mm DShKM AA MG (500 rounds)
**Crew:** 4
**Length:** 9m (inc gun), 6.45m (exc gun)
**Width:** 3.27m
**Height:** 2.40m (w/o AA MG)
**G/clearance:** 0.43m
**Weight:** 36,000kg (loaded)
**G/pressure:** 0.81kg/sq cm
**Armour:** 20mm-203mm
**Engine:** V-54, V-12, water-cooled diesel developing 520hp at 2,000rpm
**Speed:** 48km/h (road)
**Range:** 400km (road, inc external fuel tanks)
**Fuel:** 812 litres (total)
**Fording:** 1.4m, 4.486m (with snorkel)
**V/obstacle:** 0.80m
**Trench:** 2.74m
**Gradient:** 60%

*T-54 MBT captured by Israel with 12.7mm AA MG and infra-red night vision equipment removed.*
Israeli Army

## Development
The T-54 was developed from the earlier T-44 (this is still used for training). The first prototype of the T-54 appeared in 1947 and the first production models in 1949. The first models had a turret that was undercut at the rear and had an external gun mantlet. The T-54 and T-55 have been manufactured in the USSR, China (under the designation T-59), Czechoslovakia and Poland. The ZSU-57-2 is based on a modified and shortened T-54 chassis.

## Variants
*T-54:* This is the early model with the turret undercut at the rear.
*T-54A:* This has a bore evacuator, the armament is the D-10TG. Internal modifications include the stabilisation of the main armament in the vertical plane, electric oil pump, bilge pump, improved air filter, infra-red driving equipment, automatic fire extinguishers, additional fuel capacity and power elevation of the main armament.

*T-55s with laser rangefinder/designator over the main armament.* Tass

*T-54A(M):* This is the T-54 or T-54A fitted with night-fighting equipment, recognisable by the horizontal bracket for the gunner's infra-red searchlight.
*T-54B:* This model is recognisable by its infra-red searchlight for the tank commander and gunner. The commander's light is on his cupola and the gunner's light has a vertical bracket attached to the right front of the turret. The T-54B can be fitted with a snorkel; this equipment consists of two pipes which are carried on the rear decking when not required. When assembled they are placed over the loader's turret hatch, where they are supported by wire stays. A much wider pipe is used for training purposes. The T-54B has the D-10T2S gun which is stabilised in both planes.
*T-54C:* This is also known as the T-54 (X). The T-54C resembles the T-54B and has a turret dome-shaped ventilator, bracket for the gunner's infra-red searchlight is vertical as in the T-54B. No AA MG is fitted and a simple hatch replaces the loader's cupola.

*T-55:* This is sometimes called the T-55 Model 1 and was seen in public for the first time in November 1961. The T-55 has the same D-10T2S gun as the T-54B but is stabilised in both planes, other improvements include increased ammunition stowage (43 rounds of 100mm ammunition being carried) and the installation of a turret basket. It has a more powerful diesel that develops 580hp at 2,000rpm which is coupled to an improved transmission, horizontal bracket for the gunner's infra-red searchlight, no turret dome ventilator, simple hatch for the loader and no AA MG. When fitted with a 12.7mm DShKM AA MG it is known as the T-55(M).

*T-55A:* This is sometimes called the T-55 Model 2 and was first seen in May 1963. It is distinguishable by the raised hatch for the loader and smooth metal cover at the base of the commander's cupola. No bow or AA MG is fitted. Some have recently been fitted with a 12.7mm DShKM AA MG and are then designated the T-55A(M).

*Mine clearing tanks:* The T54/T-55 can be fitted with a variety of mine clearing equipment including Soviet roller models PT-3, PT-54, PT-54M and PT-55, Soviet plough system KMT-4, Soviet plough and roller system KMT-5. Czechoslovakia has developed and deployed both plough and roller mine clearing systems.

*ARVs:* The following models are known to be in service, T-54-T (spade at rear, loading platform, jib crane but no winch), T-54 (A) (East German development with push/pull bar, dismountable crane, can be fitted with snorkel for deep wading but does not have a winch or crane), T-54(B) (East German development similar to previous model but has brackets for securing ropes at rear of hull), T-54(C) (East German development with stowage platform, snorkel, rear spade, front dozer blade and heavy duty crane), Czechoslovakian T-55 ARV (loading platform, crane and commander's cupola), Poland has developed at least two ARVs on T-54 or T-55 chassis called the WZT-1 and WZT-2.

*Combat Engineer Vehicle:* Called the IMR. Is T-55 with turret replaced by a hydraulically operated crane fitted with a pair of pincer type grabs that can be used to remove trees. At front of hull is hydraulically operated dozer blade.

*Bulldozer tanks:* Two basic types of bulldozer blade can be fitted. The BTU is used for clearing topsoil and obstacles whilst the STU is used for clearing snow.

*Bridgelayer Tank MTU:* This is a T-54 with its turret removed. The bridge is carried on the top of the vehicle and winched into position over the obstacle and then lowered down into the desired position. Performance is similar to the basic T-54; some models have been seen with a 12.7mm AA MG fitted. Basic data is: *Length:* 12.30m (with bridge); *Height:* 2.865m (with bridge); *Width:* 3.27m (with bridge); *Weight:* 34,000kg (with bridge).

*Bridgelayer Tank MTU-20*: This is similar to the above bridgelayer except that it has an additional 3.85m on each end of the bridge, these fold on top of the bridge when not in use. The bridge when opened out, is 20m long and can bridge a gap of 18m. The chassis is a T-55.

*Bridgelayer Tank MT-55:* This is a Czechoslovakian development and is a T-55 with its turret removed and replaced by a scissors bridge which when opened out is 18m long and can span gap of up to 16m. Loaded weight of MT-55 is 37,000kg and the bridge can take max load of 50,000kg.

*Bridgelayer Tank BLG-60:* Joint development between East Germany and Poland. The scissors bridge is launched over the front of the vehicle and when in position is 21.6m long and can span a gap of 20m. The BLG-60 weighs 37,000kg and has a max capacity of 50,000kg.

*Indian T-54s:* These have had their 100mm guns replaced by standard 105mm L7 series weapons and their coaxial and AA MGs replaced by American type 7.62mm and 12.7mm weapons.

*Israeli T-54s:* Most of the T-54/T-55s used by the Israeli Army have been rebuilt with 105mm L7 series guns and American type coaxial and AA MGs, new fire control system and a Continental diesel engine.

*Romanian T-54s:* These have many modifications including a new suspension consisting of six road wheels either side and skirts similar to those fitted to the British Chieftain and Centurion tanks.

## Employment

Afghanistan, Albania, Algeria, Angola, Bangladesh, Bulgaria, China, Congo, Cyprus, Czechoslovakia, Egypt, Equatorial Guinea, Ethiopia, Finland, GDR, Guinea, Guinea-Bissau, Hungary, India, Iraq, Israel, North Korea (and Type 59), Libya, Mali, Mongolia, Morocco, Mozambique, Nigeria, Pakistan (and Type 59), Peru, Poland, Romania, Somalia, Sudan, Syria, USSR, Yemen (North and South), Yugoslavia, Vietnam, Zambia and Zimbabwe.

*BLG-60 bridgelayer in travelling configuration.*

# T-34/85 Medium Tank                                   USSR

**Armament:** 1×85mm M1944 (ZIS-S53), elevation +25°, depression −5° (56 rounds carried)
2×7.62mm DT or DTM MGs — bow and AA (2,394 rounds)
**Crew:** 5
**Length:** 8.076m (inc gun), 6.19m (exc gun)
**Width:** 2.997m
**Height:** 2.743m
**G/clearance:** 0.38m
**Weight:** 32,000kg
**G/pressure:** 0.83kg/sq cm
**Engine:** V-2-34, V-12 diesel, water-cooled developing 500hp at 1,800rpm OR V-2-34M V-12 diesel, water-cooled developing 500hp at 1,800rpm
**Speed:** 55km/h (road)
**Range:** 300km (road)
**Fuel:** 590 litres
**Fording:** 1.32m
**V/obstacle:** 0.73m
**Trench:** 2.50m
**Gradient:** 60%
**Armour:** 18mm-75mm

## Development

The T-34/85 was developed from the earlier T-34/76 (some of which may still be found in training units) and saw widespread service with the Soviet Army in World War 2 and was judged by many to be the best tank of the war. The chassis is similar to that used by the SU-85 and SU-100.

## Variants

*T-34/85 Bulldozer Tanks:* The vehicle can be fitted with a dozer blade.
*SKP-5 Tank Recovery Vehicle:* This is a T-34 with its turret removed and fitted with a crane capable of lifting about 5,000kg. Additional data: Length: 8.00m; Width: 3.05m; Height: 2.60m; Weight: 26,000kg.
*T-34-T Model A Recovery Vehicle:* This is simply a T-34 with no turret and therefore limited to towing operations. Some models have been seen with a superstructure or cupola in place of the turret.
*T-34-T Model B Recovery Vehicle:* The equipment fitted to this model includes rigging, jib crane and a platform that can be used to carry engines and transmissions to a max weight of 3,000kg.
*WPT-34 Recovery Vehicle:* This model has been developed by Poland and consists of a T-34 chassis with a large armoured superstructure at the front of the vehicle, a bow MG is fitted. Additional equipment includes a spade at the rear and a snorkel for deep wading.
*Czech Recovery Vehicle:* This has been developed by Czechoslovakia and is also used by Poland. It is basically a T-34 chassis with a heavy hydraulic crane mounted in place of the turret. This crane can lift a max of 5,900kg, for example a T-54 turret.
*T-34 Recovery Vehicle (Czechoslovakian):* This is fitted with spade, winch and a crane and in addition to being used as an ARV is also used by engineers in bridge construction.
*T-34 Recovery Vehicle (East German Model):* This is also known as the T-34 BG, and is similar to the T-34-T Model B but also has a push-bar on the glacis plate. It also has a winch.
*T-34 Bridgelayer (Scissors Type):* This is a Czechoslovakian design and it was first seen in 1960. Based on T-34 chassis with a scissors bridge that has a max length in position of 22.00m. Additional data is: Length: 8.5m (with bridge); Width: 3.20m (with bridge); Height: 3.70m (with bridge); Weight: 32,000kg (with bridge).
*Egypt SPG:* Syria had some T-34/85s fitted with a 100mm ATG.
*Syrian SPG:* Syria had some T-34/85s with their turrets removed and replaced by a 122mm D-30 howitzer.
*Vietnam SPAAG:* China has some T-34s fitted with a new turret armed with twin 37mm AA guns, details are given under China.

## Employment

Afghanistan, Albania, Angola, Bulgaria, China, Cuba, Cyprus, Czechoslovakia, Ethiopia, Equatorial Guinea, GDR, Guinea, Guinea Bissau, Hungary, Kampuchea, North Korea, Mali, Mongolia, Mozambique, Poland, Romania, Somalia, Vietnam, Yemen (North and South), Yugoslavia and Zimbabwe.

*T-34/85 medium tank.*

# PT-76 Amphibious Light Tank USSR

**Armament:** 1 × 76.2mm D-56T gun, elevation +30°, depression —4° (40 rounds carried)
1 × 7.62mm SGMT coaxial MG (1,000 rounds)
**Crew:** 3
**Length:** 7.625m (inc gun), 6.910m (exc gun)
**Width:** 3.140m
**Height:** 2.195m
**G/clearance:** 0.37m
**Weight:** 14,000kg (loaded)
**G/pressure:** 0.48kg/sq cm
**Engine:** V-6, in-line, water-cooled diesel developing 240hp at 1,800rpm
**Speed:** 44km/h (road), 10km/h (water)
**Range:** 260km (road)
**Fuel:** 250 litres
**Fording:** Amphibious
**V/obstacle:** 1.10m
**Trench:** 2.80m
**Gradient:** 70%
**Armour:** 10mm-15mm

## Development
The PT-76 first appeared in 1952 and is a continuation of a long line of Soviet light amphibious tanks. The PT-76 is fully amphibious, being propelled in the water by two water jets at the rear of the vehicle. Before entering the water a small trim board is folded forward at the front of the vehicle. The vehicle can lay its own smoke screen if required. The PT-76 chassis, extensively modified in some cases, is used for the following vehicles: ASU-85 SP anti-tank gun, BMP-1 MICV, MT-LB armoured tracked vehicle,

*PT-76 Model 2 amphibious light tank comes ashore from a landing craft.* Tass

BTR-50 and OT-62 (Czechoslovakian) APCs, 'FROG-2', 3, and 5 surface-to-surface missile systems, GT-T and MT-L tracked over-snow vehicles, GSP heavy amphibious ferry, Pinguin (on BTR-50 chassis), PVA amphibious crawler tractor, SAM-6 surface-to-surface missile launcher and its radar vehicle, ZSU-23-4 SP AA gun, and the 122mm M1974 SP howitzer. Production of the PT-76 has now been completed.

## Variants
*Model 1:* Is armed with the D-56T gun with no bore evacuator and a long multi-slotted muzzle brake.
*Model 2:* Is armed with the D-56TM gun with a bore evacuator and a double-baffle muzzle brake. The PT-76 Model 2 fitted with a stabilised gun becomes the PT-76B (or Model 4).
*Model 3:* This has a conventional clean barrel.

## Employment
The PT-76 is used by Angola, Benin, PR China (a modified version with an 85mm gun is built in China under the designation of the T-62), Congo, Cuba, Czechoslovakia, Egypt, Equatorial Guinea, Finland, GDR, Guinea, Guinea-Bissau, Hungary, India, Indonesia, Iraq, Israel, Korea (North), Mozambique, Pakistan, Poland, Syria, Uganda, USSR, Yugoslavia, Vietnam.

# T-10M Heavy Tank

USSR

**Armament:** 1×122mm gun, elevation +17°, depression −3° (30 rounds carried)
2×14.5mm KPV MGs — coaxial and AA (1,000 rounds)
**Crew:** 4
**Length:** 10.6m (inc gun), 7.04m (exc gun)
**Width:** 3.566m
**Height:** 2.43m (w/o AA MG)
**G/clearance:** 0.436m
**Weight:** 52,000kg
**G/pressure:** 0.78kg/sq cm
**Engine:** V-2-IS, 12-cylinder, water-cooled diesel 700hp at 2,000rpm
**Speed:** 42km/h (road)
**Range:** 250km (road)
**Fuel:** 900 litres
**Fording:** 1.2m
**V/obstacle:** 0.9m
**Trench:** 3.00m
**Gradient:** 62.5%
**Armour:** 230mm (max)

## Development

After the end of World War 2, development of the IS-3 heavy tank continued and resulted in the IS-4, IS-5, IS-6, IS-7, IS-8, IS-9 and finally the IS-10. The latter was standardised as the T-10 and entered service in 1954/55. The T-10 is distinguishable from the IS-3 by its seven road wheels, larger turret, cut-off corners on the rear hull plate and 12.7mm DShKM coaxial and AA MGs.

The T-10 was followed by the T-10M, this has 14.5mm KPV MGs in place of the 12.7mm DShKM

*T-10M heavy tank without stowage box on turret rear.*

weapons, 122mm gun has a multi-baffle muzzle brake, main armament is stabilised in both planes (horizontal and vertical), NBC system, can be fitted with snorkel for deep fording, and infra-red searchlight to right of main armament and a smaller infra-red searchlight in front of commander's hatch. Some T-10Ms have a stowage box at the turret rear.

The T-10 and T-10M 122mm gun fires separate loading ammunition which accounts for its low rate of fire.

## Employment

Small numbers of T-10 and T-10M heavy tanks remain in service with the USSR.


# IS-3 Heavy Tank

USSR

**Armament:** 1×122mm M1943, elevation +20°, depression −3° (28 rounds carried)
1×7.62mm DTM coaxial MG (1,500 rounds)
1×12.7mm DShKM AA MG (250 rounds)
**Crew:** 4
**Length:** 9.725m (inc gun), 6.77m (exc gun)
**Width:** 3.07m
**Height:** 2.44m (w/o AA MG)
**G/clearance:** 0.46m
**Weight:** 45,800kg (loaded)
**G/pressure:** 0.83kg/sq cm
**Engine:** V-2-IS, V-12 diesel, water-cooled, developing 520hp at 2,000rpm
**Speed:** 37km/h (road)
**Range:** 150km (road)
**Fuel:** 520 litres
**Fording:** 1.30m
**V/obstacle:** 1.00m
**Trench:** 2.50m
**Gradient:** 60%
**Armour:** 20mm-200mm

*IS-3 tank.*

## Development

Further development of the IS-II resulted in the IS-III which entered production in 1945. Main improvements over the earlier vehicle are increased armour arrangement and a new turret without a cupola for the commander. The engine, transmission, suspension and armament were identical to the earlier tank. The IS-4 was built in small numbers after the war and further development of this resulted in the IS-5, IS-6, IS-7, IS-8, IS-9 and finally the IS-10 which was subsequently standardised as the T-10.

**Variants using IS-type chassis:**

*ISU-122 and ISU-152 Assault Guns:* See separate entry.

*310mm M1957 SP Gun:* This was first shown in November 1957, and is based on a lengthened IS chassis with eight road wheels. This weapon is now obsolete.

*420mm M1960 SP Mortar:* This was also shown in November 1957, and has the same chassis as the above. It is now obsolete.

*IS-II-T and IS-III-T:* Either an IS-II or IS-III with its turret removed and stowage boxes fitted to the front of the vehicle. Weight 35,000kg. These are only capable of towing operations.

*'Scamp' ICBM (SS-14):* On IS chassis with eight road wheels.

*'Scrooge' ICBM:* On IS chassis with eight road wheels. It is believed that this was only an experimental missile.

*'SCUD A' and 'SCUD B'.* The 'SCUD A' is launched from a modified IS-III chassis and has a max range of 160km. The longer range 'SCUD B' (range 270km) was originally mounted on a similar chassis but is now launched from a MAZ-543 (8×8) truck.

*FROG-1:* This missile was transported and launched from a modified IS-III chassis but has now been withdrawn from service.

**Employment**

IS-II remains in service with China and Cuba. Neither tank is in front line service with any member of the Warsaw Pact but they are still used for training and held in reserve.

# BRDM-2 Reconnaissance Vehicle  USSR

*BRDM-2.*

**Armament:** 1 × 14.5mm KPVT MG, elevation +30°, depression −5° (500 rounds carried)
1 × 7.62mm PKT coaxial MG (2,000 rounds)
**Crew:** 4
**Length:** 5.75m
**Width:** 2.35m
**Height:** 2.31m
**G/clearance:** 0.463m
**Weight:** 7,000kg
**Track:** 1.84m
**Wheelbase:** 3.1m
**Armour:** 10mm
**Engine:** GAZ-41, 8-cylinder petrol engine developing 140hp at 3,400rpm

**Speed:** 100km/h (road), 10km/h (water)
**Range:** 750km
**Fording:** Amphibious
**V/obstacle:** 0.4m
**Trench:** 1.25m
**Gradient:** 60%
**Armour:** 10mm

**Development/Variants**
The BRDM-2 reconnaissance vehicle has now replaced the earlier BRDM-1 in most front line units and was first seen in public in 1966.

SA-9 'Gaskin' AA missile system on BRDM-2 chassis. Tass

The BRDM-2 is fully amphibious being propelled in the water by a hydrojet at the rear of the vehicle. A trim board is fitted under the nose of the vehicle and this is raised before the vehicle enters the water. The engine is at the rear of the vehicle and there is a winch at the front. It has four auxiliary wheels, two each side; these are lowered by the driver when required and enable the vehicle to cross trenches.

It is fitted with an NBC system and infra-red driving and fighting lights. The turret is the same as that fitted to the BTR-60PB APC and the Czechoslovakian OT-64 Model 2A armoured personnel carrier.

*BRDM-2 ('Sagger'):* This is a basic BRDM-2 with its turret removed and replaced with a launching system for six 'Sagger' ATGW. The six 'Saggers' are raised from within the vehicle complete with their overhead armour cover. In addition to the six 'Saggers' in the ready-to-launch position a further eight are carried internally and reloaded manually.

*BRDM-2 ('Swatter'):* This was first seen in 1973 and is similar in appearance to the above but has four 'Swatters' in the ready to launch position with an additional four missiles being carried internally for reloading. This version of the 'Swatter' is called the 2a, has semi-active infra-red/command guidance and a max range of 3,000m.

*BRDM-2 ('Spandrel'):* This version, sometimes called BRDM-3, was first seen in public during 1977 and has a new turret with four 'Spandrel' (AT-5) ATGWs in the ready-to-launch position with a min of five missiles being carried internally for reloading. The 'Spandrel' has a range of between 2,500 and 4,000m.

*SA-9 'Gaskin':* BRDM-2 chassis with four SA-9 AA missiles in the ready-to-launch position with a possible four missiles being carried externally for manual reloading. The missiles are infra-red homing and have a slant range of about 8,000m and a max altitude of about 5,000m.

*BRDM-2 Rkh:* this fulfils a similar role to the BRDM-1 Rkh vehicle and marks lanes through contaminated areas.

**Employment**
Algeria ('Sagger' and SA-9), Angola, Benin, Bulgaria, Cape-Verde Islands, Central African Republic, Chad, Congo, Egypt ('Sagger' and SA-9), Ethiopia, Equatorial Guinea, GDR (and 'Spandrel' and SA-9), Guinea-Bissau, Guinea, Hungary ('Sagger' and SA-9 only), Iraq (SA-9 on order), Libya, Mali, Malawi, Mozambique, Peru, Poland (and SA-9), Romania (inc 'Sagger'), Sao-Tome Principe, Seychelles, Somalia, Sudan, Syria ('Sagger' and SA-9), USSR (all versions), Vietnam (inc SA-9), Yugoslavia (inc 'Sagger' and SA-9), Yemen Arab Republic (inc SA-9), Zimbabwe, Zambia.

# BRDM-1 Reconnaissance Vehicle     USSR

**Data:** BRDM-1
**Armament:** 1 × 7.62mm SGMB MG (1,250 rounds carried) *and/or*
1 × 12.7mm DShKM MG
**Crew:** 5
**Length:** 5.70m
**Width:** 2.25m
**Height:** 1.90m (w/o armament)
**G/clearance:** 0.315m
**Weight:** 5,600kg (loaded), 5,100kg (empty)
**Track:** 1.6m

**Wheelbase:** 2.80m
**Engine:** GAZ-40P, 6-cylinder, in-line, water-cooled petrol engine developing 90hp at 3,400rpm
**Speed:** 80km/h (road), 9km/h (water)
**Range:** 500km
**Fording:** Amphibious
**V/obstacle:** 0.47m
**Trench:** 1.22m
**Gradient:** 60%
**Armour:** 10mm

## Development/Variants

The BRDM-1 (4×4) reconnaissance vehicle was first seen in public in 1959 but has now been replaced in most front line units by the BRDM-2.

The BRDM-1 is fully amphibious being propelled in the water by a single waterjet at the rear of the hull. Before entering the water a trim vane is erected at the front of the hull and the bilge pumps are switched on.

On either side of the vehicle, between the front and rear wheels, is a pair of belly wheels which are powered, these are lowered to the ground before crossing rough terrain or ditches.

The BRDM-1 is fitted with a central-tyre pressure regulation system but no NBC system.

*BRDM-1 (Rkh):* This is a specialised vehicle and is used to mark lane lines through chemical and radioactive contaminated areas. On the rear decking of the vehicles are two boxes, each containing 25 marker flags each. These flags are fired into the ground whilst the vehicle is moving without the crew leaving the vehicle.

*BRDM-1 with anti-tank missiles:*

*Model A:* This has three 'Snapper' (AT-1) anti-tank missiles carried under light armour. When required for launching the overhead doors slide down to each side of the vehicle. The range of the missiles is 2,500m

*Model B:* This has three 'Swatter' (AT-2) anti-tank missiles carried under light armour. When required for launching the overhead doors slide down to each side of the vehicle, as does an armoured cover at the rear. The range of these missiles is 3,000m.

*BRDM-1 with no armament fitted.*

*Model C:* This carries six 'Sagger' (AT-3) anti-tank missiles under armour. In this version the six missiles are raised complete with their overhead armour for launching. Maximum range is 3,000m.

*BRDM-1 (Command):* This has additional radios and is known as the BRDM-U.

## Employment

Albania, Algeria, Angola, Bulgaria, Congo, Cuba, Czechoslovakia, Ethiopia, GDR, Guinea, Mozambique, Poland, Romania, Sudan, USSR, Yugoslavia and Zambia.

# BA-64 Light Armoured Car                   USSR

**Armament:** 1 × 7.62mm DTM MG
**Crew:** 2
**Length:** 3.66m
**Width:** 1.74m
**Height:** 1.90m
**G/clearance:** 0.21m
**Weight:** 2,400kg
**Wheelbase:** 2.13m
**Track:** 1.448m
**Engine:** GAZ-MM, 4-cylinder, water-cooled, in-line, petrol engine developing 50hp at 2,800rpm
**Speed:** 80km/h (road)
**Range:** 600km
**Fuel:** 90 litres
**Fording:** 0.47m
**V/obstacle:** 0.40m
**Gradient:** 60%
**Armour:** 4mm-15mm

## Development/Employment

The BA-64 armoured car was developed during World War 2 and it is sometimes known as the Bobby. Although it is no longer used by the Russian Army the BA-64 is still used by some satellites including Albania and North Korea. The East German SK-1 armoured car is similar in appearance to the BA-64.

*BA-64 light armoured car.*

# BMP-80 MICV
USSR

In 1980 it was reported that the Group of Soviet Forces in East Germany had taken delivery of a new version of the BMP provisionally called, in the West, the BMP-80.

This is believed to have a similar chassis to the BMP but be fitted with a new two-man turret armed with a cannon, perhaps 30mm in calibre, and a coaxial 7.62mm MG.

The infantry enter and leave the vehicle via a power operated ramp in the rear of the hull. It has also been reported that late production BMPs including some of these supplied to Iran, have been fitted with a power operated ramp at the rear, similar to that installed in Western vehicles such as the M113 and M2.

**Employment**
Believed to be in service with the USSR.


# BMP-1 MICV
USSR

**Armament:** 1 × 73mm gun, elevation +33°, depression −4° (40 rounds carried)
1 × 7.62mm coaxial MG (2,000 rounds)
1 × 'Sagger' ATGW launcher (4 missiles carried inside)
**Crew:** 3 + 8
**Length:** 6.74m
**Width:** 2.94m
**Height:** 2.15m
**G/clearance:** 0.39m
**Weight:** 13,500kg (loaded), 12,500kg (empty)
**G/pressure:** 0.57kg/sq cm
**Armour:** 23mm (max)
**Engine:** V-6 6-cylinder diesel developing 290hp at 2,000rpm
**Speed:** 80km/h (road), 6-8km/h (water)
**Range:** 500km
**Fuel:** 460 litres
**Fording:** Amphibious
**V/obstacle:** 0.8m
**Trench:** 2m
**Gradient:** 60%

**Development**
The BMP-1 was first seen in 1967 and in the absence of any known Soviet designation was called

the M1967 APC and then the BMP-76B. The vehicle has now replaced the BTR-50 series in most front line Soviet units and has also been exported in large numbers.

The driver is seated at the front left with the commander to his rear and the engine compartment to his right. The one-man turret is in the centre of the vehicle and is armed with a 73mm smooth bore gun that is fed by an automatic loader, this fires HEAT-FS and HEAT-FRAG rounds and has a max rate of fire of 8rpm. Mounted coaxial with the main armament is a 7.62mm MG and mounted over the 73mm gun is a launcher rail for an AT-3 'Sagger' ATGW.

The troop compartment is at the rear of the BMP-1 and the infantry enter and leave via two doors in the rear of the hull. There are four hatches in the roof of the troop compartment and firing ports and roof mounted periscopes are also provided.

The BMP-1 is fully amphibious being propelled in the water by its tracks and is fitted with a NBC system and a full range of night vision equipment for the commander, gunner and driver.

**Variants**
*BMP-2:* Current production model with minor improvements including a lengthened bow, also called BMP-A.
*BMP M1974 (command):* Has additional radio equipment, firing ports welded shut.

*BMP-1 MICV of the East German Army.*

BMP 1975 (surveillance): Larger turret with 7.62mm MG, battlefield radar to turret rear.
BMP 1976 (Reconnaissance): Similar to M1975 but has larger two man turret with 73mm gun.
BMP 1977 (command): Command post vehicle.
BMP 1978 (command): Command and communications vehicle, large telescopic antenna, turret has no armament.

## Employment

Afghanistan, Algeria, Cuba, Czechoslovakia, Egypt, Ethiopia, GDR, Hungary, Iraq, Iran, North Korea, Libya Poland, Syria and USSR.

# BTR-70 APC                                          USSR

**Armament:** 1 × 14.5 KPV MG, elevation +30°, depression −5° (500 rounds carried)
1 × 7.62mm PKT coaxial MG (2,000 rounds)
**Crew:** 2 + 14
**Length:** 7.85m
**Width:** 2.8m
**Height:** 2.165m (hull top), 2.435m (turret top)
**Wheelbase:** 1.40m + 1.775m + 1.40m
**Weight:** 11,000kg
**Speed:** 80km/h (max road), 10km/h (max water)
**Fording:** Amphibious
**V/obstacle:** 0.4m
**Trench:** 2.1m
**Gradient:** 60%
*Note:* Above specification is provisional.

## Development

During the November 1980 parade held in Red Square, Moscow, a new 8×8 APC, provisionally called the BTR-70 in the West, made its first public appearance.

This is very similar to the current BTR-60PB but has a redesigned hull with no troop doors in either side, larger tyres and a different wheelbase with a distinct gap between the second and third axles. The BTR-70 has the same turret as the BTR-60PB but is more likely to be powered by a diesel engine in place of the two petrol engines of the earlier vehicle.

The BTR-70 is fully amphibious being propelled in the water by a water jet at the rear of the hull and is fitted with infra-red night vision equipment, NBC system and a central tyre pressure regulation system.

## Employment

In service with the USSR.

# BMD Airborne Combat Vehicle              USSR

**Armament:** 1 × 73mm gun, elevation +33°, depression −4° (40 rounds carried)
3 × 7.62mm PKT MGs — coaxial and two bow (2,000 rounds for coaxial)
1 × 'Sagger' ATGW launcher (3 missiles)
**Crew:** 7
**Length:** 5.41m
**Width:** 2.55m
**Height:** 1.77m
**G/clearance:** 0.1-0.45m
**Weight:** 8,000kg (loaded)
**G/pressure:** 0.61kg/sq cm
**Armour:** 6mm-25mm
**Engine:** V-6 liquid cooled diesel developing 290hp
**Speed:** 80km/h (road), 10km/h (water)
**Range:** 320km
**Fuel:** 300 litres
**Fording:** Amphibious
**V/obstacle:** 0.8m
**Trench:** 1.6m
**Gradient:** 60%

## Development

The BMD airborne combat vehicle entered service with Soviet Airborne Rifle Divisions and was seen for the first time in public in 1973. It was used on a large scale during the invasion of Afghanistan in 1980.

The BMD has the same turret as fitted to the BMP MICV and its seven-man crew consists of commander, driver and bow machine gunner at the front, gunner in the turret and senior gunner, grenade launcher and his assistant at the rear. The engine and transmission is at the very rear of the BMD.

The vehicle is fully amphibious being propelled in the water by two waterjets. Before entering the water a trim vane is erected at the front of the hull and the bilge pumps switched on.

Standard equipment includes an NBC system, night vision equipment, firing ports, smoke laying system and a fire extinguishing system.

An unusual feature of the BMD is its independent suspension which allows the driver to adjust the suspension to give a ground clearance of between 0.1 and 0.45m

### Variants

A command version is in service. This has a longer chassis with six instead of five road wheels each side and has no turret.

### Employment

In service only with the USSR.

BMD airborne combat vehicle. Tass

# BTR-60P   APC

**Armament:** 1 × 7.62mm SGMB MG (1,250 rounds carried)
**Crew:** 2 + 16
**Length:** 7.56m
**Width:** 2.825m
**Height:** 2.06m (w/o MG)
**G/clearance:** 0.475m
**Track:** 2.37m
**Wheelbase:** 1.35m + 1.525m + 1.35m
**Weight:** 9,980kg (loaded)
**Armour:** 10mm
**Engines:** 2 × GAZ-49B, 6-cylinder, water-cooled, in-line, petrol developing 90hp at 3,400rpm (each)

**Speed:** 80km/h (road), 10km/h (water)
**Range:** 500km
**Fuel:** 290 litres
**Fording:** Amphibious
**V/obstacle:** 0.40m
**Trench:** 2.00m
**Gradient:** 60%
**Armour:** 10mm (max)

BTR-60P (8×8) APCs come ashore from a landing craft. Tass

## Development
The BTR-60P was first seen in public in November 1961 and has now replaced the BTR-152 (6 × 6) APC in most front line Soviet units. All eight wheels of the BTR-60P are powered with steering being power-assisted on the front four wheels. The vehicle is fully amphibious, being propelled in the water by a single hydrojet at the rear of the vehicle, two smaller jets providing steering. A small trim board is erected before entering the water. The tyre pressures of all eight wheels can be adjusted from a central control to suit current ground conditions. Infra-red driving lights are fitted, later models have infra-red searchlights and most models are fitted with winches.

## Variants
*BTR-60P:* This was the original open-topped version. Some models have metal hoops over the troop compartment for supporting a canvas cover. The crew are provided with small half-doors in the sides of the vehicle and there are firing ports. Armament consists of a single 12.7mm MG and between one and three 7.62mm MGs, for example one 7.62mm MG next to the 12.7mm MG at the front and one 7.62mm MG either side of the crew compartment.
*BTR-60PA:* This version has overhead armour and three firing ports either side. There are at least three versions of this vehicle, each differing slightly in the arrangement of their roof hatches. Armament

normally consists of a single 7.62mm or 12.7mm MG mounted just behind the front two hatches. The BTR-60PA is fitted with an NBC system.
*BTR-60PB:* This is a BTR-60PA fitted with a small MG turret mounting a 14.5mm and a 7.62mm MG. The turret has a traverse of 360°, and elevation is of +30° and depression −10° and is also fitted to the BRDM-2.
**Command:** The command model has additional communications equipment and is known as the BTR-60PU. The forward air control model has the armament removed from the turret and replaced by a Plexiglass observation window; a generator is mounted on the rear deck.
*Romania:* The Romanians build a version of the BTR-60PB called the TAB-72, this has a different turret with the same armament but the weapons have a higher elevation. Whereas the BTR-60 series are powered by two 90hp petrol engine the TAB-72 has two 140hp petrol engines. There is also a version of TAB-72 which has no turret but is fitted with an 82mm mortar that fires through the roof.

## Employment
Afghanistan, Algeria, Angola, Bulgaria, Chad, Congo, Cuba, Ethiopia, Finland, GDR, Guinea, Guinea-Bissau, Hungary, Iran, Iraq, Israel, North Korea, Libya, Mali, Mongolia, Mozambique, Romania, Somalia, Syria, USSR, Vietnam and Yugoslavia.

# BTR-50P APC                                          USSR

**Armament:** 1 × 7.62mm SGMB MG (1,250 rounds carried)
**Crew:** 2 + 20
**Length:** 7.08m
**Width:** 3.14m
**Height:** 1.97m (w/o MG)
**G/clearance:** 0.37m
**Weight:** 14,200kg (loaded)
**G/pressure:** 0.51kg/sq cm
**Engine:** Model V-6, 6-cylinder, in-line, water-cooled diesel developing 240hp at 1,800rpm
**Speed:** 44km/h (road), 11km/h (water)
**Range:** 400km
**Fuel:** 400 litres
**Fording:** Amphibious
**V/obstacle:** 1.10m
**Trench:** 2.80m
**Gradient:** 70%
**Armour:** 10mm-14mm

## Development
The BTR-50 was developed from the chassis of the PT-76 light amphibious tank and was first seen in 1957. The BTR-50 series are fully amphibious being propelled in the water by two water jets at the rear of the vehicle. Later models of the vehicle are fitted with NBC equipment and infra-red lights. Czechoslovakia has built a similar model of the BTR-

50PK under the designation of the OT-62. There is a separate entry for the latter under Czechoslovakia. Soviet-built vehicles can be distinguished from Czechoslovakian built versions as the former, in the case of the BTR-50PK, have a distinct chamfer between the sides and top of the hull.

## Variants
*BTR-50P:* This was the first model to enter service and it has an open top, 57mm, 76mm and 85mm anti-tank guns can be carried on the rear decking.
*BTR-50PA:* Is BTR-50P without loading ramps at the rear and is often armed with a 14.5mm KPV MG.
*BTR-50PK:* This model has overhead protection and is provided with rectangular roof hatches. It has a projecting bay on the left. It has an improved vision device on the right front, and is often fitted with infra-red driving equipment and an infra-red searchlight. One radio aerial is fitted.
*BTR-50PU Armoured Command Vehicle:* This model has overhead protection. There are two models. Model 1 has a projecting bay on the left, Model 2 has two projecting bays. Both Model 1 and Model 2 have a hatch on the left bay, a central rotating cupola just behind the driver, two dome ventilators and two oval-shaped hatches on the roof. There are normally five radio aerials on the roof. On the Model 2 the right bay has no hatch cover and no infra-red

*BTR-50PK APC of the East German Army.*

searchlight. The Model 1 has an infra-red searchlight to the right of the driver. Both models have additional stowage boxes on the rear deck.

*Specialised models:* These include an ambulance, mortar team carrying vehicle, MTP technical support vehicle and MTK mine clearing vehicle.

**Employment**
Afghanistan, Albania, Algeria, Angola (+OT-62), Bulgaria (+OT-62), Congo, Cyprus, Czechoslovakia (OT-62 only), Egypt (and OT-62), Finland, GDR, Guinea, Guinea-Bissau, India (+OT-62), Iran, Israel (+OT-62), Iraq (+OT-62), North Korea, Libya (+OT-62), Morocco (OT-62 only), Poland (OT-62 only), Romania, Somalia, Sudan (+OT-62), Syria, USSR, Vietnam and Yugoslavia.

# MT-LB Multi-Purpose Tracked Vehicle     USSR

**Armament:** 1 × 7.62mm MG, elevation +30°, depression −5°
**Crew:** 2 + 11
**Length:** 6.454m
**Width:** 2.85m
**Height:** 1.865m
**G/clearance:** 0.4m
**Weight:** 11,900kg (loaded), 9,700kg (empty)
**G/pressure:** 0.46kg/sq cm
**Engine:** YaMZ-238V 8-cylinder diesel developing 240hp at 2,100rpm
**Speed:** 61.5km/h (road), 6km/h (water)
**Range:** 500km
**Fuel:** 450 litres
**Fording:** Amphibious
**V/obstacle:** 0.7m
**Trench:** 2.7m
**Gradient:** 60%
**Armour:** 7mm

**Development**
The MT-LB multi-purpose tracked vehicle is based on the chassis of the unarmoured MT-L amphibious vehicle and entered service in the late 1960s. For a short period it was known as the M-1970 multi-purpose tracked vehicle.

Typical roles of the MT-LB include use as a cargo carrier, APC, command or radio vehicle and a prime mover for 100mm anti-tank guns or 122mm howitzer. Max towed load is 6,500kg.

The MT-LB is fully amphibious being propelled in the water by its tracks, before entering the water a trim vane is erected at the front of the hull and the bilge pumps switched on. All vehicles have a NBC system and infra-red night vision equipment and firing ports are provided in each side of the hull and in each of the rear doors.

*MT-LB multi-purpose tracked vehicles towing 100mm T-12 anti-tank guns.*

## Variants

*MT-LBV:* This is the basic vehicle with its original 350mm wide tracks replaced by 565mm wide tracks which reduce ground pressure to 0.27kg/sq cm, making the vehicle ideal for use in snow or swampy conditions.

*MT-LBU:* This is the command version and has additional radios, generator and land navigation system. When being used in the static role a tent can be erected at the rear.

*MT-SON:* Basic MT-LB fitted with Pork Trough fire control system on roof.

## Employment

In service with Bulgaria, GDR, Hungary, Poland and the USSR.

# BTR152 APC                                      USSR

**Armament:** 1 × 7.62mm or 12.7mm MG (1,250 rounds carried)
**Crew:** 2 + 17
**Length:** 6.83m
**Width:** 2.32m
**Height:** 2.05m (w/o MG)
**G/clearance:** 0.295m
**Weight:** 8,950kg (loaded)
**Track:** 1.742m (front), 1.72m (rear)
**Wheelbase:** 3.3m + 1.13m
**Engine:** ZIL-123, 6-cylinder, in-line, petrol engine developing 110hp at 3,000rpm
**Speed:** 75km/h (road)
**Range:** 780km
**Fuel:** 300 litres
**Fording:** 0.80m
**V/obstacle:** 0.60m
**Trench:** 0.69m
**Gradient:** 55%
**Armour:** 6mm-13.6mm

## Development/Variants

The first models of the BTR-152 (6 × 6) APC appeared in 1949 and were based on the chassis of the ZIL-151 (6 × 6) truck chassis, later models, from and including the BTR-152V1, were based on the ZIL-157 (6 × 6) truck chassis. The BTR-152 APC has been replaced in most Soviet units by the BTR-60P (8 × 8) series of APC but it is still used for second line duties within the Warsaw Pact and large numbers remain in service in other parts of the world. In addition to being used as an APC it can also carry mortar teams, tow heavy mortar and anti-tank guns, and tow minelaying equipment.

*BTR-152:* First model, ZIL-151 chassis, open top, no winch and no central tyre pressure regulation system.

*BTR-152V1:* Second model to enter service, ZIL-157 truck chassis, open top, front mounted winch, central tyre pressure regulation system with external air lines.

*BTR-152V2:* Internal air-lines, no winch.

*BTR-152V3:* Internal air-lines, winch, infra-red driving lights.

*BTR-152K:* This is a BTR-152V3 with overhead armour. This increases the height of the vehicle and its loaded weight is 9,200kg.

*BTR-152U:* This is a BTR-152 converted into the command role. The roof is higher (2.72m) and additional radios have been installed.

*BTR-152A with twin 14.5mm guns:* This is a BTR-152V fitted with twin 14.5mm MG in a powered mount with an elevation of +80° and a depression of −5°, traverse is 360°. The MGs are KPVs and have an effective AA range of 1,400m. The vehicle weighs 9,600kg, height is 2.80m and it has a crew of four. The Egyptians have some BTR-152s fitted with 4 12.7mm MG53s, There is also reported to be an anti-tank model with 'Sagger' ATGWs.

## Employment

Afghanistan, Albania, Algeria, Angola, Bulgaria (reserve), Chad, China (Type 56), Congo, Cuba, Cyprus (unconfirmed), Egypt, Ethiopia, Equatorial Guinea, GDR, Guinea, Guinea-Bissau, Hungary (reserve), India, Indonesia, Iran, Iraq, Israel, Korea (Democratic People's Republic), Mali, Mongolia, Mozambique, Poland (reserve), Romania (reserve), Somalia, Sri Lanka, Syria, Sudan, Tanzania, USSR, Yemen Arab Republic (North), Yemen Arab Republic (South), Yugoslavia, Vietnam and Zaire.

*BTR-152V2 APC with rear door open.*
Michael Ledford

# BTR-40 APC

**Armament:** 1 × 7.62mm SGMB MG (1,250 rounds carried)
**Crew:** 2 + 8
**Length:** 5.00m
**Width:** 1.90m
**Height:** 1.75m (w/o MG)
**G/clearance:** 0.275m
**Weight:** 5,300kg (loaded)
**Track:** 1.588m (front), 1.6m (rear)
**Wheelbase:** 2.70m
**Engine:** GAZ-40, 6-cylinder, in-line, water-cooled petrol engine developing 80hp at 3,400rpm
**Speed:** 80km/h (road)
**Range:** 285km (road)
**Fuel:** 120 litres
**Fording:** 0.80m
**V/obstacle:** 0.47m
**Trench:** 0.70m (with channels)
**Gradient:** 58%
**Armour:** 8mm-13mm

BTR-40 APC.

### Development

The BTR-40 was developed after World War 2 and was introduced into service in 1950. It is essentially a short wheel base version of the GAZ-63 truck chassis fitted with an armoured body. Although called an APC it is widely used in the reconnaissance role.

The BTR-40 is fitted with a winch but is not fitted with an NBC system, infra-red night vision equipment or a central tyre pressure regulation system.

### Variants

*BTR-40:* This is a basic vehicle and has no roof. The data above relates to this version. The crew can fire their personal weapons through the firing ports in the sides and the rear of the vehicle.
*BTR-40K:* This model has overhead armour. This consists of two sets of hinged doors and in some vehicles these overhead doors have been provided with firing ports.

*BTR-40A with twin 14.5mm HMGs:* This is the basic BTR-40 fitted with twin 14.5mm KPV heavy MGs in a power-operated mount with a traverse of 360°, elevation between −5° and +80°. The guns have an effective AA range of 1,400m and can also be used against ground targets. The vehicle weighs 6,000kg, has a crew of four, and a height of 2.50m
*BTR-40 ('Sagger'):* East Germany has mounted triple 'Sagger' launchers on a BTR-40 as a training device.
*BTR-40kh:* This model is fitted with equipment enabling it to dispense marking pennants in nuclear contaminated area.

### Employment

Afghanistan, Albania, Algeria, Angola, Bulgaria, China (Type 55), Cuba, Egypt, Ethiopia, GDR, Guinea, Guinea-Bissau, Indonesia, Iran, Israel, North Korea, Laos, Libya, Mali, Mozambique, Somalia, Sudan, Syria, Tanzania, USSR, Vietnam, Yemen Arab Republic (North), Yemen Arab Republic (South) and Yugoslavia.

# 203mm SP Howitzer

The Soviet Union has recently deployed a 203mm tracked SP howitzer but no further details are available, but it may be based on a lengthened chassis of the 152mm M1973 SP howitzer.

# 152mm M1973 SP Howitzer

**Armament:** 1 × 152mm howitzer, elevation +65°, depression −3° (30 rounds carried)
1 × 7.62mm AA MG
30 rounds of 152mm ammunition
**Crew:** 3-5
**Length:** 7.8m (gun forward), 7.14m (hull)
**Width:** 3.2m
**Height:** 2.72m
**G/clearance:** 0.45m

**Weight:** 23,000kg
**Engine:** V-12 diesel developing 520hp
**Speed:** 50km/h
**Range:** 300km
**Fuel:** 500 litres
**Fording:** 1.1m
**V/obstacle:** 1.1m
**Trench:** 2.8m
**Gradient:** 60%

### Development

The 152mm M1973 SP howitzer, also known as the SAU-152, entered service in the early 1970s and uses many components of the SA-4 'Ganef' SAM chassis.

Main armament is a modified version of the towed D-20 gun howitzer which is mounted in a turret with a traverse of 360°. An automatic/semi-automatic loader is believed to be installed and the barrel is fitted with a double baffle muzzle brake with a fume extractor to its immediate rear. It fires a HE projectile to a max range of 18,500m, an extended range projectile to 24,000m or an HE RAP to a range of 37,000m.

The M1973 has no amphibious capability but is fitted with infra-red night vision equipment and a NBC system.

### Variants

There are no known variants of the M1973.

### Employment

GDR, Iraq, Libya and USSR.

*152mm M1973 SP howitzer from the rear.*
US Army

# 122mm M1974 SP Howitzer

USSR

**Armament:** 1 × 122mm howitzer, elevation +70°, depression −3° (40 rounds carried)
**Crew:** 4
**Length:** 7.3m
**Width:** 2.85m
**Height:** 2.4m
**G/clearance:** 0.46m
**Weight:** 16,000kg
**G/pressure:** 0.50kg/sq cm
**Engine:** Model YaMZ-238V V-8 diesel developing 240hp
**Speed:** 60km/h (road), 4.5km/h (water)
**Range:** 500km (road)
**Fuel:** 550 litres
**Fording:** Amphibious
**V/obstacle:** 1.1m
**Trench:** 3m
**Gradient:** 60%

### Development

The M1974 122mm SP howitzer, also known as the SAU-122, was first seen in public during a parade held in Poland in July 1974. It uses many automotive components, including the engine, transmission, suspension and tracks of the MT-LB multi-purpose armoured vehicle.

Main armament consists of a modified 122mm D-30 towed howitzer mounted in the turret at the rear of the vehicle that can be traversed through a full 360°. It has a semi-automatic sliding wedge breech block, power rammer, fume extractor and a double baffle muzzle brake. It fires an HE projectile to a range of 15,300m as well as chemical, HE, HEAT-FS, illuminating, leaflet and smoke. More recently a RAP has been introduced with a max range of 21,900m.

The M1974 is fully amphibious being propelled in the water by waterjets. Standard equipment includes an NBC system, infra-red night vision equipment for both the driver and commander.

### Variants

*ACRV-2:* Armoured Command and Reconnaissance Vehicle issued on the scale of one per battery of six M1974s.
*Mine clearing vehicle:* Fitted with roof-mounted rocket-propelled mine clearing system similar to British developed Giant Viper.

### Employment

Algeria, Angola, Czechoslovakia, Ethiopia, GDR, Hungary, Iraq, Libya, Poland, Syria and USSR.

*122mm M1974 SP howitzers of the Hungarian Army.* Franz Kosar

# ISU-122 and ISU-152 Assault Guns      USSR

**Data:** ISU-122 with A19S 122mm gun
**Armament:** 1 × 122mm M1931/44 (A-19S) gun,
elevation +16°, depression −3°, total traverse 14°
(30 rounds carried)
1 × 12.7mm M1938 DShKM AA MG (250 rounds)
**Crew:** 5
**Length:** 10.06m (inc gun), 6.77m (exc gun)
**Width:** 3.07m
**Height:** 2.47m (w/o AA MG)
**G/clearance:** 0.46m
**Weight:** 46,500kg (loaded)
**G/pressure:** 0.84kg/sq cm
**Engine:** Model V-2 IS, V-12 diesel, water-cooled,
developing 520hp at 2,100rpm
**Speed:** 37km/h (road)
**Range:** 150km (road)
**Fuel:** 500 litres
**Fording:** 1.30m
**V/obstacle:** 1.00m
**Trench:** 2.50m
**Gradient:** 60%
**Armour:** 19mm-110mm

**Development/Variants**
*ISU-122:* The ISU-122 SP gun entered service in
1943 and like the ISU-152 is based on the chassis
of the IS-2 heavy tank.

The first ISU-122s were armed with the M-1931/
44 (A-19S) gun which had the wartime designation
of the M-1944 and was developed from the towed
M-1931/37 (A-19). This weapon had a manually
operated screw-type breech block that reduced its
rate of fire to 3rpm.

This was followed in production in 1944 by the
ISU-122A (called ISU-122S by Soviets) armed with
the 122mm D25S gun, this had the wartime
designation of the M-1943 and was developed from
122mm M1943 (D-25) tank gun installed in the IS-2
and IS-3 heavy tanks. This had a semi-automatic
vertical sliding wedge breechblock and a max rate of
fire of 6rpm could be achieved.

Both weapons fired separate loading ammunition
with the HE projectile weighing 25.5kg, max range
was 13,400m.

*ISU-122A assault gun.*

The ISU-122 is distinguishable from the
ISU-122A by having no muzzle brake or bore
evacuator.
*ISU-152:* This has a similar hull to the ISU-122. It is
armed with a 152mm assault gun M1937/43
(ML-20S) which has an elevation of +20°, a
depression of −3°, total traverse being 10°. Only 20
rounds of 152mm ammunition are carried. The gun
is shorter than those fitted to the ISU-122, total
length including gun being 9.05m.
*Recovery Vehicles based on ISU chassis:* There are
five basic models, and all have their guns removed
and plated over.
*Model A:* This is used for the towing role and weighs
41,500kg.
*Model B:* This is similar to Model A but has a cargo
platform and a jib crane. Some models have a spade
at the rear and are fitted with a snorkel for deep
wading. Loaded weight is 44,000kg and height
3.00m.
*Model C:* This is similar to Model B but has a winch
and spade. Weight 45,000kg, length 7.825m
*Model D:* This is similar to Model C and is capable of
being fitted with a snorkel. There are two bars at the
front of the vehicle for pushing damaged tanks.
Weight 45,500kg, length 8.325m
*Model E:* This is a modified Model C. It has an A
frame spade and a jib crane, loaded weight is
45,500kg.

**Employment**
In service with Algeria (ISU-122 and ISU-152),
China (ISU-122 and ISU-152), Egypt (ISU-152), Iraq
(ISU-122), Syria (ISU-122 and ISU-152) and
Vietnam (ISU-122). There is a possibility that the
vehicles used by all these countries are in fact ARVs
and not SP guns. They are held in reserve by
members of the Warsaw Pact who also use the
ARV models.

# SU-100 Assault Gun

**Armament:** 1 × 100mm M1944 (D10S) gun,
elevation +17°, depression −2° (postwar SU-100s
have an elevation of +20° and a depression of −3°),
total traverse 16° (34 rounds carried)
**Crew:** 4
**Length:** 9.45m (inc gun), 6.19m (exc gun)
**Width:** 3.05m
**Height:** 2.245m
**G/clearance:** 0.4m
**Weight:** 31,611kg (loaded)
**G/pressure:** 0.82kg/sq cm
**Engine:** V-2-34M, 12-cylinder diesel, developing
500hp at 1,800rpm *OR* V-2-2411, 12-cylinder
diesel, developing 530hp at 2,400rpm
**Speed:** 55km/h (road)
**Range:** 300km
**Fuel:** 614 litres (inc 4 external tanks)
**Fording:** 1.3m
**V/obstacle:** 0.73m
**Trench:** 2.5m
**Gradient:** 60%
**Armour:** 10mm-78mm

## Development/Variants

The SU-100 was developed from the earlier SU-85.
The SU-100 is recognisable from the SU-85 as the
latter has a shorter 85mm gun and no commander's
cupola on the right of the superstructure. Another
wartime vehicle was the SU-122, none of which
remain in service. Most SU-85s were converted into
SU-100s or ARVs, or used for training.

The 100mm gun of the SU-100 is the same as
that fitted to the T-54 MBT and fires the same
ammunition as a number of Soviet field and AA
guns. Many postwar SU-100s have been fitted with
an additional stowage box on the right side of the
superstructure.

The SU-85 recovery vehicle is designated

*SU-100 assault gun.*

SU-85-T and is simply a SU-85 with the gun
removed and plated over. The SU-100 recovery
vehicle is similar to the SU-85-T and is designated
SU-100-T. The SU-85T is the more common of the
two models, both models may be seen with or
without winches fitted. There is also a command
model of the SU-100. This is similar to the
SU-100-T.

There is also a SU-85 with the gun removed and
plated over and a hydraulically operated dozer blade
mounted on the front.

## Employment

In service with Albania, Algeria, China, Cuba, Egypt,
Iraq, North Korea, Mongolia, Romania, North Yemen
and Yugoslavia. It is also held in reserve by most
members of the Warsaw Pact.

# ASU-85 Airportable SP Anti-Tank Gun

USSR

**Armament:** 1 × 85mm gun, elevation +15°,
depression −4°, total traverse 12° (40 rounds
carried)
1 × 7.62mm PKT coaxial MG (2,000 rounds)
**Crew:** 4
**Length:** 8.49m (inc gun), 6m (exc gun)
**Width:** 2.80m
**Height:** 2.10m
**G/clearance:** 0.40m
**Weight:** 15,500kg (loaded)
**G/pressure:** 0.50kg/sq cm
**Engine:** Model V-6, 6-cylinder in line, diesel,
developing 240hp at 1,800rpm
**Speed:** 45km/h (road)
**Range:** 260km (road)
**Fuel:** 250 litres
**Fording:** 1.10m
**V/obstacle:** 1.10m
**Trench:** 2.80m

**Gradient:** 70%
**Armour:** 10mm-40mm

## Development

The ASU-85 was developed in the late 1950s and
seen in public for the first time in 1962. It is used
only by airborne divisions and issued on the scale of
18 per division.

The barrel of the 85mm gun has a fume extractor
fitted two-thirds of the way along the barrel, and it is
also fitted with a double baffle muzzle brake. This
gun fires HE, APHE and HVAP rounds, and its rate of
fire is about 3-4rpm. The ASU-85 has a full range of
night vision equipment and many have recently been
fitted with a 12.7mm AA MG.

## Employment

Used only by the GDR, Poland and the USSR.

*ASU-85.* Tass

# SU-76 SP Gun

## USSR

**Armament:** 1 × 76.2mm M1942/43 gun, elevation +25°, depression −5° traverse 20° left and 12° right (60 rounds carried)
1 × 7.62mm Degtyarev MG
**Crew:** 4
**Length:** 5m
**Width:** 2.74m
**Height:** 2.1m
**G/clearance:** 0.32m
**Weight:** 11,200kg loaded
**G/pressure:** 0.57kg/sq cm
**Armour:** 10mm-35mm
**Engines:** 2 × GAZ-202, 6-cylinder, in-line, water-cooled petrol engines developing 70hp at 3,400rpm (each)
**Speed:** 45km/h (road)
**Range:** 360km (road)
**Fuel:** 400 litres
**Fording:** 0.9m
**V/obstacle:** 0.65m
**Trench:** 2m
**Gradient:** 60%

### Development/Variants
The SU-76 was developed during World War 2 as a tank destroyer and was based on a lengthened T-70 light tank chassis. The SU-76 was however quickly relegated to the infantry support role as its armour was very thin and the better SU-85 was entering service.

There were a number of slightly different versions of the SU-76: model with the gun in the centre of the vehicle; model with the gun to the left (data above relates to this model). This model could also be seen with a slightly different armour arrangement at the rear, and a model with fully enclosed turret. Some SU-76s were fitted with two GAZ-203 engines of 85hp, these being designated SU-76M. An anti-aircraft version was designated the SU-37. It is now obsolete. The East Germans have modified a number of SU-76s into armoured workshop and recovery vehicles. These modifications include the fitting of a new EM-6 six-cylinder diesel developing 120hp at 2,000rpm. Armament deleted, external stowage boxes added and internal equipment including a lathe, forge and welding equipment.

### Employment
Albania, China, GDR (workshop role), North Korea, Yugoslavia and Vietnam.

*SU-76 SP gun.*

# ASU-57 Airportable SP Anti-Tank Gun
## USSR

**Armament:** 1 × 57mm gun, elevation +12°, depression −5°, traverse 8° left and right (30 rounds carried)
**Crew:** 3
**Length:** 4.995m (inc gun), 3.48m (hull)
**Width:** 2.086m
**Height:** 1.18m
**G/clearance:** 0.204m
**Weight:** 3,350kg
**G/pressure:** 0.35kg/sq cm
**Engine:** Model M-20E 4-cylinder petrol developing 55hp at 3,600rpm
**Speed:** 45km/h
**Range:** 250km
**Fuel:** 140 litres
**Fording:** 0.7m
**V/obstacle:** 0.5m
**Trench:** 1.4m
**Gradient:** 60%
**Armour:** 6mm

### Development/Variants
The ASU-57 was developed for the use of airborne troops and was first seen in public in 1957. It can be para-dropped from transport aircraft and is issued on the scale of 54 per division.

The original model of the ASU-57 was of steel, weighed 5,400kg and was powered by a ZIL-123 6-cylinder petrol engine developing 110hp at 2,900rpm. The data above relates to the late production model which is of aluminium construction and much lighter.

There are two types of gun fitted, the Ch-51 which has a long thin multi-slotted muzzle brake and the Ch-51M with a double baffle muzzle brake. The gun fires fixed APHE, HE and HVAP rounds and has a max rate of fire of 6-10rpm.

### Employment
USSR and Yugoslavia.

*ASU-57 airportable SP anti-tank gun with Ch-51M gun.* Canadian Armed Forces

# ZSU-30-6 SP AA Gun
## USSR

The USSR is expected to deploy a new SP AA gun by 1982 to replace the ZSU-23-4 which has now been in service for some 20 years. This weapon has been given the provisional designation of the ADMG 680 by the USA with Soviet designation believed to be the ZSU-30-6. It is believed to be armed with a six-barrelled 30mm cannon with a max range of 3,800m and be fitted with an all weather fire control system incorporating a laser rangefinder.

# ZSU-23-4 SP AA Gun System

## USSR

**Armament:** 4 × 23mm automatic cannon, elevation +85°, depression −4°, traverse 360° (2,000 rounds carried)
**Crew:** 4
**Length:** 6.54m
**Width:** 2.95m
**Height:** 2.25m (w/o radar)
**G/clearance:** 0.40m
**Weight:** 19,000kg (loaded)
**G/pressure:** 0.69kg/sq cm
**Engine:** V-6R, 6-cylinder, in-line, water-cooled diesel developing 280hp
**Speed:** 44km/h (road)
**Range:** 260km
**Fuel:** 250 litres
**Fording:** 1.07m
**V/obstacle:** 1.07m
**Trench:** 2.80m
**Gradient:** 60%
**Armour:** 10mm-15mm

### Development

The ZSU-23-4 SP AA gun, known in the USSR as the Shilka, was seen in public for the first time at the parade held in Moscow in November 1965. The chassis, which uses automotive components of the PT-76 light amphibious tank, is almost identical to

*ZSU-23-4 with its radar up.* US Army

that used for the SA-6 'Gainful' SAM system. In recent conflicts in the Middle East, the ZSU-23-4 has proved to be a highly effective weapon system, especially when used in conjunction with surface-to-air missile systems such as the SA-6.

Main armament consists of four 23mm water-cooled cannon with a cyclic rate of fire of 800-1,000 rounds/barrel/min, although normally bursts of three to five, five to ten or a max of 50 rounds are fired. The guns fire API-T and HEI-T rounds with a muzzle velocity of 970m/sec. Max effective range in the AA role is 3,000m and max effective range in the ground role is 2,500m.

Mounted on the turret rear is the Gun Dish radar which first detects and then locks on to the target, but optical sights are also provided.

Standard equipment includes an overpressure NBC system and infra-red night vision equipment for the driver.

### Variants

There are no variants of the ZSU-23-4 but there are minor differences between production batches.

### Employment

Afghanistan, Algeria, Angola, Bulgaria, Cuba, Czechoslovakia, Egypt, Ethiopia, Finland, GDR, Hungary, India, Iran, Iraq, Libya, Mozambique, Nigeria, North Korea, Peru, Poland, Romania, Somalia, Syria, USSR, Vietnam, Yemen (North), Yemen (South) and Yugoslavia.

# ZSU-57-2 SP AA Gun

## USSR

**Armament:** 2 × 57mm AA guns (316 rounds carried)
**Crew:** 6
**Length:** 8.48m (inc guns), 7.43m (exc guns)
**Width:** 3.27m
**Height:** 2.75m
**G/clearance:** 0.425m
**Weight:** 28,100kg (loaded)
**G/pressure:** 0.63kg/sq cm
**Engine:** Model V-54, V-12, water-cooled diesel, developing 520hp at 2,000rpm
**Speed:** 50km/h (road)
**Range:** 420km (road) (595km with auxiliary tanks)
**Fuel:** 812 litres (+400 litres auxiliary fuel)
**Fording:** 1.40m
**V/obstacle:** 0.80m
**Trench:** 2.70m
**Gradient:** 60%
**Armour:** 15mm maximum

### Development/Variants

The ZSU-57-2 was developed in the 1950s and was first seen in public during a parade held in Moscow in 1957 but has now been replaced in most front line Soviet units by the ZSU-23-4 which has an all weather capability.

The chassis uses automotive components of the T-54 MBT but has thinner armour and four spaced roadwheels instead of five as in the case of the T-54. The twin S-68 guns are mounted in a open topped power operated turret with an elevation of +85° and a depression of −5°, turret traverse being a full 360°.

A total of 316 rounds of ammunition are carried of which 264 rounds are for ready use. Ammunition, which is in clips of four rounds, is the same as that used in the 57mm S-60 towed AA gun and the empty cartridge cases are ejected into a conveyor belt which deposits them in the wire cage on the turret rear. The guns, which fire APHE and HE

*ZSU-57-2 twin 57mm SP AA gun.*

projectiles, have a cyclic rate of fire of 105-120rpm, but practical rate of fire is 70rpm/barrel.

The weapon has no radar system and is therefore limited to clear weather use. Max effective range is 4,000m.

### Employment

Algeria, Angola, Bulgaria, Egypt, Ethiopia, Finland, GDR, Hungary, Iran, Iraq, North Korea, Poland, Romania, Syria, USSR, Vietnam and Yugoslavia.


# SA-4 'Ganef' SAM System

## USSR

**Crew:** 5
**Length:** 9.46m (with missiles)
**Width:** 3.2m
**Height:** 4.472m (with missiles)
**G/clearance:** 0.44m
**Weight:** 25,000kg
**Engine:** Water-cooled diesel developing 600hp
**Speed:** 50km/h
**V/obstacle:** 1m
**Trench:** 2.3m
**Gradient:** 60%

### Development

The SA-4 'Ganef' SAM system was developed in the early 1960s and was first seen in public in 1964. It was for a short period deployed in Egypt but is now found in only three of the Warsaw Pact countries.

Each 'Ganef' battery has a Pat Hand radar, three SA-4 launchers and four ZSU-23-4 SP AA guns for close defence, plus supporting vehicles. Additional radars are deployed at brigade level.

As the SA-4 has not been used in combat its exact performance capabilities are not known but it is thought to have a max range of 70,000m and a max altitude of 24,000m

The SA-4 launcher has no amphibious capability but is fitted with an NBC system. Components of the chassis are also used in the GMZ tracked armoured minelayer and the more recent 152mm M1973 SP howitzer.

### Employment

Czechoslovakia, GDR and the USSR.

SA-4 'Ganef' system with missiles elevated ready for launch.

# SA-6 'Gainful' SAM System    USSR

**Crew:** 3
**Length:** 6.8m (inc missiles)
**Width:** 3.18m (inc missiles)
**Height:** 3.45m (inc missiles)
**G/clearance:** 0.4m
**Weight:** 14,000kg
**Engine:** Model V-6R, 6-cylinder water-cooled diesel developing 280hp at 1,800rpm
**Speed:** 44km/h
**Range:** 260km
**Fuel:** 250 litres
**Fording:** 1m
**V/obstacle:** 1.1m
**Trench:** 2.8m
**Gradient:** 60%

## Development
The SA-6 'Gainful' mobile SAM system was developed in the early 1960s and was first seen in public in 1967 and first used in action by Syrian and Egyptian forces during the 1973 Middle East war. Each 'Gainful' battery has four SA-6 'Gainful' launchers each with three missiles, one 'Straight Flush' radar system and four ZSU-23-4 SP AA guns, plus supporting vehicles. Additional radars are deployed at regimental and battalion level.

The SA-6 has a max effective range of 30,000m and the max engagement height is 10,000m.

The chassis of the SA-6 launcher is based on that used for the ZSU-23-4 SP AA gun. The vehicle has no amphibious capability but has a NBC system and infra-red night vision equipment.

## Employment
Algeria, Bulgaria, Czechoslovakia, Egypt, GDR, Hungary, India, Iraq, Kuwait, Libya, Mozambique, Poland, Romania, Syria, Tanzania, Vietnam, South Yemen and Yugoslavia.

SA-6 'Gainful' SAMs in Moscow. For travelling the missiles are normally facing the rear, not the front as shown here.  Tass

# SA-8 'Gecko' SAM System

**Armament:** Four SA-8 missiles in ready-to-launch position
**Crew:** 3
**Length:** 8.99m
**Width:** 2.9m
**Height:** 4.141m (surveillance radar lowered), 1.845m (top of hull)
**Wheelbase:** 3.075m + 2.788m
**Speed:** 60-65km/h (max road)
**Fording:** Amphibious
*Note:* Above data is provisional

### Development
The SA-8 'Gecko' was seen in public for the first time during a parade held in Red Square, Moscow, in November 1975.

The system is based on a new 6 × 6 chassis that is provided with a central tyre pressure regulation

*SA-8 'Gecko' systems parade through Moscow's Red Square. Tass*

system. Before entering the water a trim vane is erected at the front of the hull and it is propelled in the water by two waterjets at the rear of the hull. It is probable that an NBC system is fitted.

When travelling, the surveillance radar which is mounted above and to the rear of the missiles is swung down 90° to the rear to reduce its overall height. The guidance group is forward of the four ready-to-launch missiles. The latter are powered by a single dual thrust solid propellant motor and have a max altitude of 12,000m and a max range of 12,000m.

More recently some SA-8 systems have been observed with six improved missiles carried in boxes in the ready-to-launch position. It is not certain if the vehicle has an on-board capability to reload the missiles once they have been launched.

### Employment
In service with the USSR. Reported to be on order for Syria.

# AT-P Armoured Tracked Artillery Tractor

**Armament:** 1 × 7.62mm SGMT MG
**Crew:** 3 + 6
**Length:** 4.45m
**Width:** 2.5m
**Height:** 1.83m
**G/clearance:** 0.30m
**Weight:** 6,700kg (loaded)
**G/pressure:** 0.47kg/sq cm
**Engine:** ZIL-123F 6-cylinder, in-line, water-cooled petrol engine developing 110hp at 2,900rpm
**Speed:** 50km/h

**Range:** 500km
**Fording:** 0.7m
**V/obstacle:** 0.7m
**Trench:** 1.22m
**Gradient:** 60%
**Armour:** 12mm (max)

### Development
The AT-Ps primary role is one of towing artillery including 85mm and 100mm anti-tank guns, 122m Howitzer D-30 and AA guns. The crew of three

consists of a commander, driver and a gunner for the MG which is on the right of the front superstructure. The rest of the men are in the rear of the vehicle. The vehicle can also be used as a personnel carrier or cargo carrier carrying up to 2,500kg of cargo.

Early models of the vehicle have the rear compartment with no overhead protection, although a canvas cover could be erected in bad weather.

**Variants**
*AT-P Command:* Fully rotating commander's cupola, overhead armour protection for rear troop compartment, rear doors with firing ports, additional communications equipment and external stowage.
*AT/P Artillery Reconnaissance:* Full width rear troop compartment.

**Employment**
In use only with the USSR.

# GMZ Armoured Tracked Minelayer
# USSR

**Armament:** 1 × 14.5mm KPV MG
**Crew:** 4-5
**Length:** 7.5m (hull), 9.1m (plough in travelling position), 10.3m (plough lowered)
**Width:** 3.2m
**Height:** 2.7m (top of searchlight), 2.5m (top of plough in travelling position)
**Weight:** 25,000kg
**Engine:** V-12 water-cooled diesel developing 520hp
**Speed:** 50km/hr
**Range:** 300km
**Fuel:** 500 litres
**Fording:** 1.1m
**V/obstacle:** 1.1m
**Trench:** 3.2m
**Gradient:** 60%
*Note:* Above specification is provisional.

**Development**
The GMZ full tracked armoured minelayer is based on a modified SA-4 'Ganef' chassis with the mine laying plough at the rear of the hull. Between 150 and 200 anti-tank mines are carried and can be laid beneath or on the surface. All vehicles have night vision equipment and it is assumed that an NBC system is fitted.

**Variants**
The SA-4 chassis, modified, is used as the basis for the 152mm M1973 (SAU-152) SP howitzer.

**Employment**
In service with the USSR.

# M-980 MICV
# Yugoslavia

**Armament:** 1 × 20mm cannon, elevation +85°, depression −5°
1 × 7.62mm coaxial MG
2 × launchers for 'Sagger' ATGW
**Crew:** 3 + 6-8
**Length:** 6.506m
**Width:** 2.89m
**Height:** 2.242m (turret), 1.8m (hull roof)
**Weight:** 12,000kg (loaded), 11,000kg (empty)
**Engine:** HS 115-2 V-8 turbo-charged diesel developing 276hp at 3,000rpm
**Speed:** 70km/h, 8km/h (water)
**Range:** 500km
**Fording:** Amphibious
**V/obstacle:** 0.8m
**Trench:** 1.85m
**Gradient:** 60%
*Note:* The above data is provisional

**Development**
The Yugoslav M-980 was first displayed at the 1975 May Day Parade in Belgrade and is now supplementing the old M-60 APC. The M-980 uses some components of the French AMX-10P MICV

including the engine and also possibly the suspension.

The engine is at the front of the hull with the driver on the left side and the commander to the rear of the driver. The turret is in the centre of the hull with the personnel compartment at the rear. The 20mm cannon is the Model M-55, this being the Swiss Hispano Suiza Type 804 cannon which has been manufactured in Yugoslavia for some years. The 7.62mm MG is mounted to the right of the main armament. The infantry is provided with firing ports and vision devices in the sides and rear of the hull which enable the crew to fire their weapons from within the hull.

The M-980 is provided with a NBC system and a full range of night vision equipment. It is fully amphibious being propelled in the water by its tracks, before entering the water a trim vane is erected at the front of the hull.

**Variants**
There are no variants of the M-980.

**Employment**
In service with the Yugoslav Army.

*Yugoslav M-980 MICV.*

# M60 APC

Yugoslavia

**Armament:** 1 × 12.7mm MG on roof
1 × 7.92mm MG in bow
**Crew:** 3 + 10
**Length:** 5.05m
**Width:** 2.75m
**Height:** 1.8m (w/o armament)
**Weight:** 9,500kg (loaded)
**G/pressure:** 0.6kg/sq cm
**Engine:** FAMOS 6-cylinder in-line water-cooled diesel developing 140hp
**Speed:** 45km/h, 6km/h (water)
**Range:** 400km
**Fuel:** 150 litres
**Fording:** Amphibious
**V/obstacle:** 0.6m
**Trench:** 2m
**Gradient:** 60%
**Armour:** 10-25mm

## Development

The M-60 APC entered service with the Yugoslav Army in the 1960s and was provisionally called the M-590. The suspension of the M-60 is based on that of the Soviet SU-76 76mm SP gun which was supplied to Yugoslavia shortly after the end of World War 2.

Main armament consists of a pintle mounted 12.7mm M2HB Browning MG mounted on the right side of the roof. In addition there is a 7.92mm M-53 MG mounted in the hull front firing forwards. The M-53 is the Yugoslav version of the German World War 2 MG42 MG.

The personnel compartment at the rear has firing ports in the sides and rear and standard equipment includes infra-red driving lights. The M-60 has no NBC system but it is fully amphibious being propelled in the water by its tracks, before entering the water a trim vane is erected at the font of the hull.

## Variants

The only known variant is an anti-tank model which is armed with twin M60 82mm recoilless guns at the rear of the hull roof. Ambulance, command and radio models of the M-60 may also be in service.

## Employment

In service with the Yugoslav Army.

*Anti-tank model of the M60 armed with twin M60 recoilless guns.*

# Other Armoured Fighting Vehicles

| Name/Designation | Type | Country | Notes |
|---|---|---|---|
| CATI | Tank destroyer | Belgium | No longer in service. |
| Charioteer | Tank destroyer | UK | No longer in service. |
| Chrysler MAC | Armoured car | USA | No longer in service. |
| Chrysler SWAT | APC | USA | Development cancelled. |
| Churchill | Tank | UK | No longer in service. |
| Conqueror | Heavy tank | UK | No longer in service. |
| Cutia-Vete | Reconnaissance | Brazil | Prototypes only. |
| ESPAWS | SPG | USA | Project for 1990s SPG. |
| Finnish (6×6) | APC | Finland | Development cancelled. |
| G-13 | Tank destroyer | Germany | No longer in service. |
| HIMAG | Trials vehicle | USA | Prototype only. |
| Hornet Malkara | Tank destroyer (ATGW) | UK | No longer in service. |
| Hotchkiss LFU | Light AFV | France | Development cancelled. |
| Hotchkiss TT A 12 | APC | France | Development cancelled. |
| HSTV(L) | Trials vehicle | USA | Prototype only, light tank. |
| HWR 42 | Armoured car | FGR | Development cancelled. |
| Indigo | SAM system | Italy | Development only. |
| Ikv-102/Ikv-103 | Tank destroyer | Sweden | No longer in service. |
| LAV | Family of vehicles | USA | For Rapid Deployment Force. |
| Lohr VPX 5000 | Light tracked vehicle | France | Announced June 1981. |
| Lohr RPX 6000 | Light wheeled vehicle | France | Announced June 1981. |
| LVA | Landing Vehicle Assault | USA | Project for 1980s/90s. |
| LVT4 | Landing Vehicle Tracked | USA | Few in service in Taiwan. |
| LVTP5 | Landing Vehicle Tracked | USA | Few in Taiwan and Philippines. |
| M2, M4, M6, M8 | APC/Armoured Car | France | Development cancelled. |
| M39 | Utility Vehicle | USA | No longer in service. |
| M50(Ontos) | Tank destroyer | USA | No longer in service. |
| M51 | Heavy ARV | USA | No longer in service. |
| M53 | SPG | USA | No longer in service. |
| M103 | Heavy tank | USA | No longer in service. |
| M114 | Reconnaissance carrier | USA | No longer in service. |
| MBT-70 | MBT | USA | Development cancelled. |
| MBT-80 | MBT | UK | Development cancelled. |
| MOWAG Puma | APC | Switzerland | Development cancelled. |
| MOWAG Shark | Reconnaissance vehicle | Switzerland | Announced June 1981 (8×8). |
| MOWAG Spy | Reconnaissance vehicle | Switzerland | Announced 1981 (4×4). |
| MPWS | Mobile Protected Weapons System | USA | Project for US Marines. |
| m/43 | SPG | Sweden | No longer in service. |
| Pbv 301 | APC | Sweden | No longer in service. |
| RDF/LT | Light tank | USA | Proposal by AAI for RDF. |
| Strv 74 | Light tank | Sweden | No longer in service. |
| Strv 40 | Light tank | Sweden | No longer in service. |
| SKP/VKP m/42 | APC | Sweden | Few still in service with Swedish Army. |
| T17E1 | Armoured car | USA | Few still in service in Africa. |
| VADAR | SRAAG | France | Development cancelled. |
| VBL | Reconnaissance vehicle | France | Under development for French Army (4×4). |
| VEAK 40 | SPAAG | Sweden | Development cancelled. |
| XM701 | MICV | USA | Development cancelled. |
| XM729 | RAMS | USA | Development cancelled. |
| XM733 | RAMS | USA | Development cancelled. |
| XM800 | Reconnaissance vehicle | USA | Development cancelled. |
| XM803 | MBT | USA | Development cancelled. |
| XM808 (Twister) | Reconnaissance vehicle | USA | Development cancelled. |
| XR-311 | Reconnaissance vehicle | USA | Development cancelled. |
| YP-104 | Reconnaissance vehicle | Netherlands | Development cancelled. |
| Yugoslav vehicle | SPAAG | Yugoslavia | Triple 20mm unveiled in 1981, APC versions will probably follow. |
| $\frac{3}{4}$ton truck | APC | Canada | No longer in service. |

# Index